Cambridge studies in medieval life and thought

WILLIAM OF TYRE

Cambridge studies in medieval life and thought
Fourth series

General Editor:
D. E. LUSCOMBE
Professor of Medieval History, University of Sheffield

Advisory Editors:
R. B. DOBSON
Professor of Medieval History, University of Cambridge,
and Fellow of Christ's College

ROSAMOND MCKITTERICK
Lecturer in History, University of Cambridge,
and Fellow of Newnham College

The series Cambridge Studies in Medieval Life and Thought was inaugurated by
G. G. Coulton in 1921. Professor D. E. Luscombe now acts as General Editor of the
Fourth Series, with Professor R. B. Dobson and Dr Rosamond McKitterick as
Advisory Editors. The series brings together outstanding work by medieval scholars
over a wide range of human endeavour extending from political economy to the
history of ideas.

For a list of titles in the series, see end of book.

WILLIAM OF TYRE

Historian of the Latin East

PETER W. EDBURY
University College Cardiff

JOHN GORDON ROWE
University of Western Ontario

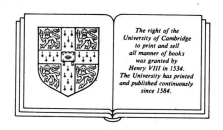

The right of the
University of Cambridge
to print and sell
all manner of books
was granted by
Henry VIII in 1534.
The University has printed
and published continuously
since 1584.

CAMBRIDGE UNIVERSITY PRESS

CAMBRIDGE

NEW YORK   PORT CHESTER   MELBOURNE   SYDNEY

Published by the Press Syndicate of the University of Cambridge
The Pitt Building, Trumpington Street, Cambridge CB2 1RP
40 West 20th Street, New York, NY 10011, USA
10 Stamford Road, Oakleigh, Melbourne 3166, Australia

First published 1988
First paperback edition 1990

Printed in Great Britain at the University Press, Cambridge

British Library cataloguing in publication data
Edbury, P. W.
William of Tyre: historian of the Latin East. – (Cambridge studies
in medieval life and thought. 4th series; 8).
1. William, of Tyre 2. Historians – Biography
I. Title II. Rowe, John Gordon
949.5'04'0072024 DF505.7.W/

Library of Congress cataloguing-in-publication data
Edbury, P. W. (Peter W.)
William of Tyre, historian of the Latin East/Peter W. Edbury.
John Gordon Rowe.
p.   cm. – (Cambridge studies in medieval life and
thought: 4th ser., 8)
Bibliography: p.
Includes index.
ISBN 0 521 26766 8
1. William, of Tyre. Archbishop of Tyre, ca. 1130–ća. 1190.
Historia rerum in partibus transmarinis gestarum.
2. Crusades – First, 1096–1099.
3. Godfrey, of Bouillon, ca. 1060–1100.
4. Jerusalem – History – Latin Kingdom, 1099–1244.
I. Rowe, John Gordon. II. Title. III. Series.
D152.W553E33 1988
940.1'8 – dc19   87-18775   CIP

ISBN 0 521 26766 8 hardback
ISBN 0 521 40728 1 paperback

For Frances and Hazel

CONTENTS

PREFACE

This is a study of a medieval historian and what he had to say. It is the fruit of a collaboration originally conceived almost ten years ago and has taken far longer to complete than it should. The distance between Cardiff and London, Ontario, and our other commitments, provide excuses, albeit rather feeble ones. More seriously, we found that the price of being engaged on a genuinely collaborative undertaking was that our labour was increased rather than diminished as points of detail were thrashed out and drafts passed to and fro across the Atlantic.

Work was already well advanced when Professor Robert Huygens' new edition of William of Tyre's history was published. It is difficult for us to express adequately our indebtedness to him for what has proved to be of enormous assistance in the final stages of our research.

Appreciation and thanks for their generous help in many different ways and at widely differing stages of our work are due to many people, not least: Dr D. R. Bates, Miss J. Buckingham, Mr Ceri Davies, Professor R. B. C. Huygens, Dr C. H. Knowles, Professor J. R. Lander, Professor J. S. C. Riley-Smith, the late Dr R. C. Smail, and Professor W. H. Stockdale; also the staff of the Bodleian Library, Oxford and the libraries at University College Cardiff and the University of Western Ontario, where in particular we would mention Dr R. E. Lee, the chief librarian, and his colleagues Mr R. Gardiner and Mr G. Malcahy. However, the responsibility for the mistakes remains our own, and for these the authors will no doubt blame each other.

We dedicate this volume to our wives, who have endured patiently and been a constant source of support and encouragement.

University College Cardiff   P. W. E.
University of Western Ontario   J. G. R.

ABBREVIATIONS AND FORMS OF REFERENCE

B/K	William Archbishop of Tyre. *A History of Deeds Done Beyond the Sea*. Translated and annotated by E. A. Babcock and A. C. Krey. 2 vols. New York, 1941.
EHR	*English Historical Review.*
PL	Patrologiae cursus completus. Series Latina. Compiled by J. P. Migne. 217 vols. with 4 vols. of indexes. Paris, 1844–64.
RHC	*Recueil des historiens des croisades.* Paris, 1841–1906.
Arm	*RHC Documents arméniens.* 2 vols. 1869–1906.
Lois	*RHC Lois. Les Assises de Jérusalem.* 2 vols. 1841–3.
Occ	*RHC Historiens occidentaux.* 5 vols. 1844–95.
Or	*RHC Historiens orientaux.* 5 vols. 1872–1906.
RRH	*Regesta Regni Hierosolymitani (1097–1291).* Compiled by R. Röhricht. Innsbruck, 1893. *Additamentum.* 1904.
TRHS	*Transactions of the Royal Historical Society.*
WT	*Willelmi Tyrensis Archiepiscopi Chronicon.* Edited by R. B. C. Huygens. 2 vols. Corpus Christianorum Continuatio Mediaevalis. 63–63A. Turnholt, 1986.

Citations from William of Tyre are from Professor Huygens' edition rather than from the nineteenth-century *Recueil des historiens des croisades*. Our practice has been to use roman numerals for the books and arabic numerals for the chapters, without giving page numbers, but providing line numbers to the chapters where appropriate. Where page numbers are given, these refer to the editor's introduction.

INTRODUCTION

Historians are unanimous: the work by William II, archbishop of Tyre, which until recently has been known as the *Historia rerum in partibus transmarinis gestarum*, but which might better be entitled *Historia Ierosolymitana*, is important and influential. William flourished in the kingdom of Jerusalem during the reigns of King Amaury (1163–74) and his son, Baldwin IV (1174–85), and he provided the Latin kingdom with an account of its foundation and history, spanning the period from the preaching of the First Crusade in 1095 until the year 1184. The *Historia* begins with a brief survey of the background to the First Crusade, going back to the recovery of the True Cross by the Byzantine emperor Heraclius early in the seventh century, before proceeding to recount the story of the Crusade (Books I–VIII) and the fortunes of the Latins in the lands they conquered (Books IX–XXIII). It is a long work: in the most recent edition William's Latin text fills just under a thousand pages.[1] Its very size makes it difficult to view as a whole, and for this reason scholars have been far more ready to use it as a quarry for historical information than to try to assess its strengths and weaknesses as an example of twelfth-century historiography or to seek to examine the presuppositions and attitudes of its author. As a quarry for historical information it has long been recognized as being of the utmost importance. From the late 1120s until the point at which it ends it is the only contemporary or near-contemporary account of the history of the Latin East written in Latin by a Christian resident

---

[1] *Willelmi Tyrensis Archiepiscopi Chronicon*, ed. R. B. C. Huygens. Identification des sources historiques et détermination des dates par H. E. Mayer et G. Rösch (Turnhout, 1986). As Huygens demonstrated (*WT*, pp. 33–4), William's own title for his work is unknown; Huygens himself opted to supply the neutral *Chronicon*. We, however, prefer *Historia Ierosolymitana* which, although not William's usage, is indicated as a possible title in the incipits of two English manuscripts. We shall frequently use the shorthand form, *Historia*.

in that area. For the reigns of Amaury and Baldwin IV it is of particular interest, since at that period its author was a prominent man of affairs, and so might reasonably be expected to have been well informed about his subject-matter.

William's subject, the Crusades to the eastern Mediterranean and the history of the lands conquered by the crusaders, is in any reckoning of major importance for an understanding of the central middle ages. The success of the First Crusade in capturing Jerusalem from the Muslims in 1099, the fact that the Christians could go on to consolidate their achievement and extend the territory under their control, and their continued presence in parts of Syria and Palestine for almost two centuries, have often evoked surprise and admiration. Modern historians may emphasize the importance of the Crusade in things such as the history of the medieval papal monarchy, the beginnings of the systems of national taxation, or the growth of international trade, but William's interests as a contemporary were in political events – battles and the deeds of kings. Other matters, such as the deeds of popes or the activities of traders from the Italian maritime republics, were only incidental to his story. As an archbishop and churchman he allowed himself to digress from time to time and write about the doings of the secular Church in the East, but ecclesiastical history was not his main theme. The *Historia* tells of the successes and achievements of the crusaders and Latin settlers, but, especially towards the end, there is also a sense of foreboding. In William's own day the Muslims under Saladin were posing a serious threat, and the Christians lacked the resources to sustain their resistance. William saw the danger and wrote about it. Within a short time of his death his fears passed in to reality with the defeat of the Christians at Hattin on 4 July 1187 and the subsequent collapse of the Latin kingdom.

William addressed his work to 'his venerable brothers in Christ',[2] in other words, to his fellow-members of the higher clergy, and it goes without saying that the appeal of his lengthy Latin narrative would have been restricted to clerically educated circles. The title as it appears in some manuscripts, *Historia rerum in partibus transmarinis gestarum*, might be construed as indicating that he was writing for people who regarded the Latin East as being beyond the seas and who were thus themselves living in western Europe, but there are sound textual reasons for supposing that this title is not William's

---

[2] R. B. C. Huygens, 'La tradition manuscrite de Guillaume de Tyr', *Studi medievali*, 3rd ser., v (1964), 313; *WT*, p. 32.

own and so proves nothing. More likely, he imagined that his work would be of interest to other Latins resident in the East – he anticipated his readers being able to consult another of his writings in the cathedral archive at Tyre – but after his visit to Europe for the Third Lateran Council of 1179 came to regard it as having a potential readership throughout Christian Europe as well.[3]

The fact that William died soon after laying down his pen suggests that he had little part in the diffusion of his *magnum opus*. Presumably it circulated in the East before finding its way to Europe: two of the surviving manuscripts contain orthographical peculiarities which might perhaps point to their exemplars having been copied in the East, and James of Vitry, bishop of Acre (1216–28), certainly knew the work.[4] In the West, as we know from its colophon, one of the surviving manuscripts was given by Anseau, bishop of Meaux (1197–1207), to the Cistercian abbey of Barbeaux near Melun, and the Cistercian house at Pontigny also apparently acquired a copy in the thirteenth century. A French participant in the Third Crusade, Guy of Bazoches, who died at Châlons-sur-Marne in 1203, had access to the work and copied excerpts from it into his *Cronosgraphia*. He is thus the earliest known person to have made use of the *Historia*.[5] In England the *Historia* was used by the mid-thirteenth-century St Albans chronicler, Matthew Paris. In a marginal note Matthew recorded that Peter des Roches, bishop of Winchester, brought a manuscript containing one of William's works back from the Crusade – this would have been in 1231 – but it seems that it was probably of his lost work, the *Gesta orientalium principum*, and that Matthew had used a copy of the *Historia* in a version already in circulation in England before that date.[6] Two manuscripts of the *Historia* copied in England in the thirteenth century survive, one evidently belonging to the first quarter of the century, and there is what could be a reference to a copy in the library of the Priory of St Andrew, Rochester, as early as 1202.[7] But insofar as the number of extant manuscripts can serve

---

[3] Huygens, 'Tradition manuscrite', p. 315; *WT*, p. 32–3.
[4] Huygens, 'Tradition manuscrite', pp. 322–3, 335; *WT*, pp. 77–8.
[5] Huygens, 'Tradition manuscrite', pp. 290, 291–2; *idem*, 'Pontigny et l'*Histoire* de Guillaume de Tyr', *Latomus*, xxv (1966), 139–42; *WT*, pp. 15, 16–18, 76–7.
[6] *WT*, pp. 78–87.
[7] Huygens, 'Tradition manuscrite', pp. 287–8; *WT*, pp. 19–21. One manuscript belonged to Waltham Abbey; the provenance of the other is unknown. The 1202 catalogue of the Rochester library (BL MS Royal 5.B.xii, f. 2v) lists a 'Hystoria ierlm' which could denote William's *Historia*, since both the extant thirteenth-century English manuscripts describe the work in their incipits as *Historia Ierosoly-*

as an indication, William's work was not widely read. Only nine copies and a fragment of a tenth are known; they date from the thirteenth century, or perhaps the very end of the twelfth, to the fifteenth, and a thorough analysis shows that the manuscript tradition they embody was limited in its geographical scope to France and England.[8]

The *Historia* may not have circulated widely in the form in which William wrote it, but translated into French it proved to be a major success. The French translation is said to have been made in France in the years leading up to 1223.[9] The translator followed his Latin text fairly closely but was not above embroidering or making cuts in what he found. The manuscript at the translator's disposal was certainly no nearer William's original than the copies of the Latin text which survive to this day, and, although on occasion he could add informed comment, the translator is unlikely to have had extra information on historical matters, and his embellishments generally need to be treated with reserve.[10] At least fifty-nine manuscripts or fragments of manuscripts survive from the medieval period. Many were produced in the West, others in the East, at Acre or elsewhere. A substantial proportion include continuations, some of which carry the narrative well into the second half of the thirteenth century.[11] The French translation would have appealed to laymen as well as to clerics, and in this connection it may be significant that

mitana (*WT*, p. 33). We are indebted to Professor D. E. Luscombe for first drawing our attention to the Rochester entry, but, as Huygens has pointed out (*WT*, p. 21 note 37), this reference could equally be to another history of the Crusade with the same title.

8 Huygens, 'Tradition manuscrite', pp. 282, 284–313 *passim*; *WT*, pp. 3–31.

9 'L'Estoire de Eracles empereur et la conqueste de la terre d'Outremer', *RHC Occ*, I–II; M. R. Morgan, *The Chronicle of Ernoul and the Continuations of William of Tyre* (Oxford, 1973), pp. 119, 172.

10 Huygens, 'Tradition manuscrite', p. 334. The value of the translator's embellishments is a matter of some debate. Morgan (pp. 185–7) was highly critical of the use made of the translation by J. Prawer (especially in his 'Colonization Activities in the Latin Kingdom of Jerusalem', *Revue belge de philologie et d'histoire*, XXIX (1951), 1074). For other examples of a positive attitude to the historical value of the translation, see H. E. Mayer, 'Studies in the History of Queen Melisende of Jerusalem', *Dumbarton Oaks Papers*, XXVI (1972), 107; R. H. C. Davis, 'William of Tyre', in D. Baker (ed.), *Relations between East and West in the Middle Ages* (Edinburgh, 1973), pp. 72–3; B. Z. Kedar, 'Gerard of Nazareth, a Neglected Twelfth-Century Writer in the Latin East', *Dumbarton Oaks Papers*, XXXVII (1983), 62 and note 36. The date, manuscript tradition and content of the French translation deserve systematic investigation.

11 J. Folda, 'Manuscripts of the *History of Outremer* by William of Tyre: A Handlist', *Scriptorium*, XXVII (1973), 90–5. For the complex relationship of the continuations, see Morgan, *Chronicle of Ernoul*.

some of the passages of purely ecclesiastical interest were omitted or compressed. Its popularity is evident both from the number of manuscripts which have come down to us and also in the influence it had on other writers. An early fourteenth-century compiler at work in Cyprus could refer his readers to the translation and its continuations, calling it the *Livre dou conqueste*, and his contemporary, the Armenian Hayton of Gorhigos, also knew it by that name.[12] Another early fourteenth-century writer, Marino Sanudo, used it in his *Liber Secretorum Fidelium Crucis*. In the thirteenth century, at the behest of Alphonso X of Castile (1252–84), it was translated from French into Spanish, and in the fourteenth an Italian, Francesco Pipino, even translated parts of it back into Latin. In the fifteenth century William Caxton rendered excerpts into English, and it was probably also then that other excerpts were paraphrased into Italian and incorporated into the compilation known as the *Chronique d'Amadi*.[13]

William's Latin original was first printed in 1549 at Basel, where it was reissued in 1564. In 1611 J. Bongars included an edition of the *Historia*, based on three different manuscripts, in his compendium of chronicles of the Crusades entitled *Gesta Dei per Francos*. Bongars's edition was reprinted in 1855 by J. P. Migne in the Patrologia Latina (volume 201), although in 1844 A. Beugnot and A. Le Prévost had made a fresh edition for the project sponsored by the Académie des Inscriptions et Belles Lettres under the title of *Recueil des historiens des croisades*. The *Recueil* edition established a text which was not markedly better than Bongars's, but it is nevertheless the edition that modern scholars have hitherto normally used.[14] In 1986, however, the distinguished Dutch scholar, Professor R. B. C. Huygens of the University of Leiden, published a splendid new edition which undoubtedly will now become accepted as standard. Thanks to his detailed and painstaking examination of the manuscripts, we now have a dependable text, and the value of his work is further enhanced by the useful historical notes contributed by Professor H. E. Mayer and Dr G. Rösch.

[12] 'Les Gestes des Chiprois', *RHC Arm*, II, 654, 657, 663, 744; Hayton of Gorhigos, 'La Flor des estoires de la terre d'orient', *RHC Arm*, II, 176, 306. In the thirteenth century John of Ibelin may have had some other work in mind when he used this title (John of Ibelin, 'Livre des assises de la haute cour', *RHC Lois*, I, 429).

[13] For Sanudo, Pipino and Caxton, see Morgan, *Chronicle of Ernoul*, pp. 22–5; *La Gran Conquista de Ultramar*, ed. Pascalis de Goyangos (Madrid, 1858); 'Chronique d'Amadi', ed. R. de Mas Latrie, in *Chroniques d'Amadi et de Strambaldi* (Paris, 1891–3), I.

[14] Huygens, 'Tradition manuscrite', pp. 318–22; *WT*, pp. 87–91.

Introduction

Modern scholarship on William of Tyre and the *Historia* may fairly be said to have begun with Heinrich von Sybel, who in 1841 published an extended essay on the work in the preface to his *Geschichte des ersten Kreuzzüges*.[15] Despite his outdated views on certain aspects, von Sybel's discussion can still be read with profit. He has some valuable and sensitive comments on William's handling of his sources and the manner in which he collected his materials. He drew attention to the fact, that despite his belief in the divine ordering of the affairs of men, William could adopt an essentially human-centred approach, and he was critical of the *Historia*, pointing out obscurities in its chronology and stressing its lack of originality as a source for the First Crusade.

Von Sybel's work was continued later in the nineteenth century by Hans Prutz, who made a careful examination of the materials then available which bear on William's career and writings.[16] But after Prutz, although many scholars used the *Historia*, few directed their attention to examining the problems that it presents. T. A. Archer and W. B. Stevenson each attempted to straighten out some of William's misleading statements with regard to chronology; H. Propst looked at his information on Syrian and Palestinian geography; F. Lundgreen wrote an over-critical study on his treatment of the Order of the Temple; R. Grousset discussed the incident recorded in Book XVII, chapter 20.[17] But when in 1941 August C. Krey came to write what he elsewhere described as 'an effort to summarize our present knowledge of the subject', we find a heavy dependence on Prutz with a strong dose of fanciful speculation.[18] Krey's chief contribution to the study of William of Tyre lies in his edition of the English translation made by E. A. Babcock,

---

[15] We have consulted the English translation by Lady Duff Gordon, *The History and Literature of the Crusades* (London, n.d.), pp. 197–238. Von Sybel (pp. 252–72) also gave a résumé of crusade historiography from the mid-fifteenth century to his own day, with some tart comments on the use made of the *Historia*.

[16] H. Prutz, 'Studien über Wilhelm von Tyrus', *Neues Archiv der Gesellschaft für ältere deutsche Geschichtskunde*, VIII (1883), 91–132. See *idem*, *Kulturgeschichte der Kreuzzüge* (Berlin, 1883), pp. 458–69.

[17] T. A. Archer, 'On the Accession Dates of the Early Kings of Jerusalem', *EHR*, IV (1889), 89–105; W. B. Stevenson, *The Crusaders in the East* (Cambridge, 1907), pp. 361–71; H. Propst, 'Die geographischen Verhältnisse Syriens und Palästinas nach Wilhelm von Tyrus, Geschichte der Kreuzzüge', *Das Land der Bibel*, IV:5/6 (1927), 1–83, continued in V:1 (1927), 1–40; F. Lundgreen, *Wilhelm von Tyrus und der Templerorden* (Berlin, 1911); R. Grousset, 'Sur un passage obscur de Guillaume de Tyr', *Mélanges syriens offerts à M. René Dussaud*, Bibliothèque archéologique et historique, 30 (Paris, 1939), II, 937–9.

[18] A. C. Krey, 'William of Tyre: The Making of an Historian in the Middle Ages', *Speculum*, XVI (1941), 149–66. See B/K, I, 3–44.

published in 1943. In the period since Prutz's day study of the Crusades and the Latin East had proceeded by leaps and bounds, but the study of William had not made marked progress.

In recent years, however, there has been a renewed interest and some substantial advances have been made. Without doubt the most considerable contribution has been the work of R. B. C. Huygens. It had always been assumed that a chapter in the *Historia* describing William's early career had been lost; the existence of such a chapter was known from the lists of rubrics, but in the text of the manuscripts hitherto used by the various editors it was missing. Huygens rediscovered this chapter (Book XIX, chapter 12) in a previously little used Vatican manuscript and at a stroke solved many of the questions surrounding William's studies in the West.[19] His rediscovery came in the course of the systematic examination, preparatory to his edition, of all the surviving manuscripts of the Latin version of the *Historia*, and his researches into the manuscript tradition have yielded many important insights into its transmission and diffusion.[20]

Discoveries of fresh materials which bear on William's career and writings are rare, and so it came as an agreeable surprise when in 1978 Rudolf Hiestand drew attention to an otherwise unnoticed obit giving the day of the month, but not the year, of William's death.[21] Other scholars who in various ways have added to our understanding of William and the *Historia* in recent years include R. H. C. Davis, who has offered some shrewd comments on the purposes and influence of the *Historia* and on the ways in which it has been misunderstood; D. W. T. C. Vessey, who has contributed an important article on William's use of literary conventions and has challenged his claims to be impartial; Hans Mayer, who, besides examining the problems surrounding the date of William's death, has tried in his study on Queen Melisende of Jerusalem to bring a section of the *Historia* describing events from the 1120s to the 1150s under critical control; W. Giese, who has examined the character sketches and topographical descriptions; and R. C. Schwinges, who has sought to place William in the context of the Twelfth-Century

---

[19] R. B. C. Huygens, 'Guillaume de Tyr étudiant. Un chapitre (XIX, 12) de son "Histoire" retrouvé', *Latomus*, XXI (1962), 811–29.

[20] Huygens, 'Tradition manuscrite', pp. 281–373; *idem*, 'Pontigny', pp. 139–42; *idem*, 'Editing William of Tyre', *Sacris erudiri*, XXVII (1984), 461–73. The substance of these articles is repeated in the introduction to his edition.

[21] R. Hiestand, 'Zum Leben und zur Laufbahn Wilhelms von Tyrus', *Deutsches Archiv*, XXXIV (1978), 345–80.

Renaissance and to examine his attitude to Islam and his Muslim neighbours.[22]

It might be thought that with so much literature on the subject a further appraisal is unnecessary. A number of the relevant articles, however, have been published in foreign periodicals, and no one has ever attempted a full-scale analysis of William's work in English. More importantly, there are, we believe, many questions about William and his writings which remain either unasked or not answered sufficiently. Our intention is twofold: first we shall explain our views on William's approach to the writing of history and how he used his sources of information, both written and oral, and we shall then examine his attitudes to particular institutions or topics – the monarchy in the Latin East, the relations of Church and State, the papacy in its dealings with the East, the Byzantine empire and, lastly, Christian warfare in the East – trying to gauge his presuppositions and assumptions and so understand his prejudices and beliefs about the past. It is not part of our purpose to make an exhaustive, line-by-line critique of the *Historia* to test the accuracy of each statement contained in it, although we shall have occasion to comment on William's reliability in particular instances. Still less in discussing the work will we use it as a springboard for a reinterpretation of twelfth-century Latin Syrian history. Rather, we hope to provide the groundwork whereby the context of William's information can be better understood and so to make an appreciation of his strengths and weaknesses easier. No one can ever hope to say all there is to be said about this author and his work – certainly not us – and we have chosen to leave on one side a number of topics which might yield interesting conclusions: for example, his view of Islam, which has been discussed by R. C. Schwinges, or his attitude to the indigenous Christian communities in the East or the Italian merchants, about neither of which – and this is no doubt significant in itself – William had much to say. Instead we shall concentrate on

---

[22] Davis, 'William of Tyre', pp. 64–76; D. W. T. C. Vessey, 'William of Tyre and the Art of Historiography', *Mediaeval Studies*, xxxv (1973), 433–55; *idem*, 'William of Tyre: Apology and Apocalypse', in G. Cambier (ed.), *Hommages à André Boutemy* (Brussels 1976), pp. 390–403; H. E. Mayer, 'Zum Tode Wilhelms von Tyrus', *Archiv für Diplomatik*, v–vi (1959–60), 182–201; *idem*, 'Melisende', pp. 93–182; W. Giese, 'Stadt- und Herrscherbeschreibungen bei Wilhelm von Tyrus', *Deutsches Archiv*, xxxiv (1978), 381–409; R. C. Schwinges, *Kreuzzugs-ideologie und Toleranz. Studien zu Wilhelm von Tyrus* (Stuttgart, 1977); see *idem*, 'Kreuzzugsideologie und Toleranz im Denken Wilhelms von Tyrus', *Saeculum*, xxv (1974), 367–85. Note also P. W. Edbury and J. G. Rowe, 'William of Tyre and the Patriarchal Election of 1180', *EHR*, xciii (1978), 1–25.

themes which, though not necessarily central to his own interests, do reveal his outlook. No medieval writer of history ever wrote without some axe to grind. So what were William's purposes in writing? And what was his message?

PART I

WILLIAM OF TYRE AND THE WRITING OF THE *HISTORIA*

Chapter 1

WILLIAM'S CAREER

Most of what we know about the life and work of William, archbishop of Tyre, comes from what he himself recorded in the
Historia Ierosolymitana. The *Historia*, both by what it is and by what
it tells us about its author, makes it abundantly clear that he was a
gifted man, and thanks to its survival more is known about him
than about any of his contemporaries in the ecclesiastical hierarchy
in the East. William enjoyed a successful career, but one which
followed a well-trodden path, familiar to many successful churchmen in twelfth-century Latin Christendom. What is distinctive
about him was that he added the vocation of historian to the
vocations of royal servant and prelate. His legacy is among the
more memorable and important pieces of historical writing from
the entire medieval period.

   A detailed reconstruction of his life is not possible, and there are
major questions, in particular about the nature of his political role in
his closing years, which remain unanswerable. However, the discovery of the autobiographical chapter in which he described his
early career has done much to illuminate his life before the mid-
1160s.[1] We now know for certain that he was born in the city of
Jerusalem and that he spent almost twenty years studying in the
Schools of western Europe. The date for his return to the East can
be established as 1165, and this would put the date for his departure
to Europe as *c.* 1146. On the basis of these dates historians are
agreed in placing his birth in or around the year 1130. Of his
childhood and early education little is known. Presumably he had
had some elementary schooling before he went to the West, and it
could be that he had attended the school attached to the Holy

---

[1] *WT*, XIX, 12. Cf. Huygens, 'Guillaume de Tyr'; Schwinges, *Kreuzzugsideologie*,
pp. 19–29.

Sepulchre, where there was a *magister scholasticus* as early as 1103.[2] William recorded that in his youth, evidently in the late 1130s, he himself had seen Patriarch Ralph of Antioch,[3] and another possible childhood reminiscence is provided by the remark that 'we saw' ('vidimus') Manasses of Hierges acting as royal constable – he had acquired the post soon after the death of King Fulk in 1143.[4] It has also been suggested that William's gross exaggeration of Fulk's age – he believed him to have been over sixty at the time of his accession in 1131 – could well be the result of a distorted impression dating from his own boyhood.[5] Such memories do not amount to very much, but they do serve to reinforce the belief that William's early years were spent in Jerusalem in the 1130s and early 1140s.

Apart from a single reference to his mother,[6] William said nothing about his family and background. The essential clue to his social origins is provided by a document, dated December 1175, which includes among the witnesses a certain Ralph, who is described as 'the brother of the Lord W. archbishop of Tyre'. From his position in the list of witnesses it is clear that Ralph was a burgess of Jerusalem,[7] and the inferences to be drawn are that William was of non-noble, burgess stock and that members of his family continued to live in Jerusalem itself. When the family first settled there and where they came from originally – France or Italy are the most plausible suggestions – are matters for speculation.[8] Whether William's silence about his background can perhaps be ascribed to a sense of embarrassment about his relatively humble origins in one who was in regular contact with kings and princes must also remain uncertain, although he was in good company: of the twelfth-century clerical careerists who rose to great heights in both Church and State, and who might be described as his counter-

---

2 *Le Cartulaire du chapitre du Saint-Sépulcre de Jérusalem*, ed. G. Bresc-Bautier (Paris, 1984), no. 19, p. 74; *RRH*, no. 40.
3 *WT*, xv, 17, lines 19–20.
4 *WT*, xii, 1, lines 19–20. For Manasses' appointment, see Mayer, 'Melisende', p. 116.
5 *WT*, xiv, 1, lines 13–14; B/K, ii, 47 note 1.
6 *WT*, xix, 12, lines 8–9.
7 *Cartulaire du Saint-Sépulcre*, no. 160, p. 312; *RRH*, no. 531. For examples of other witnesses in this list described as burgesses or jurats of the *cour des bourgeois* of Jerusalem, see *RRH*, nos. 492, 516, 561, 651. Abū Shāma ('Le livre des deux jardins', *RHC Or*, iv, 202) quoted a letter recording the death of a brother of the 'bishop of Tyre' in 1179, but whether this was Ralph or a third brother, or indeed the brother of another archbishop altogether, is not known.
8 Schwinges, *Kreuzzugsideologie*, pp. 19–20; Huygens, 'Editing William of Tyre', pp. 461–2. Cf. *WT*, p. 1 and note 3.

parts in the West – Peter of Blois, John of Salisbury, Thomas Becket, Rainald of Dassel, Robert Pullen – only Rainald was of noble birth.[9]

In the chapter recording his autobiography William wrote of his teachers and education in Europe. He had spent ten years studying the liberal arts and six studying theology in Paris and Orleans; the remaining years he spent at Bologna with the leading masters of civil law.[10] He claimed to have studied both canon and civil law, yet none of the teachers he named were canonists, and it may be wondered how much instruction in canon law he in fact received. He also asserted that he spent his time in the West 'willingly poor'.[11] No doubt he intended his readers to imagine him as a hungry scholar, eschewing bodily comforts in his quest for learning. How far this statement is to be taken at face value is unclear, but it does raise the questions of how William supported himself over such a long period of study, whether he received subventions from the East, and, if so, from whom. Again, we do not know, but the immediate granting of a benefice on his return and his rapid preferment thereafter do arouse the suspicion that his presence in the leading European centres of education had not passed unnoticed in high places in the Latin kingdom.

In 1165, now probably in his mid-thirties, William returned to Jerusalem. On his arrival William, bishop of Acre, acting with the consent of his chapter, gave him a prebend in his cathedral.[12] Perhaps Bishop William, himself a Lombard, was anxious to recruit someone trained in the Bolognese school of civil law to his staff. There is no mention of royal patronage as early as this, but in the course of the next two years King Amaury intervened actively to advance his career. According to William, the king had said that he would gladly bestow on him any benefice in his gift were it not for the objections of certain persons. Amaury then set about persuading

---

[9] Schwinges, *Kreuzzugsideologie*, p. 34.
[10] *WT*, XIX, 12, lines 1–61; cf. XIX, 4, lines 21–5. For William's teachers, see Huygens, 'Guillaume de Tyr', pp. 814–15, 825–9; Schwinges, *Kreuzzugsideologie*, pp. 26–8; R. W. Southern, 'The Schools of Paris and the School of Chartres', in R. L. Benson and G. Constable (eds.), *Renaissance and Renewal in the Twelfth Century* (Oxford, 1982), pp. 129–33. The fact that most of William's Parisian masters were also mentioned by the author of the *Metamorphosis Goliae* dated to 1142/3 lends support to the belief that his studies in the West stretched back to the 1140s. Four of William's masters were also among those John of Salisbury listed in the account of his studies during the years 1136–47.
[11] *WT*, XIX, 12, line 13: 'in paupertate voluntaria'.
[12] *WT*, XIX, 12, lines 62–8.

the bishops to provide for him from the benefices at their disposal, doing so, William would have us believe, without his knowledge.[13] Amaury's solicitations bore fruit when in August 1167 he returned victorious from his campaign in Egypt to marry the Greek princess, Maria Comnena. Shortly after the festivities Archbishop Frederick of Tyre granted William the vacant archdeaconry of Tyre 'in the presence and at the request of the king and many other distinguished men'.[14]

From then until after Amaury's death in 1174, William was employed as a trusted servant of the crown. His education in the West equipped him for international diplomacy, and almost at once, in 1168, he was sent on an important mission to the Byzantine emperor, Manuel Comnenus. King Amaury had embarked upon the conquest of Egypt; he looked to the Byzantines for support, and William's task was to reach agreement with Manuel on the detailed plans for a joint expedition. He found the emperor in Serbia and completed his negotiations with no apparent difficulty, returning to Jerusalem towards the end of the year.[15] In the event the expedition, which took place late in 1169, ended in fiasco. Amaury's 1167 campaign had been a success, but his failure to strengthen his hold on Egypt in the campaigns of 1168 and 1169 marked a significant reverse. Saladin, nominally the representative of the Syrian ruler, Nūr al-Dīn, gained control of Egypt in 1169, and the threat of Muslim encirclement of the Latin kingdom of Jerusalem was henceforth much more real.

In 1169 William was again in the West. Archbishop Frederick had set off on a diplomatic mission to Europe in May of that year to seek aid for the Latin East after the failure of the 1168 Egyptian campaign. William, in a tantalizingly elusive sentence, then recorded that 'having been occupied with private affairs and countering ("declinantes") the unmerited anger of my lord archbishop, I had gone to the Church of Rome'.[16] It may be that Frederick had laid charges against him at the papal *curia*. Alternatively some serious matter concerning the see of Tyre may have arisen after Frederick's

[13] *WT*, XIX, 12, lines 68–75. See Huygens, 'Guillaume de Tyr', pp. 815–16.
[14] *WT*, XX, 1, lines 23–7.
[15] *WT*, XX, 4.
[16] *WT*, XX, 17, lines 32–5: 'Nam nos eo anno, familiaribus tracti negociis et domini archiepiscopi nostri declinantes indignationem inmeritam, ad ecclesiam nos contuleramus Romanam.' The phrase 'familiaribus . . . negociis' could be understood to mean either private business or family business; cf. *WT*, p. 1 note 4. For Frederick's mission, see R. C. Smail, 'Latin Syria and the West, 1149–1187', *TRHS*, 5th ser., XIX (1969), 13–14.

departure, and William, perhaps fearing to act on his own initiative, may have sought the archbishop's approval for the course of action to be taken. Whatever the truth, it would appear that he was back in the East before the end of 1170, for in that year King Amaury appointed him tutor to his son and successor, the future Baldwin IV.[17] The embassy of 1168 and the appointment as tutor are evidence enough of the trust that Amaury placed in him, and his new appointment presumably ensured that he spent much of his time in the royal entourage. No doubt he owed his rise to his training and ability, but it must be remembered that for as long as Amaury was alive his position at court was totally dependent on continuing royal patronage.

King Amaury died in 1174 and was succeeded by the young Baldwin IV, then aged thirteen. Baldwin was thus a minor at the time of his accession. Worse than that, he was already known to be suffering from leprosy; indeed William claimed to have been the first to notice that anything was wrong with him.[18] Baldwin's reign was to be a period of growing difficulties for the Latin kingdom of Jerusalem. Externally, pressure from the Muslims grew as Saladin, who in 1174 had added Damascus to his rule, tightened his control on the neighbouring territories. Internally, the fact that the king was ill and often incapable of ruling meant that there were struggles over who should exercise power and patronage on his behalf, and the fact that he could have no children of his own prompted concern and disagreement over who should succeed him. Not surprisingly under these circumstances, factions developed. King Amaury had married twice. By his first wife, Agnes of Courtenay, the daughter of Count Joscelin II of Edessa, he had had two children – a daughter, Sibylla, and a son, the future Baldwin IV. At the time of his accession in 1163 Amaury had divorced Agnes, and then in 1167 he married the Byzantine princess Maria Comnena, who bore him a second daughter, Isabella. Both Agnes and Maria survived their husband. Prominent in the faction which then grew up around Agnes were her brother, Joscelin III, titular count of Edessa, and Raynald of Châtillon, who early in Baldwin's reign married the heiress to the lordship of Oultrejourdain; they were joined by Guy of Lusignan, who in 1180 married Baldwin's sister Sibylla, Eraclius the archbishop of Caesarea, who also in 1180 became patriarch of Jerusalem, and Gerard of Ridefort, from 1185 master of

---

[17] *WT*, XXI, 1, lines 12–16. For the date, see B/K, II, 397 note 3.
[18] *WT*, XXI, 1, lines 16–32.

the Templars. Ranged against this group were Maria Comnena's second husband, Balian of Ibelin, his brother Baldwin, Raymond III, count of Tripoli, whose wife had inherited the lordship of Tiberias, and a number of other leading barons. It is clear that personal rivalry played a major role in the formation of these factions – it is difficult to imagine Agnes and Maria having any mutual affection – but it is also broadly true that Agnes's was a 'court party' made up of her kinsmen and a group of *curiales* and newcomers to the East, while their opponents were largely the party of the old-established aristocracy.

It was impossible for any one in public life to remain neutral in these disputes, and William in the *Historia* showed a clear preference for the faction of Maria Comnena and Count Raymond of Tripoli. As a curial servant in King Amaury's reign, it might be thought that his connections would incline him to sympathize with the court faction, especially since in the *Historia* he was at pains to defend Baldwin's rights to exercise kingly office. But in fact he did not do so. Various reasons why he took sides against Agnes and her faction can be suggested. Although a *curialis*, William's period of royal service under Amaury coincided with the years of the king's marriage to Maria, and so Agnes would have been a distant figure. Similarly, he can have had no contact at all with her leading supporters, Joscelin of Edessa and Raynald of Châtillon, since they had both languished in Muslim captivity for virtually the whole of Amaury's reign. It would also seem that he had been a supporter of the idea that Jerusalem needed to ally with Byzantium, in which case he would have had a natural rapport with Maria Comnena. But a far more compelling explanation of why his sympathies belonged where they did is provided by the simple fact that Raymond of Tripoli, who had managed to get himself accepted as regent of Jerusalem during Baldwin IV's minority within a few months of Amaury's death, took him under his wing and brought him considerable advancement.

Towards the end of 1174 Raymond, 'with the advice of his *principes*', appointed William to the office of chancellor, which had recently fallen vacant.[19] Further and final promotion followed in May or June 1175, when he was elected archbishop of Tyre. Here

[19] *WT*, XXI, 5, lines 63–7. The Latin text leaves no doubt that it was Raymond and not Baldwin who made the appointment (contrary to B/K, II, 404). The first charter issued under William's name to survive is dated 13 Dec. 1174 (*RRH*, no. 518). He is there described as archdeacon of Nazareth as well as archdeacon of Tyre.

again, although William was to write only of election by the clergy and people followed by the formal royal ratification,[20] we can presumably see the hand of Raymond of Tripoli, who as regent would have wielded such influence as the king normally had in senior church appointments. As chancellor William had charge of the royal writing office, being responsible for the drafting of the king's written *acta* and official correspondence. As archbishop of Tyre he ranked second only to the patriarch of Jerusalem in the ecclesiastical hierarchy of the kingdom. He combined both offices from 1175 until at least as late as 1184, the date at which he was making his last additions to the *Historia*.

Despite his high office we should be wary of assuming that William was deeply involved in the secular politics and decision-making processes of government during these years. In 1177 he evidently had a role in the abortive negotiations with Count Philip of Flanders over the regency of Jerusalem and with the Byzantines for further joint military action against the Muslims, and in 1180 he appears to have acted in some capacity on behalf of the emperor Manuel in his dealings with the principality of Antioch.[21] But otherwise his diplomatic experience seems not to have been drawn upon. From 1177 until 1183 Raymond of Tripoli's rivals held the reins of government, and William's political position may have diminished as a direct consequence. Certainly he was not present for the important decision taken in the first half of 1183 to give Guy of Lusignan viceregal powers,[22] and it is generally assumed that it was his association with Raymond and the fact that Agnes of Courtenay was dominant at court that prevented William obtaining for himself the patriarchate of Jerusalem in 1180.[23] True he held the office of chancellor throughout this period, but the evidence of the surviving royal diplomas suggests that this position was not particularly onerous. Those from the years 1175, 1176 and 1177 indicate that he was not directly involved in their drafting but that his duties as chancellor were being performed by deputies.[24] After the latter part of 1177 all the charters to survive from Baldwin's reign bear William's name as chancellor, but it is not clear that he was responsible for these either. From October 1178 until July 1180 he

[20] *WT*, xxi, 8, lines 75–81.
[21] *WT*, xxi, 13–17 *passim*; xxii, 4, lines 56–8.
[22] *WT*, xxii, 26, lines 24–36 *passim*. But in Feb. 1183 he had been given responsibilities as a receiver of taxes (*WT*, xxii, 24, lines 4–5).
[23] Edbury and Rowe, 'Patriarchal Election', pp. 18–25 *passim*.
[24] *RRH*, nos 525, 537, 538, 552. See Hiestand, 'Zum Leben', p. 356.

was absent from the Latin kingdom attending the Third Lateran Council, yet several diplomas belonging to this period survive. Unless he superintended their drafting after his return, dating them retrospectively, the inference must be that during his absence the chancery operated without him, albeit using his name.[25] In the Prologue to the *Historia* William referred to the burdens of the office of chancellor, but they may not have been as great as his readers might imagine.[26]

Much of what William himself recorded about his career after he became archbishop suggests that he concentrated his energies on church affairs. He consecrated suffragan bishops to vacancies within his province, conducted the funeral of the king's brother-in-law, William of Montferrat, attended the Third Lateran Council and built up the library of his cathedral church.[27] At Christmas 1182 he entertained King Baldwin at Tyre, and this example of hospitality, together with the fact that earlier that same year the king had made a grant of tithes to his archbishopric, suggests that the two men continued to enjoy amicable relations.[28]

But it is precisely at this point in William's career that we move into uncertain terrain. His last mention in a royal diploma as chancellor is dated March 1183; in 1184, when he wrote the last parts of the *Historia*, he made it clear that he was still archbishop and chancellor, but by 10 May 1185 Peter, archdeacon of Lydda, had become chancellor, and by 26 October 1186 Archbishop Joscius had succeeded him at Tyre.[29] So much is certain. A later writer asserted that William was excommunicated one Maundy Thursday by Patriarch Eraclius, his successful rival for the patriarchal chair in 1180; that he appealed to Rome and was poisoned at Eraclius' bidding. Allegations of poisoning rarely deserve credence, and perhaps the entire story should be rejected out of hand as the invention of someone out to blacken Eraclius' memory. But it may contain a kernel of truth even if it is overlaid by a measure of fanciful distortion. If indeed William was excommunicated towards the end of his life, a date before 1183 is improbable, since he continued to

---

[25] For the period of William's absence, see *WT*, XXI, 25, lines 1–5; XXII, 4, lines 58–62. The charters dated to this period are *RRH*, nos. 562, 577, 579, 582, 587, 588, 591, 593. But see *WT*, XXII, 5, lines 17–18, where William's personal involvement in the routine of chancery (*c.* 1180) is indicated.

[26] *WT*, Prologue, lines 106–12.

[27] *WT*, XXI, 10, lines 62–6; 12, lines 36–8; 25; XXII, 7, lines 60–3.

[28] *RRH*, no. 615; *WT*, XXII, 23, lines 45–8.

[29] *RRH*, nos. 625, 643, 653; *WT*, Prologue, lines 106–12.

function as chancellor and archbishop. Maundy Thursday 1185 is ruled out as Eraclius was then in the West, and 1184 and 1186 are both unlikely as William's patron, Raymond of Tripoli, was then in control of the kingdom. Thus, by a process of elimination, it would appear that the most plausible year would seem to be 1183 when Maundy Thursday fell on 14 April. But why? Allegedly William had spoken out against the patriarch's unsavoury personal reputation – he was said to keep a mistress and also to be the lover of the queen-mother – but this was supposedly common knowledge anyway and so would seem insufficient reason in itself. The most obvious explanation is that the excommunication was a political act directed against a protégé of Raymond of Tripoli. If Eraclius' election as patriarch in preference to William in 1180 was the direct result of the patronage of Agnes of Courtenay, William's excommunication, if it occurred at all, might be regarded as a piece of deliberate victimization emanating from Agnes, Eraclius and their circle against a well-placed man in their opponents' camp. Indeed, the excommunication could be seen as coinciding with an increase in the control exercised by William's enemies and signalled by the appointment early in 1183 of Guy of Lusignan to be regent for the now incapacitated king.[30]

The story of the excommunication raises an important question in interpreting William's career. If it is accepted, then it follows either that his political influence in the time of Baldwin IV was considerable, sufficient to warrant the attack, or at least that his enemies saw him as posing a threat to themselves. But if it is rejected, the remaining evidence for his participation in political affairs would indicate that he played only the modest, indirect role already outlined. In this case the question then arises as to whether he chose to concentrate on his duties as archbishop and on his writing and take only a small part in politics and diplomacy, or whether his apparent absence from the political forefront for much of Baldwin's reign was dictated by Agnes and her supporters during their period of ascendancy. The self-evidently garbled account of the excommunication, William's own reticence and the absence of other sources for his activities in these years make it impossible to resolve these problems with any degree of certainty. But the frequent assumption that he was consigned to a 'political wilderness' by the opponents of Raymond of Tripoli is not necessarily correct. Eraclius' appointment as patriarch in preference to him need not be

---

[30] Edbury and Rowe, 'Patriarchal Election', pp. 5, 7–11.

seen as having had any sinister overtones: it could be that at the time he was simply regarded by the court as being the stronger candidate. Nor is there any need to conclude that William failed to obtain the patriarchate because he supported the 'wrong' party or that he was generally cold-shouldered by those in power.

These are intractable difficulties. The same sort of problem surrounds the date of William's death. Clearly he had died before 21 October 1186, when his successor as archbishop was already installed, but did he die before 10 May 1185, when his successor as chancellor first appears, or was he relieved of his post during his lifetime? If he was replaced as chancellor before his death, this too might perhaps be seen as evidence that his career in public life was curtailed. We do not know. Professor Hiestand has drawn attention to an obit which gives William's death as occurring on 29 September.[31] But 29 September of which year? There is no certain evidence showing him alive beyond the early part of 1184, and so 1184, 1185 and 1186 are all technically possible. 29 September 1186 is unlikely, since this would mean that his successor was elected, confirmed and enthroned within the space of three weeks. For what it is worth, an obviously muddled statement in the excommunication story suggests that William died while Eraclius was in the West. Eraclius did visit Europe between mid-1184 and mid-1185, and so this could be a pointer to 1184 being the year of William's demise.[32] If so, he died on 29 September 1184, presumably retaining the chancellorship until the end. But, in the absence of further evidence, this question too must be left undecided.[33] It is a measure of the value of his writings to modern scholars that, although biographical details of many laymen and clerics are known thanks to his recording them, William found no clerical historian of comparable stature to succeed him, and so the year of his own death is unrecorded and remains uncertain.

[31] Hiestand, 'Zum Leben', p. 351 *et passim*.
[32] Edbury and Rowe, 'Patriarchal Election', pp. 10–11.
[33] Mayer ('Zum Tode') argued on the basis of a document dated 17 Oct. 1186 (*RRH Additamentum*, p. 44) that William died in 1186. His view has since been refined by Hiestand ('Zum Leben') and, following him, by B. Hamilton (*The Latin Church in the Crusader States: The Secular Church* (London, 1980), pp. 81–2), who believe he died on 29 Sept. 1186. However, Hamilton (p. 81 note 4), rightly in our opinion, has questioned the validity of the 1186 document, apparently without realizing that, as B. Z. Kedar ('The Patriarch Eraclius', in B. Z. Kedar, H. E. Mayer and R. C. Smail (eds.), *Outremer: Studies in the History of the Crusading Kingdom of Jerusalem* (Jerusalem, 1982), p. 181 note 9) has pointed out, the case for 1186 hinges on it. The effect of rejecting this piece of evidence is to re-open the possibility that William died in 1184 or 1185.

Chapter 2

WILLIAM'S HISTORICAL WRITINGS

Besides the *Historia*, William informs us that he had written two other works: an account of the decrees of the Third Lateran Council of 1179, with a list of participants, and a history of the Muslim world perhaps entitled *Gesta orientalium principum*. Both are now lost. William claimed that he wrote his account of the Lateran Council at the request of the other clergy present on that occasion, and he referred his readers to a copy in the cathedral archive at Tyre.[1] The Muslim history was said to have been written at the behest of King Amaury, who had enabled him to carry out his task by providing him with copies of Arabic historical writings including one by the tenth-century patriarch of Alexandria, Sa'īd ibn Baṭrīk. William alluded to this other work of his no fewer than five times in the *Historia*, making it clear that in it he had covered the entire span of Muslim history from the time of Muhammad down to his own day. He made contradictory statements about the date at which it ended: twice he stated that it stopped in the year 570 A.H. (i.e. 1174/5), but he wrongly gave the equivalent year of the Christian era as, on one occasion, 1182 and, on the other, 1184; on a third occasion he said that the work ended in 577 A.H., which he correctly identified as A.D. 1181. This confusion can be explained by assuming that he added to the work from time to time to bring it up to date and failed to make adequate corrections to his allusions to it in the *Historia*, on which he was evidently working simultane-

---

[1] *WT*, XXI, 25, lines 73–9. See Huygens, 'Tradition manuscrite', p. 283 note 4. William was almost certainly also responsible for a passage of commentary contained in the *Ordinatio sedum*, a list of bishoprics in the patriarchates of Antioch and Jerusalem evidently derived from a much earlier Byzantine list. This document is contained in a number of manuscripts of the *Historia* and is printed in *RHC Occ*, I, 1135–7. See Huygens, 'Tradition manuscrite', p. 285. Note the use of the phrase 'Dei cultrix civitas' (at p. 1136, lines 13–14) to denote Jerusalem, and the appearance of the same phrase in the *Historia*, I, 3, line 49; VIII, 4, line 1.

ously.[2] The *Gesta orientalium principum* was known to James of Vitry and also, so it has been suggested, to the later thirteenth-century Dominican writer, William of Tripoli. Matthew Paris had access to a copy at St Albans but appears not to have drawn material from it for his own historical writings. Compared to the *Historia* it was a failure: to the best of our knowledge, after the second half of the thirteenth century no one read it. As Professor R. H. C. Davis has aptly commented, to Christians in medieval Europe 'crusades were interesting, but Muslims were not'.[3]

William's one extant work of scholarship is the *Historia Ierosoly-mitana*. In three places he recorded that it too was written at the suggestion or command of his patron, King Amaury, and, by way of adding colour to this assertion, he noted elsewhere that Amaury in common with Baldwin III and Baldwin IV had had historical interests.[4] In recording the king's involvement William was no doubt hoping to bolster the reputation of his work and provide himself with a pretext for writing; he may also have wanted to remind those of his readers who were aware of the bitter in-fighting of Baldwin IV's reign that his own credentials dated from what would by then have seemed the relatively untroubled days of Baldwin's predecessor. One commentator, however, has called in question the extent to which Amaury can be said to have commissioned the *Historia*, pointing out that the assertion that a work was composed in obedience to the command of someone in a position of authority was a commonplace medieval literary convention. The king could well have encouraged William to write both the *Historia* and the *Gesta orientalium principum* and may well have been so pressing in his encouragement that William viewed it as being tantamount to a command. But to go further and suggest as some have done that Amaury's commission was bound up with William's promotion to the archdeaconry of Tyre in 1167, or that his original brief had been to write simply a history of Amaury's own reign, is to strain the available evidence too far. The idea that the king shared the intellectual pleasures of historical enquiry may too be no more

[2] *WT*, Prologue, lines 85–7 (570 A.H. = 1184 A.D.); I, 1, lines 31–8; 3, lines 50–5 (570 A.H. = 1182 A.D.); XIX, 15, lines 37–40; 21, lines 55–61 (577 A.H. = 1181 A.D.).

[3] Davis, 'William of Tyre', p. 71. For further discussion and references, see Huygens, 'Tradition manuscrite', pp. 322–3, 333–4; Schwinges, *Kreuzzugsideologie*, pp. 41–2, 108–10; H. Möhring, 'Zu der Geschichte der orientalischen Herrscher des Wilhelm von Tyrus', *Mittellateinisches Jahrbuch*, XIX (1984), 170–83.

[4] *WT*, Prologue, lines 80–4; XIX, 12, lines 75–9; XX, 31, lines 42–3. For the kings' interest in history, see *WT*, XVI, 2, lines 16–18; XIX, 2, lines 17–18; XXI, 1, lines 50–1.

than one element in a series of rhetorical exercises in which William characterized the kings in imitation of Einhard's characterization of Charlemagne.[5] But just because William followed established literary conventions is no reason in itself for doubting the truthfulness of his statements.

In fact the question of whether or not William started work in response to a royal command is largely irrelevant, since the *Historia* in the form in which it survives is in no sense an 'official' history of the Latin East. He completed it a decade after Amaury's death and addressed it not to the king or members of the royal family but to his 'venerable brothers in Christ', his fellow-prelates of the Church.[6] It is true that he showed himself to be an upholder of the principles of monarchical government and hereditary right and was anxious to give a generally favourable impression of the achievements of the royal house of Jerusalem. But the *Historia* contains criticism of the kings, both direct and implied, and indeed his patron, King Amaury, emerges from its pages as perhaps the least attractive of the dynasty.[7] As we shall see when we come to examine William's motivation and message, his task was one not simply of flattering the dynasty, but of presenting a favourable portrait of the Latin East to his readers and of seeking to understand the current misfortunes of the Latin East by delving into its history. In the Prologue to the whole work, written in 1184, he stated that it had been love of his native land that had prompted him to write, and he expatiated on this theme at some length before mentioning Amaury's commission.[8] In another passage he indicated that he himself had conceived the idea of recording past events, a remark which may in fact be nearer the truth.

1169, the year of the unsuccessful joint expedition with the Byzantines against Egypt, saw William in Rome. At the end of his account of that campaign he explained that on his return to the East he made careful enquiries as to what had happened and how this setback had come about, for, as he put it, 'We had already decided to commit all these things to writing.'[9] This would seem to indicate that his vocation as a historian dated from before 1170, and also that it was William himself who had taken the decision to write. There is nothing in this passage to suggest that he was at work on a commis-

[5] Vessey, 'William of Tyre', pp. 436–9.
[6] For the salutation, see *WT*, Prologue, p. 97.
[7] See below, pp. 75–6.   [8] *WT*, Prologue, lines 66–80.
[9] *WT*, xx, 17, lines 38–9.

sion. Exactly when he had started and whether he had always intended to write a full-length history of the Latin East from the time of the First Crusade are questions which admit no definite answers. But beginning with his account of the year 1167, the year of Amaury's victorious Egyptian campaign, the narrative is far more detailed and far better informed than it had been for the earlier years of his reign; and there can be little doubt that it was with that campaign, and so within a short time of his return from the West in 1165, that William had begun to assemble information and take note of contemporary events.

William worked on the *Historia* from about 1170 until 1184, the year to which the preface and the sole chapter of Book XXIII evidently belong and the year in which, as he himself recorded, he wrote the Prologue.[10] Throughout this period he was involved in secular and ecclesiastical affairs, and it is reasonable to assume that the writing of the *Historia* was of secondary concern to him and proceeded intermittently. No doubt as time wore on his outlook on events and institutions shifted: his changing attitude to the Byzantine empire provides a clear case of how events in train while he was writing modified his perception.

In so large a work, composed over the course of a number of years, it comes as no surprise to find on close examination flaws and unevenness. Chronology is sometimes confused and dates are given wrongly; thus historians have long recognized that many of the accession dates William supplied for the kings of Jerusalem and their regnal years are inaccurate.[11] In places the connection between events described is inadequately explained. What, for example, was William doing in Constantinople during the winter of 1179–80, and why did he then travel to Antioch at the emperor's behest? He noted his journeyings but made no attempt to set them in context.[12] There are also abrupt changes in tempo, the most dramatic being the sudden switch to detailed narrative for the Egyptian campaign of 1167 (occupying eighteen chapters in Book XIX) after the extremely sketchy reporting of the events of the previous four years. William clearly subjected the work to revisions, some of which proved more effective than others, but his insertions, especially the documentation relating to the ecclesiastical province of Tyre in Book XIV, are

[10] *WT*, Prologue, lines 85–6.

[11] For the classic discussions of this point, see Archer, 'Accession Dates', pp. 91–105; Stevenson, *Crusaders in the East*, pp. 361–71.

[12] *WT*, XXII, 4. William's silence is made all the more tantalizing since he had evidently travelled to Constantinople direct from the Third Lateran Council.

sometimes clumsy. What is remarkable – and this is testimony to his mastery of the craft of historical writing – is that these blemishes and inconsistencies are not far more numerous.

The fact that there are blemishes and inconsistencies preserved in the text as it has come down to us allows us to detect something of how William set about writing and how, over the years, his own vision as a historian developed. But only to a limited extent. What they do not do is give much indication of how rapidly his composition of the *Historia* progressed or when precisely he wrote a particular passage. In the years 1181–2 he introduced fresh material in the course of his revisions. The problem, however, remains that, whereas a number of the alterations and insertions made at that time can be identified with some degree of confidence, it is by no means always clear where they begin and the original drafting ends, and so the task of dating the surrounding material is made all the more difficult. It is therefore hazardous to attempt to link William's understanding of past events with specific incidents in his own day which could have had a bearing on his writing.

However, various scholars, in particular Prutz and Krey, have noted anachronisms in the narrative which allow for some tentative hypotheses about William's progress in working on the *Historia* to be put forward. One suggestion is that his account of King Amaury's Egyptian campaign of 1167 was one of the first sections to be written. In support of this contention is the fact that his account is disproportionately detailed by comparison with those of the campaigns of 1163 and 1164, although this feature may signify no more than that William had returned to the East in the meantime and was now noting current events. Perhaps more telling is a remark in the course of the description of the 1167 campaign which seems to indicate that the Fatimid caliphate, suppressed in 1171, was still in existence at the time of writing, thus making the original version of this section very nearly contemporary with the events themselves.[13] The idea that the Fatimid caliphate was still in existence is also implied in the preliminary material at the beginning of Book I, although here the question is complicated by a further hypothesis that the passage in question has been lifted out of the *Gesta orientalium principum*.[14] Writing of the events of 1116, William

---

[13] *WT*, XIX, 21, lines 52–5. See Krey, 'William of Tyre', p. 154 note 2. For another passage perhaps suggesting that the Fatimid caliphate was still in existence, see *WT*, IV, 24, lines 3–7.

[14] *WT*, I, 4, lines 2–7.

stated that from that date until the present the Sicilian Normans had done nothing to succour the Latin East; it may well be that this passage was written before 1174, when, as he himself records, a Sicilian fleet attacked Egypt.[15] In the course of the narrative for the year 1124 he mentioned the constable, Humphrey of Toron, who died in 1179, in a way which perhaps implies he was still alive.[16] These clues, slender in themselves, point to him having drafted large sections of the *Historia* before his departure to the West in 1178 for the Third Lateran Council and his absence from the Latin East for almost two years.

In the period immediately after his return to Jerusalem in 1180, William resumed writing and made extensive revisions to his existing draft. He appears to have reworked the opening chapters of Book 1, drawing material from his Muslim history for this purpose, and it may be that he inserted other passages concerned with the Islamic background to his narrative at that time.[17] He also seems to have introduced a number of sections dealing with purely ecclesiastical matters. Apropos the death of the previous archbishop in 1158, he noted that the present holder of the see of Nazareth, Letard, was now in the twenty-third year of office; elsewhere he stated that he himself had now been archbishop of Tyre for six years. Both statements point to the passages in question as having been written in 1181.[18] Writing of King Amaury's divorce in 1163, William mentioned Patriarch Amaury 'of good memory' – a sure sign that this passage too was written or at least revised after the latter's death in 1180.[19] In addition there are a number of other, less clear-cut examples of indications that William was inserting material of ecclesiastical interest at about this time: when he came to write of the papal schism of 1159, he was aware that it was now at an end – he was thus giving this episode his attention after 1177;[20] in passages dealing with the ecclesiastical history of his own archbishopric in the 1120s and 1130s he made it clear that he himself was the present archbishop – they thus belong to a date after 1175.[21]

---

[15] *WT*, XI, 29, lines 31–40; cf. XXI, 3, lines 1–8. See B/K, I, 514 note 99.

[16] *WT*, XIII, 13, lines 46–8; cf. XXI, 26, lines 35–44. See B/K, II, 19–20 and note 30.

[17] Krey, 'William of Tyre', pp. 159 note 1, 160; B/K, I, 61 note 4, 71 note 29. William specifically mentioned the date of writing I, 3, lines 52–3 as 1182 and of XIX, 21, lines 58–9 as 1181.

[18] *WT*, XVIII, 22, lines 5–8; XXI, 25, lines 77–8.

[19] *WT*, XIX, 4, lines 13–14. *WT*, XXI, 11, dealing with Manuel Comnenus' defeat at Myriokephalon in 1176, was written after the emperor's death, also in 1180.

[20] *WT*, XVIII, 26, lines 17–22; cf. XXI, 24, lines 44–6.

[21] *WT*, XIII, 23, lines 20–1; XIV, 11, line 18; cf. XIX, 25, lines 54–6.

Almost certainly William inserted all the material on the problems which had beset his see since the beginning of the twelfth century in the years after 1180, and he may well have included other ecclesiastical material such as Baldwin I's foundation charter for the see of Bethlehem at the same time.[22] Maybe some of the topographical descriptions of the cities and the character sketches of the various rulers and princes were also composed at this stage, and it has been suggested that the autobiographical chapter describing his studies in the West belongs to the early 1180s as well.[23]

A simple explanation as to why he should have revised his work in the way he did at this period readily presents itself. What had happened at the Lateran Council was that he had met his counterparts among the higher clergy of western Europe, and, as a result of his experiences there and the conversations he would have had, his conception of his purpose in writing and his appreciation of his potential audience had greatly increased. He now hoped that these westerners would read the *Historia*: they were clearly included among the 'venerabiles fratres' to whom it was addressed. William had discovered what they needed to be told about the Latin East and he also knew what sort of things would hold their interest – local ecclesiastical politics being prominent among them.

By the time he came to write up the events of Baldwin IV's reign, the *Historia* was becoming a record of contemporary developments, and his descriptions have an immediacy which testify to this fact. The final chapter of Book XXII takes the narrative down to a point late in 1183. Book XXIII consists of a single chapter containing an account of events which apparently belong to the early part of 1184, together with a full-length preface. The gist of this preface is that the fortunes of the Latin East were in such a parlous state that William had decided to give up writing about them but was nevertheless persuaded to continue, fortified by the example of the ancient historians Livy and Josephus. It is an extravagant exercise in rhetoric. Certainly it is not to be accepted at face value; rather, it should be seen as an attempt to confront the reader as forcibly as possible with the message that the Latin East was in dire straits. Perhaps significantly the chapter that follows related the replacement of Guy of Lusignan as regent by William's patron, Raymond of Tripoli, and it ends on an optimistic note, now that the man whom William would have his readers believe was the most capable figure in the kingdom had taken charge; the kingdom had

---

[22] *WT*, XI, 12.   [23] Huygens, 'Guillaume de Tyr', pp. 819–20.

been in peril, but thanks to Raymond's presence the potential for recovery and salvation was still there.

Why then does the *Historia* stop at this point, so soon after the beginning of a new book? It could be that William, who wrote in the Prologue that he had divided it into twenty-three books, had in fact completed Book XXIII but that some folios had become detached from the end of his autograph manuscript and their contents lost for ever.[24] We, however, incline to a different view. William had stopped writing because there was no more to write; he was up to date. His plan, as outlined at the end of the preface to Book XXIII and repeated in the Prologue, was that for as long as his life should allow he would attend diligently to committing to writing whatever future times would bring.[25] In other words, having dealt with time past, he would continue to write his history as events occurred, adding to it from time to time for as long as he was able. As it happened he was not to add any more. But it was at this point, in 1184, that he wrote the Prologue to the *Historia*, echoing within it the high-flown rhetoric, though not the sentiment, of the preface to Book XXIII.

The *Historia Ierosolymitana* is thus complete in the sense that when William laid down his pen there was nothing more he then wished to record, incomplete in the sense that he intended to go on writing. But his achievement is impressive, and the work as it stands possesses a clear organizational scheme. The first eight books deal with the history of the First Crusade. Thereafter the work is divided by reign: each king of Jerusalem being allotted two books except the uncrowned Godfrey of Bouillon, who is given one; Baldwin III, whose twenty-year reign (1143–63) was the longest of any of the twelfth-century kings, who is given three; and Baldwin IV, who is given two plus what little there is of Book XXIII. Book XI covers the longest span, fourteen years; most of the others cover between five and eight years. Taken as a whole, the narrative of the years 1099–1184 is remarkably evenly spaced. The account of the period from 1165, when William himself was living in the East, is not given in appreciably greater detail – the years 1167 and 1168 are the exception – nor is it disproportionately expansive. There is unevenness; there are places where William seems to be spinning

---

[24] Huygens, 'Tradition manuscrite', pp. 313–14. But see *WT*, p. 34 note 64.
[25] *WT*, XXIII, preface, lines 50–2: 'que subsequentia ministrabunt tempora . . . vita comite, scripto mandare curabimus diligenter'. Cf. *WT*, Prologue, lines 118–25. See also Hiestand, 'Zum Leben', pp. 368–9.

out inadequate information; there are periods for which his narrative is unaccountably thin; there are clumsily executed insertions; but there is much that stands in its own right as polished twelfth-century historical writing at its best.

Chapter 3

CLASSICAL AND CHRISTIAN
INFLUENCES IN THE *HISTORIA*

Even if the autobiographical chapter in which William described his studies in western Europe had remained lost to view, there would be no questioning the nature of his educational background. The *Historia* itself provides ample testimony to the breadth of his learning and to the influences which bore upon him. In the light of his long sojourn in the Schools of the West it comes as no surprise to find evidence throughout his work of his indebtedness to the authors of pagan antiquity and the earlier Christian centuries, whether in his choice of words and his use of quotations, in the information he wished to impart, or indeed in the form and genre of his historical writing itself.

In a masterly fashion his modern editor has provided us with a scholarly apparatus, identifying the sources of his quotations and classical allusions and also drawing attention to a large number of instances in which his phraseology is reminiscent of those ancient or Christian writers whose works were widely read and admired in the twelfth century. Frequently, as we might expect from an educated churchman, William quoted the Vulgate version of the Bible or used expressions which call to mind phrases from it, and he also echoed the wording of the liturgy.[1] The list of pagan authors Professor Huygens has noted as providing the origins for other verbal echoes is long – Plautus, Terence, Cicero, Sallust, Virgil, Horace, Livy, Ovid, Quintilian, Statius, Persius, Lucan, Juvenal and Suetonius – as is the list of Christian writers – Jerome, Augustine, Orosius, Prudentius, Sulpicius Severus, Boethius, Benedict of Nursia, Cassiodorus, Gregory the Great and Einhard.[2] William's legal grounding too is indicated by the inclusion from time to time

---

[1] For examples of liturgical phrases, see *WT*, 1, 12, line 22; 13, line 14; 15, line 3.
[2] For references, see *WT*, Index général.

of phrases culled from the principal texts of civil law.[3] But the use of these literary allusions and the occasional quotation testifies not so much to any particular erudition as to his general literacy. Many of these allusions and quotations were probably drawn sub-consciously from his reading, especially if they belonged to those passages he had committed to memory as part of his education. In some instances he may have known the lines concerned only at second hand – perhaps, for example, thanks to their inclusion among the *exempla* of the grammarians he would have studied in his youth. Indeed, a quotation from a pagan or Christian author, or even the mention of an author by name, cannot in itself be regarded as proof that a writer in the middle ages had any direct acquaintance with the work concerned. Many medieval writers cited ancient authors at second or third hand while creating the illusion that they had first-hand familiarity with them, and William was no excep-tion. On one occasion he referred grandiloquently to 'our Aris-totle', but his phraseology gives him away, and it is clear that he was simply adapting a passage from Boethius.[4] Elsewhere he men-tioned Lucan, 'the distinguished *prosecutor* of the civil war', and repeated two lines of his, but this was in a section where he had derived his information from the *Etymologiae* of Isidore of Seville, who in his turn had both named the poet and quoted these same lines.[5]

Taking the *Historia* as a whole, specific references to the pagan authors of classical antiquity are few. Apart from Aristotle and Lucan, William mentioned Cicero, Virgil, Horace, Livy, Ovid, Juvenal and also Plato (whose *Timaeus* he knew from Calcidius' Latin translation), and he correctly ascribed individual quotations to Book I of Virgil's *Aeneid* and to Ovid's *Metamorphoses* and *Hero-ides*.[6] But more commonly lines are quoted without attribution, in such a way as to suggest that they formed part of his general know-ledge rather than that he had a close familiarity with the authors' works. For example, he quoted lines from Terence, Sallust, Horace and Ovid, describing them as proverbs, and it may be wondered

---

[3] For references, see *WT*, Index général, s.v. *iuridica*.
[4] *WT*, XXI, 7, lines 40–1.
[5] *WT*, XIII, 1, lines 21–4; cf. apparatus to lines 13–27.
[6] *WT*, Prologue, lines 23–6; cf. lines 42–6 (Cicero); XVI, preface, lines 14–18 (Horace); XXIII, preface, line 36 (Livy); VII, 1, lines 22–4 (Juvenal); XIX, 24, lines 29–36 (Plato). For Virgil, see XIII, 1, lines 33–5 (*Aeneid*); XX, 2, lines 7–8. For Ovid, see IV, 10, lines 28–34 (*Metamorphoses*); XV, 16, lines 28–30; XVI, 24, lines 8–11 (*Heroides*); XX, 23, lines 15–16.

how far he was aware of their actual origin.[7] Normally he introduced classical quotations simply to embellish the text rather than to furnish information, although on occasion he drew on both Ovid and Plato for specific points.[8]

On the other hand he did make use of the factual material to be gleaned from post-classical and Christian writers. In several places he cited Ulpian's chapter 'De censibus' from the *Digest* for historical or topographical data,[9] and he also named Bede (the *De locis sanctis*), Eusebius (whose work he knew from Rufinus' translation), Hegesippus, Jerome and Orosius as authorities for other pieces of information.[10] Four sources in particular provided him with material, and he incorporated extended passages from each into the *Historia*: Josephus' *Antiquitates Iudaicae* he knew from the Latin translation made in the circle of Cassiodorus in the late sixth century;[11] the third-century Roman geographer Solinus, an author widely used in the middle ages, he quoted or alluded to on a number of occasions;[12] the *Historia tripartita*, a work compiled by Cassiodorus from the Greek historians Socrates, Sozomenus and Theodoretus, and translated into Latin by Epiphanius in the sixth century, also finds a place in William's *Historia*,[13] as does Einhard's *Vita Caroli*, which he used when describing Charlemagne's relations with Hārūn al-Rashīd and his concern for the Christians in the East.[14] In quoting these works William demonstrated that he stood in the mainstream of medieval historical endeavour. Cassiodorus had set the tone in recommending, among others, Josephus, Eusebius and Rufinus, the *Historia tripartita* and Orosius as suitable Christian reading, and his list maintained a lasting influence throughout the middle ages. Indeed, Orosius, Josephus, the *Historia tripartita* and also Einhard were

---

[7] *WT*, Prologue, line 18; VII, 24, lines 50–1; XIV, 6, lines 10–11; XVIII, 10, lines 43–4; XX, 15, lines 48–9; XXII, 26, lines 45–6; cf. XV, 16, lines 28–30.

[8] *WT*, IV, 10, lines 28–34; XVI, 24, lines 8–11; XIX, 24, lines 26–36.

[9] *WT*, X, 22, lines 24–6; XI, 13, lines 10–14; XIII, 1, lines 1–9; XXI, 10, lines 21–3.

[10] *WT*, XIII, 18, lines 20–7 (Bede); IV, 2, lines 15–20; XVI, 5, lines 36–45 (Eusebius); cf. IV, 10, lines 57–62 (a quotation from Rufinus' continuation of Eusebius); VIII, 2, lines 18–23 (Hegesippus); IV, 10, lines 17–18; VIII, 9, lines 16–19; XIII, 1, lines 84–7 (Jerome); II, 7, lines 38–42 (Orosius).

[11] *WT*, XIII, 1, lines 65–79; 4, lines 16–48; XIV, 22, lines 39–44. Cf. VIII, 2, line 18; XXIII, preface, line 38, and Index général, s.n. Iosephus. William was evidently more familiar with the *Antiquitates* than with the *Bellum Judaicum*.

[12] *WT*, II, 7, lines 15–24; III, 20, lines 16–20; IV, 10, lines 35–40, 66–73; VIII, 4, lines 29–31, 55–60; 9, lines 6–15; cf. XIX, 18, lines 35–6; 27, lines 8–13; 31, lines 16–20. For Solinus' popularity in the middle ages, see B. Guenée, *Histoire et culture historique dans l'Occident médiéval* (Paris, 1980), pp. 168–9, 303.

[13] *WT*, IV, 10, lines 52–6; VII, 24, lines 8–18.   [14] *WT*, I, 3, lines 21–34, 38–47.

evidently among the most widely read historians, to judge by the number of surviving medieval manuscripts, and by the same token it would seem that in the twelfth century they were as popular as ever.[15]

In view of the length of the *Historia*, the number of direct citations from ancient or Christian authors is not particularly large. Many of the references are concentrated into particular passages, and so only rarely can William be accused to trying to dazzle his readers with the virtuoso display of learning. Still less was he adopting a style of writing which comprised a pastiche of phrases and passages culled from his favourite ancient authors. What we have is an educated churchman sharing with his peers their common intellectual background. There was nothing unusual about the choice of reading-matter, and many of his allusions were, as he said, proverbs or sayings. In fact some of these twelfth-century clichés, for example, 'quot homines, tot sententiae' and 'timeo Danaos et dona ferentes', have continued to be sufficiently commonplace to find their way into modern dictionaries of quotations.[16] There are, however, a few places in which, in marked contrast to the *Historia* as a whole, he did indulge in some self-conscious erudition, notably in the Prologue, the preface to Book XXIII and the various descriptions of towns and cities.

At suitable points in the narrative, he provided accounts of the location and history of the cities of the East,[17] three of the most notable being those of Jerusalem, Antioch and Tyre. The description of Jerusalem comes at the beginning of his account of the siege of 1099 and consists of a description of the Holy Places, with a large number of biblical references to its history; William cites Hegesip-

---

[15] See Guenée, *Histoire et culture*, pp. 250, 271–3, 301–3. The contents of William's own library in Tyre are unknown. An undated catalogue of a library which is probably that of the Augustinian chapter of Nazareth (where William had for a short time been archdeacon) survives (J. S. Beddie, 'Some Notices of Books in the East in the Period of the Crusades', *Speculum*, VIII (1933), 240–1). It contained, besides biblical commentaries and theological works, a number of pagan authors including Cicero (the *De amicitia*), Virgil, Horace, Ovid, Persius, Statius, Lucan and Juvenal. See H. E. Mayer, 'Das Pontifikale von Tyrus und die Krönung der lateinischen Könige von Jerusalem', *Dumbarton Oaks Papers*, XXI (1967), 144; Schwinges, *Kreuzzugsideologie*, p. 63.

[16] For examples, see *WT*, IX, 1, lines 35–7; XIV, 6, lines 10–11; XV, 16, lines 28–30; XVIII, 10, lines 43–4; XX, 15, lines 48–9; XXII, 26, lines 45–6.

[17] For a discussion of the genre and William's descriptive techniques, see Giese, 'Stadt- und Herrscherbeschreibungen', pp. 383–96, and, more generally, P. Kletler, 'Die Gestaltung des geographischen Weltbildes unter dem Einfluß der Kreuzzüge', *Mitteilungen des österreichischen Instituts für Geschichtsforschung*, LXX (1962), 294–322.

pus and Josephus for the destruction by Titus, the canons of the First Council of Nicaea for the continued use of the Roman name Aelia, and Solinus, whose statement that Judaea was renowned for its waters he contradicted, no doubt on the strength of his own experience.[18] In the case of Antioch, William provided a brief résumé of the biblical references to the city and history of the Church there, supplementing them with a quotation from the canons of the Council of Constantinople. He followed Fulcher of Chartres and ultimately Jerome in mistakenly identifying Antioch with the Old Testament Riblah. When he came to describe the location of the city he launched into an extended discussion, with citations from Ovid's *Metamorphoses*, Solinus, Theodoretus in the *Historia tripartita* and Rufinus as authorities for questions concerning the identification of Mount Parnassus and the Castalian Spring.[19]

The great *tour de force*, however, is the description of Tyre. William quoted Ulpian's chapter 'De censibus', Virgil, Ezekiel, Isaiah, Josephus' *Antiquitates* (from which he copied verbatim at length) and Jerome, and he clearly made use of the *Etymologiae* of Isidore of Seville, whence he obtained the two-line quotation from Lucan mentioned previously. In addition, there are allusions to information gleaned from other parts of the Bible, from Ovid and from Jerome's *Liber interpretationis Hebraicorum nominum*.[20] It is instructive to compare William's use of his authorities with Fulcher's. Both authors introduced their descriptions apropos the siege of 1124. William appears to have drawn on Fulcher – as the juxtaposition of his references to Tyrian purple and the supposed etymologies of the city's name would suggest – but in each instance William expanded Fulcher's statements. Fulcher also had quoted from or alluded to Isaiah, Virgil and Josephus, but William did not simply copy his use of his authorities, as his own fuller quotations from Josephus testify. On the other hand, he ignored Fulcher's discussion of Hazor and the founding of Carthage (the latter based on Orosius), presumably judging them irrelevant. Both writers devoted a section to the history of the earlier sieges of Tyre, and

---

[18] *WT*, VIII, 1–4. The criticism of Solinus is at VIII, 4, lines 29–34. For another example of William contradicting geographical information from antiquity (the number of the mouths of the Nile), see XIX, 23, lines 15–26.

[19] *WT*, IV, 9–10. Note that in his statistics for the dependent provinces of the patriarchate, William contradicts his later statement (XIV, 12, lines 11–22; cf. apparatus *ad loc.*) and the figures given in the *Ordinatio sedum* (*RHC Occ*, I, 1135–6). See above, p. 23 note 1. For Riblah, see Fulcher of Chartres, *Historia Hierosolymitana*, ed. H. Hagenmeyer (Heidelberg, 1913), pp. 216, 709.

[20] *WT*, XIII, 1–4.

both used their descriptions of Tyre as a springboard for a general description of the geography of Syria. But, where Fulcher had given a geographical survey which owed much to Josephus' *Bellum Judaicum*, William gave an account based on the late Roman provincial structures.[21] So William took his cue from Fulcher for his description of Tyre, but, while Fulcher's account is no mean display of learning in its own right, William, with his wider learning and his superior command of his materials, was both more expansive and more impressive.

The Prologue to the *Historia* begins with a reference to the twin perils of Scylla and Charybdis, a classical proverb which originated with Terence, and two quotations from Cicero. But although it starts with a show of classical humanism, it ends on a note of Christian humility and the awareness of human fallibility, with quotations from St Matthew and the Book of Proverbs. The preface to Book XXIII has specific allusions to Virgil's *Eclogues* and references to Livy and Josephus, as well as quotations from the Bible, introduced by William to lament the current misfortunes facing the Latin East. But these two passages are not typical of his writing as a whole. Although there are a number of echoes of phrases from their works scattered in the *Historia*, neither Cicero nor Livy is referred to or quoted directly elsewhere, and it may be suspected that William was not as familiar with these authors as he would have liked his readers to believe. Livy was not widely diffused in the West until after 1300,[22] and as for Cicero, our confidence in William's direct knowledge of his work is not enhanced by the discovery that one of the two quotations he used was also employed by Einhard in his preface to the *Vita Caroli*.[23] It is possible that William composed or at least revised his descriptions of Jerusalem, Antioch and Tyre after 1180 as part of his scheme of alterations and insertions designed to increase the appeal of the *Historia* to his western audience. The Prologue and the preface to Book XXIII were certainly among the last sections to have been written, and so perhaps his employment of allusions to classical and earlier Christian writers in these pas-

[21] Cf. Fulcher, *Historia Hierosolymitana*, pp. 713–20.
[22] See Guenée, *Histoire et culture*, pp. 304–5. Cf. B. Smalley, *Historians in the Middle Ages* (London, 1974), p. 19.
[23] See the apparatus to *WT*, Prologue, lines 43–6. The proverb from Terence is cited by Cicero in the other passage quoted. Cf. apparatus to Prologue, line 18. For an analysis of classical influences on William's prologue, see B. Lacroix, 'Guillaume de Tyr: Unité et diversité dans la tradition latine', *Études d'histoire littéraire et doctrinale*, IV (1968), 201–15. See also Vessey, 'William of Tyre', *passim*.

sages should be seen as something of an afterthought, supplying a veneer of literary scholarship to an otherwise largely unadorned text as a means of satisfying his readership.[24]

To the ancients history had been a species of rhetoric, and in the *Historia* William followed classical rules for historical writing.[25] In his Prologue he declared his intention of telling the whole truth without suppression, partiality or malice: a classical prefatory topos which necessarily would be difficult to sustain in practice. Reading between the lines, especially in the sections dealing with his own day, it can be seen that he had a distinctly partisan view of events; on occasion, as in the cases of Miles of Plancy, Odo of St Amand or Agnes of Courtenay, he could make savage attacks on individuals he disliked.[26] But in general he presented his material in such a way that his readers would not be immediately conscious that they were being given a slanted account, unless, like those modern historians who have attempted to get to the bottom of the events of the period concerned, they were already on their guard. Another classical canon he obeyed was the chronological presentation of his material. In the Prologue he spoke of following the order of events, and, a few involuntary lapses apart, he succeeded. Only rarely did he make allusions to events out of sequence, and even then he tied them into the narrative framework in such a way as to enhance our understanding. So, for example, writing of the papal schism of 1159, he mentioned that it was healed nineteen years later.[27] William was also careful to place the events he described in their geographical context and present them in a logical and coherent manner. Thus he explained that in building the castle of Montreal, Baldwin I's intention had been to extend the frontiers of the kingdom and protect the fields from the ravages of the enemy; he then described the building of the fortress and the installation of the garrison and concluded by stating that the castle dominated the entire region.[28] Presentation of the bare facts was insufficient. His narrative technique allowed him scope for explanation and occa-

[24] For the 1180s revisions, see above, pp. 26–9. The use of classical quotations in the later sections to be written was noted by Krey, 'William of Tyre', p. 158 note 2.

[25] For Cicero's statement in his *De Oratore* II, xv, of the classical rules for the writing of history, see Smalley, *Historians*, p. 18; D. Hay, *Annalists and Historians: Western Historiography from the Eighth to the Eighteenth Century* (London, 1977), p. 4. Cf. Lacroix, 'Guillaume de Tyr', *passim*.

[26] *WT*, xx, 9, lines 1–13; xxi, 28, lines 40–6; xxii, 10, lines 24–5. For William's treatment of Miles, see Vessey, 'William of Tyre', pp. 446–50.

[27] *WT*, xviii, 26.   [28] *WT*, xi, 26, lines 15–33.

sionally, as for example in the discussion of the reasons for the failure of the siege of Damascus in 1148 or the reasons why by the time of Baldwin IV the Muslims were more powerful than previously, he provided an extended examination of causation.[29]

William also followed classical precedent in his conception of his role as a moralist. He indicated his approval or disapproval of past events; he provided character sketches of the principal *dramatis personae* in which he described both their physical and their moral traits. The character sketches were based squarely on classical models, transmitted from antiquity via Einhard,[30] but although the *Historia*, after the conclusion of the account of the First Crusade, is structured around the reigns of successive kings of Jerusalem, it is far more than simply a series of royal biographies written after the fashion of the *Vita Caroli* in the manner of Suetonius. As a moralist, William was aware of the need to edify as well as condemn, and his awareness of classical forms in this respect is made clear when at one point he contrasted the writing of history with the writing of satire, the literary form concerned solely with identifying and castigating evil.[31] And as a moralist he showed restraint, never allowing himself to adopt the persona of the repetitive and mawkishly self-righteous preacher, although he did ascribe lack of success to the absence of divine assistance because of sin. It is here that the classical tradition and Christian teaching met, for in equating moral decay, or sin, with political decay, he was embracing a classical topos as well as giving a Christian explanation.[32]

Before moving on to consider William as a Christian writer of history, it is as well to mention aspects of the classical tradition of historiography which he avoided. Although he adopted a moral stance, he was concerned chiefly with sin against God and lacked Sallust's preoccupation with corruption and self-indulgence. Contrasting him again with Sallust, we find that from time to time he employed dates and copied documents into his text, and when he provided fictionalized speeches or letters he did not normally take the opportunity to treat his readers to an exercise in set-piece

---

[29] *WT*, XVII, 7; XXI, 7.
[30] See Vessey, 'William of Tyre', p. 438. For further discussion, see Giese, 'Stadt- und Herrscherbeschreibungen', pp. 396–409.
[31] *WT*, XXI, 7, lines 21–5.
[32] For example, *WT*, XX, 22, lines 5–13; XXI, 7, lines 12–37; XXIII, preface, lines 20–32. See B. Smalley, 'Sallust in the Middle Ages', in R. R. Bolgar (ed.), *Classical Influences on European Culture, A.D. 500–1500* (Cambridge, 1971), pp. 165–8.

rhetoric.[33] Indeed, his use of fictionalized speeches and letters is sparing after his account of the First Crusade, and when he did employ this device it was frequently in places where the source he was using had already done so.[34]

In a broad sense the *Historia* was written in accordance with the canons of classical historiography, although William evidently did not set out to imitate the style of any one writer. But if the form of the *Historia* owes much to pagan antiquity, the content, necessarily because of the nature of its subject–matter, owes much to Christianity. However, we must be wary of assuming that he was greatly influenced by earlier Christian historians. He was not writing universal history; he was not writing church history; nor was he writing the history of a nation or *gens*. Rather, the *Historia* conforms to the definition given by Isidore of Seville: it is a *narratio rei gestae*, an account of past events, which in this instance are the events of the First Crusade and the doings of its leaders and their successors.[35] In so far as William had models, they were Fulcher of Chartres and other historians of the First Crusade and its aftermath.

There is no hint anywhere in the *Historia* that William subscribed to an apocalyptic view of history: the idea, associated with Augustine and Orosius, that world history can be divided into seven ages with the present lying somewhere in the sixth and the seventh being the Christian millennium, finds no echo; nor is there any suggestion that he accepted the Christian periodization of world history into four empires, a view based on an interpretation of the Book of Daniel. Only once, early in Book I, is there a reference to the expected Second Coming of Christ.[36] Gone is much of the chiliasm of previous twelfth–century accounts of the Crusade; a classical, linear view of human history has prevailed. Although William's subject is the Crusade and the subsequent struggles to defend what had been won, the *Historia* is in no sense an ecclesiastical history. Eusebius had written church history within a framework of secular history; what William wrote was Christian political history with the ecclesiastical information inserted often as an afterthought. So, although William quoted from Rufinus' Latin version of Eusebius,[37]

---

[33] For an exception, see *WT*, XVII, 29, lines 16–43.
[34] For Sallust as a model for medieval writers, see Smalley, 'Sallust', pp. 165–75.
[35] Isidore of Seville, *Etymologiae*, PL, 82, col. 122; cf. Guenée, *Histoire et culture*, p. 18.
[36] *WT*, I, 8, lines 7–9. Cf. Vessey, 'Apology', p. 395.
[37] *WT*, IV, 2, lines 15–20; XVI, 5, lines 33–45 (both passages refer to the same piece of information in Eusebius). See also IV, 10, lines 56–62.

he had not been influenced by him. Another writer whom William cited was Orosius,[38] but he was clearly unmoved, either by his periodization of history or by his message, totally at variance with his own outlook, that 'wars are cruel and futile but rulers, being fools or criminals, never stop fighting'.[39]

The idea of supernatural intervention in the affairs of men was allowed by the writers of history in pagan antiquity, but in Christian historiography divine intervention and divine causation can come to dominate. In the case of the *Historia* we find a juxtaposition of a Christian, theological world-view in which God controls the course of events and intervenes directly in human history, and a human view of history as exemplified by William's phrase at the beginning of the Prologue, where he wrote of 'describing the deeds of kings'. Except at the end, where he lamented his own inadequacy and asked prayers for forgiveness, the Prologue is largely secular in tone. Only in one place did William allude to a theocentric view of history when he mentioned

the departure of those brave men and princes, beloved of God, who, at the call of the Lord, went out from the kingdoms of the West and appropriated with a strong hand the Land of Promise.[40]

But early in Book I, at the end of what may have been an earlier draft of the Prologue, he wrote:

In the present work, we intend to set down as an everlasting memorial to the faithful in Christ the means and ordering of the divine plan by which He purposed to relive the long-standing affliction of His people (the Christians in Jerusalem).[41]

In the *Historia* there are numerous references to God giving or withholding victory, to God answering prayer, to God guiding or commanding the Christians, to God punishing sin, or to the idea that God has entrusted the lands conquered in the East to their Christian rulers. The affairs of men are subject to God's will. There are also examples of divine intervention in human history, as evinced by miracles, visions and portents. But these instances are noticeably infrequent,[42] especially when the *Historia* is compared

---

[38] *WT*, II, 7, lines 36–40. See Vessey, 'William of Tyre', pp. 439–40, for a clear echo from Orosius (not noted by Huygens) at *WT*, Prologue, lines 76–7.

[39] Smalley, *Historians*, p. 46.   [40] *WT*, Prologue, lines 92–5; cf. lines 1–2.

[41] *WT*, I, 10, lines 56–9. Cf. X, 11, lines 1–10.

[42] The principal references are *WT*, I, 12, lines 20–8; VI, 14, lines 3–17; 19, lines 1–19; VIII, 16, lines 11–14, cf. 17, lines 11–12; VIII, 22; XI, 5, lines 35–41; XIII, 26, lines 40–81; XVI, 8–13; 17, lines 8–13; XX, 21, lines 40–4.

with the earlier histories of the First Crusade which William used, and it is clear that he suppressed much of the supernatural material at his disposal. Only once after these earlier histories had been left behind did he offer his readers a concentrated dose of the miraculous, in his account of the ill-fated expedition to Bostra in 1147.[43] So if the *Historia* is an account of the *Gesta Dei per Francos*, it is an account of God ordering, commanding, guiding, not of God suspending the laws of nature and introducing a supernatural or irrational element into human history. The Christian humanism of the twelfth-century Schools has set a limit to William's credulity.

William's interpretation of God's place in history, and in particular his attitude to the divinely appointed role of Christians to participate in the war against the infidel, will be examined more fully in a later chapter. But the more secular side of his writing deserves some comment. Although he often explained events as turning out the way they did because God has so willed, he was equally capable of giving simple, mundane explanations, sometimes of the same event. For example, in explaining the failure of the joint crusader–Byzantine expedition to Egypt of 1169, he suggested that 'this undertaking had been begun in the face of divine anger', but then in the next chapter he told of his own investigations into the failure and explained that one reason was that the Byzantine forces had been insufficiently supplied.[44] There are, however, passages in which God's involvement with human affairs is almost entirely absent. The two prime examples are the account of the siege and capture of Tyre in 1124 and the account of the 1167 expedition to Egypt. In each section – the latter spread across eighteen chapters – the idea of God governing the course of events received but one passing mention, even although both enterprises had ended in success and we might well have expected William to ascribe victory to God's favour.[45] The contrast between his account of the capture of Tyre and his account of the other major successful siege of the twelfth century, the siege of Ascalon of 1153, in which divine assistance figures prominently, is striking.[46]

So, in common with other twelfth-century historians, William

---

[43] *WT*, XVI, 8–13.   [44] *WT*, XX, 16–17 (at 16, line 67).

[45] For 1124, see *WT*, XIII, 6–14 (and note XIII, 9, lines 36–7). Cf. XIV, 14, line 35, where Tyre's capture is said to have been due to the mercy of God. For 1167, see *WT*, XIX, 13–32 (and note XIX, 22, line 27). For examples of other passages where the theme of God's control of events is surprisingly absent, see *WT*, I, 22–6; VII, 1–8.

[46] *WT*, XVII, 21–5, 27–30.

was indebted to pagan antiquity for the genre and form of his historical writing, while allowing his Christian belief to influence its content. He was writing Christian history in a classical mould. Although well educated, he did not normally make a display of erudition, and when he introduced quotations, more often than not they were from the Bible. Many of his quotations and allusions illustrated the biblical setting of the events he described and so reminded his readers of the sacred associations of the places concerned, but generally he used the Bible as he used the Latin classics, as a means of sharing with his audience their common heritage. Well read as he was in Scripture, scriptural phrases flowed naturally from his pen. William, typically of educated men of his generation, combined the two strands in his background, Christianity and pagan classical learning. An earlier Christian writer, Einhard, had written a life of Charlemagne in which the idea of God's control of human affairs was totally excluded. Whether William consciously tried to emulate Einhard in those passages where he too saw events in purely human terms is far from certain, but anyway it was impossible in the twelfth century to write a purely 'secular' history of the Crusade. Without doubt he did believe in God's commanding presence in history, but his reluctance to record concrete manifestations of the supernatural, together with a tendency to deal in stereotyped expressions of his belief in the ways in which God had aided or withheld His aid from the Christians, points to the conclusion that he himself was poised between an acceptance of divine grace and of man's dependence on God and a belief in human capacity for achievement and in man's ability to formulate a rational understanding of events.

Chapter 4

WILLIAM AND HIS SOURCES

William of Tyre took the view that his personal experience provided the key for writing about the events of his own lifetime. Some events he had witnessed in person; others he had learnt of from others. But the very fact that he had been alive at the time, could remember his own immediate reactions and those of his contemporaries and had known many of the leading figures personally gave him a critical understanding and appreciation of what had been going on. By contrast, his perception of the events of preceding generations depended largely on unverifiable traditions, and from remarks in the preamble to Book XVI it is clear that he felt less secure about the adequacy of his account of them. He chose to signal the transition from his narration of past events to the account of his own generation with the accession of King Baldwin III in 1143.[1] At that date he would have been in his teens, just a few years before his departure to the West to study in the Schools of France and Italy. To the modern historian there is nothing very different about the tone and content of the *Historia* for the decades either side of 1143, and we might prefer to divide the work at 1127, the point at which his last extant literary source, the *Historia Hierosolymitana* of Fulcher of Chartres, breaks off, and again at 1165, when William returned to the East and began his career in the hurly-burly of Latin Syrian public life. But to William it was the threshold of manhood that formed the dividing line, and his consciousness of the dichotomy between his perception of the events of his own day and his necessarily less satisfactory perception of earlier events provides another instance of his debt to the legacy of classical historiography.

In the Prologue William had something to say about how he set about gathering information. He stated that he had had access to no Greek or Arabic written sources and, excepting the few things he

[1] *WT*, XVI, preface, lines 1–11.

had witnessed in person, he had been informed solely by traditions ('solis traditionibus instructi').[2] What in fact he had were his own experiences, the memories of others, oral traditions passed on from one generation to another, a certain amount of formal documentation preserved in the archives, the writings of those earlier Christian or pagan authors referred to in the previous chapter, and some earlier narrative histories of the Crusade. At first sight it may seem strange that he should either leave these earlier Crusade histories out of the reckoning or should lump them together with the oral sources of information as *traditiones*. But it is important to see these remarks in context. William had just been describing his Oriental History and had made it clear that he had relied largely on the work of Sa'īd ibn Baṭrīk. We may surmise that, in the absence of other information on the course of Muslim history, he had followed this author closely and had regarded his work as authoritative. In contrast, when he wrote the *Historia* he not only used no Greek or Arabic text, he lacked any work he could treat as an authority. It is true he used older narrative materials, but he did not feel obliged to accept their every detail: they were traditions which happened to be in written form, not definitive statements to be regarded as the inviolable truth. In consequence the *Historia* is not a compendium of information consisting of a received body of material from the periods before William's own generation and then his account of his own day. Instead it is in its entirety a work of critical perception. William could handle the events of the present generation to his own satisfaction; as for the events of earlier generations, he had to use his historical acumen as best he might to gain his understanding from the *traditiones* at his disposal.[3]

For his account of the First Crusade, William had the works of Albert of Aachen,[4] Raymond of Aguilers, Fulcher of Chartres and

---

[2] *WT*, Prologue, lines 89–91. In a sense William did employ Arabic materials in the *Historia*, to the extent that he may have incorporated material from his own Oriental History, notably in the early chapters of Book I: see *WT*, I, 1–2. The assumption that he was familiar with Greek and Arabic has recently been challenged: see *WT*, pp. 2–3.

[3] Note the contrast between William's approach and the less sophisticated medieval historiographical tradition which made a much sharper distinction between the historian's perception of events in his own lifetime and his dependence on his authorities for earlier events. On this point, with reference to the earlier twelfth-century writer William of Malmesbury, see M. Chibnall, *The World of Orderic Vitalis* (Oxford, 1984), pp. 170–1.

[4] William's knowledge of Albert did not extend beyond the capture of Jerusalem. It has been suggested that he had at his disposal not Albert's work, which in any case was written in the West between 1119 and c. 1140, but a lost Lotharingian chronicle which served as a basis for them both. In support of this contention it has been

Baldric of Dol, as well as the anonymous *Gesta Francorum* or another closely related text.[5] A large proportion of his statements can be traced to these histories. For the early years of the twelfth century he used Fulcher and occasionally the Antiochene writer Walter the Chancellor, but increasingly we find him including material which cannot be identified as coming from his extant literary sources. How far he had access to other narratives which have not survived is a matter for speculation. One possibility is that he had a history of Antioch for the second quarter of the century which provided information on the dynastic problems in the principality following the death of Bohemond II in 1130, on the career of Patriarch Ralph of Antioch and on the interventions of Emperor John Comnenus in the East, interrelated subjects about which he seems well informed. But it is equally likely that he composed his version of these events by drawing on the reminiscences of men older than himself. The problem is that, here as elsewhere, he covered his tracks well. His method of working means that it would not, for example, be possible to reconstruct the texts of his sources for the First Crusade from an examination of the *Historia* had they not survived; nor is it possible to detect where his last extant source, Fulcher of Chartres, breaks off.[6]

William was no plagiarist. In the early books of the *Historia* he drew on the sources just mentioned, using them as a quarry for facts and the sequence of events, but he simplified and clarified his material, reconciling conflicting accounts and omitting incidents which tried his credulity or which for some other reason did not appeal to him. In reworking his information he managed to avoid copying passages verbatim, and it is remarkable how infrequently his phraseology echoes that of his sources. This is not to say that he

calculated that there are only about thirty verbal echoes of Albert's text to be found in William's *Historia*: see P. Knoch, *Studien zu Albert von Aachen* (Stuttgart, 1966), pp. 29–63; E. O. Blake and C. Morris, 'A Hermit Goes to War: Peter and the Origins of the First Crusade', in W. J. Sheils (ed.), *Monks, Hermits and the Ascetic Tradition* (Oxford, 1985), pp. 91–2, 98–104. This attractive theory is unproven; we shall continue to assume that it was Albert's text, presumably in a manuscript which lacked the later books, that William used. Mayer and Rösch (see the following note) did not discuss this point but evidently made a similar assumption.

5 H. E. Mayer and G. Rösch have identified William's extant literary sources for Huygens's edition: see *WT*, p. 93. They make the intriguing suggestion that William used William of Malmesbury's *Gesta regum Anglorum* for his knowledge of European events. Cf. *WT*, IX, 13; XII, 8.

6 Fulcher of Chartres's narrative closes with the events recorded by William at XIII, 21. Specific allusions in the *Historia* to literary sources for the First Crusade are rare, but see *WT*, III, 17, lines 10–14; VIII, 19, lines 27–8.

invariably succeeded in giving an account which is more coherent and convincing than his original. Take the example of the background to the First Crusade as described in Book 1. William followed Albert of Aachen, who alone of the earlier writers he was using had given pride of place to Peter the Hermit's distinctive contribution to the summoning and launching of the Crusade. But he reorganized and modified Albert's version of events, introducing the idea that Peter was already preaching the Crusade before the Council of Clermont, while at the same time removing much of the supernatural element and using the material to point the contrast between the deficiencies of the Byzantine empire and the strengths of the Latins. Modern writers generally agree in rejecting the prominence afforded Peter by Albert, but, allowing for the fact that William was heir to this historical tradition, he employed his information in a way which reveals his own broader perspective.[7] When, however, we move on to his description of the condition of western Europe just prior to the Crusade, we find that he did not appreciate as clearly as Fulcher of Chartres the relationship between the Investiture Contest, the papal schism and the preaching of the Crusade. In consequence, although his version of Pope Urban's speech is more sophisticated than Fulcher's, it is also more artificial.[8]

Three episodes can serve to illustrate how William handled his literary sources and combined them with other documentation and oral tradition. For the siege of Antioch (1097–8) he had the *Gesta Francorum*, Raymond, Baldric, Fulcher and Albert, but he did not utilize them all to the same extent. Here as elsewhere, he drew most heavily on Albert, the writer whose account had given the greatest prominence to the role of Godfrey of Bouillon as a leader of the Crusade. There is much detail provided by these sources which William left out, and he evidently concentrated his efforts on giving an overview of developments. Raymond had given an account of the siege as seen from the count of Toulouse's army, but William's concern was rather to give a general narrative. In consequence, with the exception of the series of events surrounding the Holy Lance, William made comparatively little use of Raymond, although it may be noted in passing that Raymond's down-to-earth, eyewit-

---

[7] *WT*, 1, 11–14; cf. Albert of Aachen, 'Historia Hierosolymitana', *RHC Occ*, IV, 272–3. For a recent attempt to call the accepted views into question, see Morris and Blake, 'A Hermit goes to War'.

[8] *WT*, 1, 13–15; cf. Fulcher, *Historia Hierosolymitana*, pp. 119–43.

ness description of the geographical setting of Antioch gives a clearer picture than does William's more fulsome, classically inspired account.[9]

With the Holy Lance, William was in difficulty. He felt obliged to take Raymond's account seriously, but his own retelling was much abridged, and it may be wondered whether he had doubts as to the authenticity of the relic. He would have known that, according to Raymond, Adhemar had disbelieved at first, and also he would have seen that Fulcher was openly sceptical. His own attitude may have been complicated by his ambivalence towards Raymond's lord, Count Raymond of Toulouse. In the end he came down on the side of caution and hesitation, unsure of his verdict on Peter Bartholomew, the central figure in this episode. It was no easy decision. He may have allowed himself to be swayed by the fact that, by the time he was writing, the Lance was an established part of the tradition, even although elsewhere he normally shied away from the miraculous.[10]

On occasion, however, William showed that he had understood things better than his sources. Thus, although Albert, Raymond and the *Gesta Francorum* had all mentioned the Fatimid embassy which visited the crusaders at Antioch, none of them seems to have appreciated its significance in terms of the political and religious divisions in Islam as well as he did.[11] In other words, William culled his information from the sources but used his own insight to form his interpretation. Another example of the same sort of understanding is his appreciation that it was Kerbogha's abortive attack on Edessa in June 1099 that had given the Christians the requisite breathing-space to establish themselves inside Antioch.[12]

It is not difficult to see how William selected and modified the information from his sources for the siege of Antioch, and, indeed, for the other episodes of the First Crusade. Far more problematical is his treatment of the origins of the Latin patriarchate in Jerusalem.

---

[9] Raymond of Aguilers, *Le "Liber" de Raymond d'Aguilers*, ed. J. H. and L. L. Hill (Paris, 1969), pp. 47–8; cf. *WT*, IV, 9–10.

[10] Raymond, *Le "Liber"*, pp. 68–76, 84–5, 120–4; cf. *WT*, VI, 14; VII, 18. Cf. *Gesta Francorum et aliorum Hierosolimitanorum*, ed. and trans. R. Hill (London, 1962), pp. 59–60; Fulcher, *Historia Hierosolymitana*, pp. 235–41; Albert, 'Historia Hierosolymitana', pp. 419–20, 452.

[11] *WT*, IV, 24; VII, 19. Cf. *Gesta Francorum*, pp. 37–8, 42; Raymond, *Le "Liber"*, p. 58; Albert, 'Historia Hierosolymitana', pp. 379–80.

[12] *WT*, V, 14, lines 18–49. Cf. Fulcher, *Historia Hierosolymitana*, pp. 242–3; Albert, 'Historia Hierosolymitana', pp. 396–7.

In telling of the election of Arnulf as patriarch, his deposition, the election of Daimbert of Pisa and Daimbert's relations with Godfrey and Baldwin I, William showed himself friendly to Daimbert and hostile to Arnulf. The ecclesiastical politics of the period were complex, and discrepancies in the sources add to the confusion.[13] William's penchant for Daimbert and animosity towards Arnulf were at variance with the line taken by Albert of Aachen; but, as he evidently did not know Albert's account of events after the capture of Jerusalem, this conflict should not be regarded as an example of a deliberate rejection of his testimony. Previously William had taken Albert's lead in reporting that Arnulf, together with Peter the Hermit, preached before the final assault on Jerusalem.[14] On the other hand, it was Raymond of Aguilers, whose narrative broke off before the arrival of Daimbert at Christmas 1099, that William was following when he made scandalous allegations about Arnulf's private life; and he also used Raymond's account for his own description of Arnulf's election as patriarch.[15] In this he rejected the more favourable notice of the election given by the *Gesta Francorum*.[16] As for Daimbert, William had at his disposal the account of Fulcher of Chartres, who had recorded his arrival in the East and his election to the patriarchate and had alluded to his quarrel with Baldwin I and to their reconciliation, which led to Baldwin's coronation on Christmas Day 1100. But Fulcher was brief, made no value-judgements on Daimbert's career, although later he was laudatory, and said nothing of Arnulf's previous election as patriarch. William echoed Fulcher's account of Daimbert's arrival, his withdrawal to the church of Mount Zion following his quarrel with Baldwin I, and the reconciliation, but he gave a much fuller and more circumstantial account of Daimbert's relations with Godfrey and Baldwin.[17] Fulcher also stated, although in a totally unrelated context, that Godfrey and Bohemond had received their lands from Daimbert, another point taken up by William.[18]

[13] See H. E. Mayer, *Bistümer, Klöster und Stifte im Königreich Jerusalem* (Stuttgart, 1977), pp. 1–43; Hamilton, *Latin Church*, pp. 12–16, 53–7.

[14] For William and Albert, see above, note 4. Before the assault Albert (p. 470) referred to Arnulf as 'clerus magnae scientiae et facundiae', and William, in the equivalent passage (VIII, 11, lines 6–7), spoke of him with apparent approval as 'vir litteratus'.

[15] Raymond, *Le "Liber"*, pp. 153–4; *WT*, IX, 1, lines 25–42; 4, lines 1–13.

[16] *Gesta Francorum*, p. 93.

[17] Fulcher, *Historia Hierosolymitana*, pp. 333, 368–9, 383–4; *WT*, IX, 15; X, 7; 9, lines 1–8.

[18] Fulcher, *Historia Hierosolymitana*, pp. 741–2; *WT*, IX, 15, lines 8–11.

So how did William obtain his additional information and form his own distinctive view? Writing of Daimbert's dealings with Godfrey, he stated that the details 'had been derived from the account of others and indeed had been committed to writing' – an indication that he possessed written materials which have not survived. He later quoted in full a letter purporting to have been sent by Daimbert to Bohemond and retailing the patriarch's version of his agreement with Godfrey and the *coup d'état* by Baldwin's supporters immediately after Godfrey's death in July 1100. It is, however, difficult to accept that the letter as it stands is genuine, and it may be that William himself composed it on the basis of a report of such a letter having been sent which he had found in the writings just referred to.[19] It is also likely that he would have been aware of the traditional views handed down among the clergy at the Holy Sepulchre, and it could well be that in Holy Sepulchre tradition Daimbert was respected and Arnulf denigrated. In any case, his information on Arnulf's later career would have reinforced his view of Arnulf's worthlessness. But, besides the rather insubstantial statements of Raymond of Aguilers and Fulcher of Chartres, Daimbert's letter and the traditions of the Holy Sepulchre, William had his own views on the issues these events exemplified: the relationship between *regnum* and *ecclesia* and the standing of the monarchy of Jerusalem, which Daimbert, in crowning Baldwin I on Christmas Day 1100, had been instrumental in inaugurating. William's presuppositions on these subjects will be examined later, but there can be no doubt that in assembling his data and constructing his account he had allowed his own views to influence his version of events.[20]

The description of the siege of Antioch shows William using the material in his narrative sources in conjunction with his own historical insight. On the other hand, his account of the origins of the patriarchate of Jerusalem shows him combining narrative sources with other information, some of it perhaps handed down orally, and shaping it in accordance with his own views. This combination

---

[19] *WT*, IX, 16, lines 19–21. Daimbert's letter is at X, 4. For some recent comments, see Mayer, *Bistümer*, pp. 11, 29. The precise nature of the letter is open to question. The information contained in it does not quite tally with what William says elsewhere, but this perhaps may be explained by suggesting that he revised his narrative at some stage and failed to make the necessary adjustments to the letter. It is further possible that the letter or the document on which it was based could have been concocted as ammunition in a later quarrel between Church and State – perhaps that of Patriarch Stephen and Baldwin II in the late 1120s.

[20] See below, pp. 99–105.

of narrative, oral and also documentary materials can again be seen in the description of the siege and capture of Tyre in 1124. William's one extant written source was Fulcher, and he followed him in his general outline.[21] But he also had other sources. Somehow he had acquired precise figures for the composition and size of the Venetian fleet.[22] Fulcher had indicated that some of the Venetian ships arrived in Acre and then set sail to engage the Egyptian fleet off Jaffa; William had them sail direct to Jaffa from Cyprus – but did he have different information which he thought superior to Fulcher's or was he merely tidying up his narrative by making it simpler and more logical?[23] In the naval engagement which followed, William described the doge's own galley ramming and sinking a ship bearing the Egyptian commander. Fulcher had had nothing of this. The anecdote has all the appearance of a *conte*, and it could well have been part of an oral tradition that William had picked up.[24] He explicitly stated that he had acquired information from 'certain elderly men' who had been present at the discussion as to whether to attack Tyre or Ascalon. Fulcher had mentioned that the Venetians had agreed to attack one or the other but gave no indication as to why Tyre was selected. William, on the basis of his oral information, told of counter-representations from the Christian-held towns in the vicinity of these places, and went on to describe the drawing of lots by an innocent child to determine which it should be. This detail invites the scepticism of the modern reader, and it is rather difficult to see why William included it, as it is so out of keeping with the predominantly rational tone of the *Historia* and does nothing to enhance the reputation of the rulers of Latin Syria for wise leadership.[25] That he was concerned with the reputation of the Latin East at this point is shown by his suppression of Fulcher's story that to pay for the campaign the church plate of the Holy Sepulchre had had to be pledged; presumably this sounded too much like an unjustifiable infringement of ecclesiastical liberty.[26]

But there are two important areas in which William's superior historical acumen showed itself. The first was in his topographical and historical description of Tyre, which has been discussed already.[27] The other was in his accounts of the various attempts by

[21] Fulcher, *Historia Hierosolymitana*, pp. 693–720, 728–35; *WT*, XII, 22–5; XIII, 1–14.
[22] *WT*, XII, 22, lines 3–4.
[23] Fulcher, *Historia Hierosolymitana*, pp. 669–71; *WT*, XII, 22, lines 5–11.
[24] *WT*, XII, 23, lines 1–5.   [25] *WT*, XII, 24, lines 22–52.
[26] Fulcher, *Historia Hierosolymitana*, p. 694.
[27] See above, pp. 36–7.

neighbouring Muslim rulers to raise the siege or launch diversionary attacks, where William, in part using data furnished by Fulcher, made better sense of their strategy.[28] A final feature of his account of the siege which deserves comment is the incorporation into his narrative of the full text of the treaty between the Venetians and the Christians in the East, a reminder that as archbishop of Tyre and as chancellor of the kingdom he had access to archival materials.[29]

These comments on a few selected sections in the *Historia* give an indication of how William used the older narratives in combination with other information to construct his *magnum opus*. In the early books he seems generally to have relied on first one and then another source, using others to supplement his information, but his methods probably varied according to the nature of his material. For the First Crusade he relied on written sources for his factual data, which then served as a springboard for his historical imagination. As the *Historia* progressed and as the range of his narrative sources diminished, he came increasingly to rely on orally transmitted accounts. There are signs that he was aware of oral traditions for events as far back as the battle of Dorylaeum (1097) and the siege of Antioch,[30] but by the time he was writing, the collective memory of the events of the First Crusade and the early years of the Latin East probably contained much that was fanciful and fantastic. Just as he rejected much of the supernatural element he found in his written sources, so presumably he would have sifted and rejected much that was passed on to him by word of mouth. The possibility that he had other written narratives which have not survived means that there is no way of knowing precisely how much he owed to the memories of his elders. But what is clear is that he was at pains to acquire his information and record only what he believed to be correct.[31] As he said in the preamble to Book XVI, the point at which he passed from the history of the previous generations to the history of his own day,

[28] *WT*, XIII, 8–9; 12; 13, lines 13–30. Cf. Fulcher, *Historia Hierosolymitana*, pp. 731–2.
[29] *WT*, XII, 25. Cf. G. L. F. Tafel and G. M. Thomas (eds), *Urkunden zur älteren Handels- und Staatsgeschichte der Republik Venedig mit besonderer Beziehung auf Byzanz und die Levante* (Vienna, 1856–7), I, 84–9.
[30] *WT*, III, 16, lines 35–9; VI, 7, lines 48–51.
[31] For examples in the early part of the *Historia* of William informing his readers that he had made a careful enquiry into a particular episode, see VI, 12, lines 22–5; IX, 16, lines 26–31; 17, lines 5–6.

What we have hitherto set down in this present history we have assembled only from the account of others who have preserved to this day a fuller memory of time past; and so it has been with great difficulty, begging ('mendicantes') as it were other people's information, that we have attained a true picture, the correct sequence of events and the right dates; however, we have committed this account to writing as faithfully as we can.[32]

William was aware of the difficulties of using recollections of events which had taken place half a century or more before the time he was at work; what is surprising is that he did not preserve more stories which would appear to have belonged to a questionable oral tradition, such as the anecdote that the decision to attack Tyre and not Ascalon in 1124 was made by drawing lots.

If William is to be believed, it was with something of a sigh of relief that he could move from his description of past events to an account of his own times. His preamble to Book XVI continues:

But what follows from now on is in part what we have observed as an eye-witness and in part what has been passed on to us by the trustworthy account of those who were present at the events. And so, relying on this two-fold support, with the aid of God, we shall set down what remains for future reading more easily and more faithfully. For the memory normally recalls recent times more accurately, and the impression that things seen make on the mind is not so easily forgotten as things learnt of solely by word of mouth.[33]

But the problem still remains of the extent to which he himself was an eyewitness. In the Prologue he spoke of the 'few things which we ourselves have beheld with our own eyes',[34] and it is likely that this is not just an example of false modesty. From the mid-1140s until 1165 William was in the West, and so, except for childhood reminiscences such as his sighting of Patriarch Ralph of Antioch, he was totally dependent on hearsay until his return.[35] But even for the years of his public life in the Latin kingdom as described in Books XIX to XXIII he may not have observed many events at first hand.[36] For example, he never to our knowledge actually participated in a military campaign or carried the relic of the Cross into war.[37] Yet

---

[32] *WT*, XVI, preface, lines 1–6.   [33] *WT*, XVI, preface, lines 6–14.
[34] *WT*, Prologue, line 91.
[35] See above, p. 14.
[36] Specific allusions to William as an eyewitness are rare. For an example, see *WT*, XVIII, 3, lines 53–6.
[37] Note his dependence on his informants for the Egyptian campaigns of 1167 (XIX, 18, lines 1–5; 25, lines 13–15), 1168 (XX, 7, lines 25–6), and 1169 (XX, 17, lines

these books are full of accounts of military activity. What we have, therefore, are his informants' reports leavened by his own insight and imagination. It may also be wondered whether he spent as much time at the court of King Baldwin IV as is commonly supposed. As we have seen, there is reason to believe that, even although he held the office of chancellor, he was not in regular attendance on the king.[38] But the difficulty lies partly in the manner in which he reported events. Thus it is only the fact that three days later he was appointed archdeacon of Tyre that leads us to suspect that he had been present at the marriage of King Amaury and Maria Comnena: otherwise, except possibly for his remarks about Amaury's attire at the wedding, there is nothing to indicate that he was an eyewitness.[39]

The difficulty in establishing how far William provided first-hand testimony may be further illustrated by considering his account of the visit of the Byzantine envoys in 1168. A careful reading of this episode shows that, although he subsequently returned with them to Constantinople and then sought out the emperor in Serbia, William had not been a party to the secret negotiations which had taken place in Tyre. The fact that he could only offer a paraphrase of the contents of the Byzantine emperor's message, as well as the fact that he only joined the returning ambassadors when they had reached Tripoli, is a clear pointer to his absence from the royal council. So here he has juxtaposed second-hand material with his own experiences. Yet his telling of his participation in this diplomatic exchange could easily leave the impression that he had been involved from the outset.[40]

William related a certain amount about his own activities, but only so much. The result is that the historian cannot always be certain whether his impersonal account of a particular event means that he only knew of it at second hand or that he was directly involved but was reticent about pushing himself to the forefront of his narrative. Occasionally, as in the description of the visit of Count Philip of Flanders to the Latin East in 1177, the tell-tale first person is introduced.[41] Perhaps the fact that his account of this episode is difficult to disentangle testifes to his personal involvement; had he not been there the account might have been more

---

28–40), and for the Mont Gisard campaign of 1177 (xxi, 22, lines 5–8), with the clear implication that he himself was not present.
[38] See above, pp. 19–20.   [39] *WT*, xx, 1.   [40] *WT*, xx, 4.
[41] *WT*, xxi, 13, lines 40–50.

coherent, being simply his own reconstruction of eyewitness reports. Similarly, it is instructive to compare William's rather impressionistic and incomplete account of his own seven-month sojourn in Constantinople in 1179–80 with the more rounded and clearly directed account of King Amaury's visit there in 1171, an account which almost certainly he had based on the reports of others.[42] When William was close to the events he described, he was not necessarily at his best.

So if William was not strictly speaking as an eyewitness of most of what he recorded, how did he gather his information? Of the failure of the Second Crusade to capture Damascus, he wrote:

> I recall that I frequently enquired of the more generally prudent men and of those whose memory of that time was still quite fresh, so that by taking the greatest care to find out the facts I might set down in the present history the reason behind so great an evil and the identities of the authors of so great a crime.

But for all his questioning he could obtain no satisfactory answer.[43] In the case of the Second Crusade it may well be that by the time he was writing memories were confused and scanty; certainly his information on the Crusade seems thin by comparison with his knowledge of the Egyptian campaigns in the late 1160s. Occasionally he named his informants: Stephany of Courtenay, abbess of St Mary Major, had provided him with detailed information on royal genealogy and the affinity between King Amaury and Agnes of Courtenay; Hugh of Caesarea had provided details about the Egyptian campaign of 1167.[44] Other probable informants include King Amaury himself and Humphrey of Toron, constable of Jerusalem. But if for some incidents such as the failure of the Second Crusade William had asked many people for their recollections, for the most part we might suppose that he was content with the versions of just a few. The material gleaned from his interrogations would have been kept for subsequent sifting, rearrangement, expansion and development in written form. His aim, as he explained in another passage in which he described gathering infor-

[42] *WT*, XX, 22–4; XXII, 4. There is no concrete evidence to suggest that William accompanied Amaury to Constantinople in 1171. For a contrary assumption, see S. Runciman, 'The Visit of King Amalric I to Constantinople in 1171', in B. Z. Kedar, H. E. Mayer and R. C. Smail (eds.), *Outremer: Studies in the History of the Crusading Kingdom of Jerusalem* (Jerusalem, 1982), p. 153.
[43] *WT*, XVII, 7, lines 1–5. See A. J. Forey, 'The Failure of the Siege of Damascus in 1148', *Journal of Medieval History*, X (1984), 13–23.
[44] *WT*, XIX, 4, lines 25–31; 19, lines 44–5; 30, lines 6–7.

mation and interviewing the principal participants, was the discovery 'de rei veritate' – of the truth of the matter[45] – a quest he pursued by extrapolation from the various pieces of information he had been able to collect. It was a complex process, and it is remarkable how frequently he brought to it a great deal of imagination and vividness.

What we cannot know, once William's literary sources are behind us, is how carefully he walked that invisible line between legitimate imagination and serious distortion. This problem becomes acute when we consider his reliance on information gathered at second or third hand and the role of rumour and hearsay in the construction of the *Historia*. That he recorded things he understood simply as rumour is unquestioned. Alphonse of Toulouse's death in 1148 was due to poison. William signalled that his statement was based on rumour by the phrase 'ut dicitur', but the fact that he bothered to record it at all conveys with it a sense of probability.[46] Twice he used this same phrase, 'ut dicitur', in his account of the election of Amaury of Nesle as patriarch of Jerusalem in 1157: the election was irregular, 'so it is said', and the papal confirmation was secured by bribery, 'so it is said'.[47] Here there is a genuine difficulty. William may have been unsure of the truth behind the rumour, or it could be that he chose to disguise firm information as rumour owing to the delicate nature of the allegations. On the other hand, scepticism is aroused by some of the things he presented as hearsay: was Baldwin III's character really transformed when he married Theodora Comnena? Was Manuel Comnenus really so generous to all and sundry on his visit to northern Syria in 1158–9?[48]

William's account of the death of Baldwin III in 1163 is important in this context, if rather disillusioning. The king, who was away in Antioch at the time, seeing the approach of winter had asked a native physician for a tonic and was given some pills. He died subsequently after a long illness. William inveighed against native doctors and the willingness of the Franks to place themselves in their care. He was in no doubt that Baldwin was poisoned and repeated a ridiculous story about a dog who ate some of the same medicine and died within a few days. William was clearly lost in a maze of hearsay, and the whole story displays a total lack of discretion and judgement. The dog died too quickly; the physician,

45 *WT*, xx, 17, line 36.   46 *WT*, xvi, 28, lines 14–18.
47 *WT*, xviii, 20, lines 4–5, 18–19.
48 *WT*, xviii, 22, lines 47–56; 24, lines 52–7.

so it would seem, went unpunished; why anyone should have wanted to kill Baldwin was not discussed. Read critically, it is a story of Baldwin's lingering death and the suspicion of poison. But William saw it as a case of murder and used it as a vehicle for his own prejudice against native medicine.[49] He was rarely so intemperate. Consider the loss of Banyas in 1164. Allegations and rumours as to who had been responsible were rife, but in the end he was unable to apportion blame. Rumour was not turned into fact: 'We have not learnt anything definite about these things . . .'[50]

Except where he himself was an eyewitness, William was dependent on the written or oral information he had been able to acquire. But in assessing this information he relied on his own expertise and education, and it was only after he had brought his own critical scrutiny to bear upon it that, suitably refashioned, it could pass into writing. Significantly, there are few miracle stories in the *Historia* and few incidents, such as the circumstances of the death of Baldwin III, which not only arouse disbelief but also leave us wondering how he could have allowed himself to present his material so unconvincingly. Not much that is miraculous or self-evidently fictitious has got through William's grid. His intellect, insight and training in rhetoric combined to set criteria by which he could evaluate his data. The problem, as he himself perceived, was that the reliability of his information varied considerably. Inevitably this carried over into the *Historia* itself, with the result that not all his statements are of equal authority. So, before accepting his information and standpoint on any particular incident, historians have to be on their guard and consider carefully the nature and reliability of his own sources. It is dangerous to cite him indiscriminately and out of context. What William had set out to do was to divine the truth from his sources and his own experience. The originality of his presentation in the course of so large a work, and the consistency with which, a few lapses apart, his sober narrative unfolds, attest his success and achievement. But, for all his preoccu-

---

[49] *WT*, XVIII, 34, lines 1–28.
[50] *WT*, XIX, 10, lines 53–4. For other examples of William admitting his uncertainty in the face of conflicting reports or being unwilling to commit himself, see VII, 1, lines 43–54 (causes of plague at Antioch, 1098); XX, 25, lines 67–75 (reasons for murder of bishop of Acre, 1172); XXI, 4, lines 31–7 (background to the murder of Miles of Plancy, 1174); XXII, 26, lines 34–6 (circumstances of the appointment of Guy of Lusignan as regent, 1183); XXII, 27, lines 78–80 (reasons for failure to engage Saladin's army, 1183).

pation with the establishment of truth and the recital of accurate information, he had a point of view. What that point of view was, and how it affected the shape and content of the *Historia*, is the subject of the second part of this study.

PART II

WILLIAM OF TYRE AND THE MEANING OF THE *HISTORIA*

Chapter 5

THE MONARCHY

In the preceding books we have, after a fashion, described the remarkable deeds of those brave men who for eighty years and more have held dominion in our part of the East and in particular in Jerusalem.

Thus William of Tyre, writing in the preface to Book XXIII of the *Historia*, surveyed his work.[1] The deeds of rulers, especially the kings of Jerusalem, had featured prominently. The early books had recorded the events of the First Crusade, giving the limelight to its leaders. The Crusade over, it had been the same men, Godfrey, Baldwin of Boulogne, Raymond, Bohemond and Tancred, who ruled in the territories that had been won, and so the transition from the description of the Crusade to the description of what followed worked smoothly. In his Prologue, William had spoken of the *Historia* as a *gesta regum*, and so in large measure it is. But, as he went on to say, writing of the deeds of kings poses moral problems for the historian: should he tell the truth or engage in flattery? After all, descendants of these men might read what he had written and take offence.[2]

Part of William's intention was to inspire people to renewed efforts by recounting the achievements of past rulers. These men had had a role to play in the unfolding of divine providence, but William made some attempt to give them individual characteristics and not to portray them simply as stereotypes. However, in presenting the monarchy of Jerusalem to his readers he was on the defensive. The king at the time he was writing was Baldwin IV (1174–85). Baldwin was a leper and had been known to be suffering from leprosy even before his accession. At the time of his accession he had been a minor. It is not hard to imagine people asking why, at

---

[1] *WT*, XXIII, preface, lines 11–14.
[2] *WT*, Prologue, lines 1–54. See also XX, 31, lines 42–3.

Table 1. *The royal house of Jerusalem in the twelfth century*[a]

[a]Capital letters denote rulers of Jerusalem.

62

a time when the Muslim threat to Jerusalem was perhaps greater than ever and the need for outside assistance correspondingly more pressing, the Latins in the East should deliberately saddle themselves with a king who would be incapable of ruling, incapable of defending his kingdom and incapable of begetting a successor. In an age in which the personal ability of the monarch was of primary importance, ineffectual leadership accompanied by dynastic uncertainty was a recipe for trouble.[3]

There was too a moral dimension to Baldwin's leprosy. In his crusade encyclical of January 1181, *Cor nostrum et*, Pope Alexander III had this to say when describing the difficulties facing the kingdom of Jerusalem:

For there is no king who can rule that land, since he, namely Baldwin, who holds the government of the kingdom is so gravely scourged by the just judgement of God ('justo Dei judicio flagellatus') . . . that he is scarcely able to bear the continual sufferings of his body.[4]

Alexander's purpose in issuing this bull was to gain support for the Latin East, but it may be wondered how far equating the king's illness with God's judgement on sin had the effect of casting a slur on the Jerusalemite royal house and was counter-productive. People in the West might have been put off sending aid if they thought God's wrath had fallen on the monarchy. Baldwin himself and those around him must surely have taken exception to the pope's remark.

More specifically, it would seem that there were fears that the direct royal line might be supplanted. William recorded that in 1180 Baldwin had been afraid that Raymond III of Tripoli and Bohemond III of Antioch were out to dethrone him and seize power for themselves,[5] and a contemporary chronicler related that in 1176 King Henry II of England believed Count Philip of Flanders, who was about to set out for Jerusalem, had ambitions to become king.[6]

---

[3] The reign of Baldwin IV is to be the subject of a study by Dr Bernard Hamilton.

[4] Alexander III, *Opera omnia*, PL, 200, col. 1294. The bull was reissued by Lucius III in 1184/5 at the time of Patriarch Eraclius' visit to the West. See R. Hiestand (ed.), *Vorarbeiten zum Oriens Pontificius*, I–II: *Papsturkunden für Templer und Johanniter* (Göttingen, 1972–84), I, nos. 165, 175.

[5] *WT*, XXII, I, lines 1–5; cf. XXII, 10, lines 13–15. The same ambition was attributed to Miles of Plancy in 1174 (XXI, 4, lines 33–6).

[6] W. Stubbs (ed.), *Gesta Regis Henrici Secundi*, I, 116. Writing of Philip's visit to the East in 1177, William stated that he 'in supplantationem domini regis hec moliri attemptaret' (XXI, 13, lines 49–50). This remark could be understood as confirming the *Gesta Regis Henrici*, but the context, Philip's attempt to meddle in the marriages

It is difficult to know how much truth there was in these statements or how seriously the threats they embody were taken at the time. Raymond and Bohemond were cousins of Baldwin IV, being like him descended from Baldwin II, while Philip, and also Henry, were the grandsons of King Fulk and his first wife, Aremburg of Maine. Philip's father, Thierry of Alsace, had come to the East on four occasions and had clearly entertained territorial ambitions there, while Henry II had, since the early 1170s, been sending substantial sums of money to the Holy Land in preparation for the Crusade he had undertaken to lead.[7] Baldwin's relatives were certainly taking an interest in what was happening in Jerusalem.

It was also true that in their desperation to get the rulers of the West, in particular the kings of France and England, to bring military aid to the East, both Amaury and Baldwin IV had been prepared to sacrifice elements of their own sovereignty. In the mid-1160s Amaury had promised King Louis VII of France that if Louis came to the Holy Land he would place himself at his command. In 1184–5 an embassy from the East led by Patriarch Eraclius had offered King Philip Augustus the keys of the Holy Sepulchre and had then offered the keys and also the banner of the kingdom to Henry II of England. It may be that the keys of Jerusalem had previously been offered to Louis VII by an embassy in 1169. Exactly what these gestures signified is a matter for debate, but at the very least they would appear to indicate that the resources of the Latin East were to be at the disposal of the western kings, should they choose to come.[8]

---

of Baldwin's sisters, would indicate that in fact William was accusing him of trying to usurp royal prerogatives and not of trying to seize the throne.

[7] For William's own description of the relationships, see *WT*, xiv, 1. For Thierry, see xv, 6; xvii, 1, lines 32–4; xviii, 16–17; 24, lines 3–4; xix, 10, lines 1–11; 11, line 7; and especially xvii, 7, lines 7–26; xviii, 18, lines 45–68. For Henry's financial preparations, see H. E. Mayer, 'Henry II of England and the Holy Land', *EHR*, xcvii (1982), 721–39.

[8] See R. C. Smail, 'Latin Syria and the West', pp. 8–20 *passim*; *idem*, 'The International Status of the Latin Kingdom of Jerusalem, 1150–1192', in P. M. Holt (ed.), *The Eastern Mediterranean Lands in the Period of Crusades* (Warminster, 1977), pp. 23–8, 31–2. For a suggestion that in 1184/5 the leaders of Latin Syria were attempting by sending Eraclius to western Europe to find a prince of one of the royal houses of the West who would displace their own dynasty, see H. E. Mayer, 'Kaiserrecht und Heiliges Land', in H. Fuhrmann, H. E. Mayer and K. Wriedt (eds.), *Aus Reichsgeschichte und Nordischer Geschichte* (Stuttgart, 1972), pp. 204–6. His views have been challenged by Smail, 'International Status', pp. 41–2 note 38, and by J. B. Gillingham, 'Roger of Howden on Crusade', in D. O. Morgan (ed.), *Medieval Historical Writing in the Christian and Islamic Worlds* (London, 1982),

The king was unsuitable, his rule was in question and the kingdom was in such dire straits that he was prepared to humiliate himself by trading his sovereign prerogatives for military assistance. In short, the credibility of the monarchy was in doubt. It is against this background that William, in writing the *Historia*, should be seen as an apologist for the dynasty and in particular for Baldwin IV. How far he was motivated by affection for the king whose tutor he had been, by the *amor patriae* which in the Prologue he asserted had spurred him to write,[9] or simply by the consideration that, unsatisfactory though the situation might be, it would be made far worse by the disputes and upheavals attendant on a change of ruler, we do not know. To William, the credentials of the dynasty were impeccable and the right of successive kings to rule unquestioned. Nevertheless, legitimacy had to be coupled with ability and success: in constructing his *apologia*, he wanted both to vindicate the monarchy and to present it as an inspiration for the future.

Something of William's innate respect for legitimate rule can be gauged from his denunciation of usurpers. Book I opens with a description of the events of the early seventh century. Jerusalem had been laid waste by Chosroes II, but, contrary to what we might expect, William had no word of condemnation for what he could easily have viewed as an act of sacrilege. Instead he concentrated attention on the idea that this invasion was retribution on the Byzantine emperor, Phocas, who had treacherously killed his predecessor, Maurice, in 602. Chosroes' action was justifiable because 'he abhorred the perfidy of those who were prepared to have a wicked man even yet stained with the blood of his lord to rule over them'.[10] William used the same sort of language to describe that 'worthless and deceitful man' Alexius I. 'Striking treacherously against his lord and benefactor [Nicephorus III] . . . he had seized the empire and was presuming to hold it by force.'[11] The only ruler in the history of Latin Syria whom William considered a usurper

---

pp. 62–4 and note 26. But Mayer is unmoved: Mayer, 'Henry II', p. 732; see also Kedar, 'Patriarch Eraclius', pp. 191–4.

9 *WT*, Prologue, line 67. For *amor patriae* as a literary topos, see Lacroix, 'Guillaume de Tyr', p. 209; Vessey, 'William of Tyre', pp. 439–40.

10 *WT*, I, 1–2, at 2, lines 14–16.

11 *WT*, II, 5, lines 1–2, 7–10. See also XX, 26. Cf. I, 9, lines 41–5, where William by contrast appears to sympathize with the seizure of power by Michael VII after the defeat of Romanus Diogenes in 1071.

was Alice, the widow of Bohemond II of Antioch (d. 1130), who had attempted to seize power for herself and disregard the rights of her own infant daughter. To William Alice was a wicked woman, and he recorded with apparent satisfaction how her repeated efforts were thwarted by, in turn, her father, King Baldwin II, King Fulk, and then Patriarch Ralph of Antioch working in co-operation with Raymond of Poitiers.[12] In this context it is instructive to read his account of the acquisition of Edessa in 1098 by Baldwin of Boulogne, the future Baldwin I. The legitimate ruler, the Armenian Thoros, had been murdered by his own people, but William was at pains to make it clear that Baldwin, although the beneficiary of this deed, had tried to save him and had then been given the rule despite protestations of reluctance. He had come to power following a *coup d'état* but was blameless.[13]

In contrast to rulers who had usurped power, legitimate rulers were those who were the rightful heirs of their predecessors and whose reigns had been inaugurated in the correct manner. But, before we examine William's treatment of these themes as applied in the Latin East, his ideas about how the monarchy of the kingdom of Jerusalem had come into being in the first place deserve consideration. Early in Book I he had given a mythical account of the origins of the Seljük dynasty. The only obstacle preventing the Seljük Turks from seizing lands was that they had no king, so they determined to elect one, which they did by lots:

By common decree they placed this man [Seljük, the eponymous founder of the dynasty] in authority over them and raised him to the royal throne, showing him the reverence which is due to kings and binding themselves by general agreement and by the common swearing of oaths to carry out his commands.[14]

There are several elements here which foreshadow William's story of the election of Godfrey of Bouillon to rule in Jerusalem. Then too it was military need, in this case the need to defend Jerusalem, that precipitated the choice of ruler.[15] Godfrey was chosen by the leaders of the crusading army, not by the drawing of lots, but after an investigation into the personal suitability of the various contenders out of which he emerged as the unanimous choice.[16] William still

---

[12] *WT*, XIII, 27; XIV, 4–5; 20. [13] *WT*, IV, 5. [14] *WT*, I, 7, lines 83–7.
[15] *WT*, VIII, 21, lines 1–8.
[16] *WT*, IX, 1, lines 1–7; 2; 3, line 1. William spoiled the effect by stating in apparent self-contradiction that the majority of the electors had agreed on Raymond of Toulouse but had backed down, and he ended by repeating that Godfrey had been

had the problem of explaining why Godfrey was not anointed and crowned king: he had royal responsibility, and William wanted his readers to think of him as if he were a king but one who had declined the crown for reasons of pious humility.[17] Godfrey was thus ruler by virtue of election, just like Seljük. But Godfrey also had to be shown to have held his lands in trust from God, and to this end he accepted investiture at the hands of God's representative, Patriarch Daimbert.[18]

The establishment of the monarchy in Jerusalem was completed by the coronation of Baldwin I as king on Christmas Day 1100. William was careful to introduce several salient points into his account: Baldwin was designated by Godfrey on his death-bed, was elected 'by the unanimous advice of the leaders', came to power by hereditary right, and was acclaimed by the populace.[19] The insistence on the idea that Godfrey had been king in all but name means that it comes as no surprise that as soon as Baldwin's differences with Daimbert had been patched up he should be crowned. William was explicit that he was consecrated and anointed and 'crowned with the royal diadem'.[20] The coronation thus conformed to the rites common in western Europe, and Baldwin's right to rule was vindicated by the norms current in the West: designation, election, acclamation and hereditary succession.[21]

But if Baldwin was created king in the western European tradition, there still remains the question of by what right the monarchy in Jerusalem could be called into existence at all. Later the papacy was to confirm Baldwin I in his kingship, but William made no reference to this fact.[22] Instead he left his readers with the impression that the piety of the individuals concerned and their God-given success in recapturing Jerusalem had been sufficient warrant for the inception of kingly office. There is no suggestion

---

the unanimous choice. He had clearly been caught between conflicting accounts in his sources. See Raymond, *Le "Liber"*, pp. 152–3.

[17] *WT*, Prologue, lines 95–9; IX, 5, lines 1–2; 9, lines 14–33.

[18] *WT*, IX, 15, lines 8–13. See below, pp. 103–4.

[19] *WT*, X, 1, lines 4–9; 6, lines 57–61.

[20] *WT*, X, 9, lines 6–8.

[21] For a discussion of coronation rites in the Latin kingdom of Jerusalem, see Mayer, 'Das Pontifikale von Tyrus'.

[22] *RRH*, no. 122. Almost a century later it required the authority of the western emperor to bring the Latin monarchy in Cyprus into being (G. Hill, *A History of Cyprus* (Cambridge, 1940–52), II, 48–9).

in the *Historia* that the kingdom of Jerusalem was anything other than totally autonomous.

Once the monarchy was inaugurated, William repeated apropos each new king down to and including Baldwin V that he was anointed and crowned.[23] His consistency on this point is an indication that to him, as to his contemporaries, it was the formal ecclesiastical ceremony that created the king. King Fulk was consecrated and crowned jointly with his wife, Melisende, the daughter of his predecessor, and Theodora and Maria Comnena were both consecrated queen before their marriages to the reigning monarchs, respectively Baldwin III and Amaury.[24] But William was less consistent in mentioning designation, election and acclamation. Baldwin II ascended the throne after an *electio* by prelates and lay magnates. Fulk of Anjou, Melisende and their infant son, the future Baldwin III, were designated by Baldwin II on his death-bed, although it may be added that Fulk had only come to the East to marry Melisende and thus succeed to the throne after the leading laymen and ecclesiastics had unanimously decided to invite him.[25] It was only in the case of Baldwin V that William gave full play to the various elements he had referred to in his description of the accession of Baldwin I. Baldwin V's coronation was unique, since his uncle, Baldwin IV, was still alive at the time. The decision to crown him king (he was in any case unable to exercise authority in person as he was a minor) was confirmed by Baldwin IV in consultation with his barons. The coronation 'had the support of the entire people and was agreed to by the clergy who were present'.[26] So the young Baldwin was designated by the king, elected by the magnates and acclaimed by the people as well as being anointed, and on this occasion, for once, William mentioned homage and fealty being performed after the ceremony. But, although William did not mention all the relevant points on each occasion, the reader is left in no doubt that each new reign commenced with the correct legal procedures being followed.

If what made a king was consecration and coronation, what entitled a man to be king was election and hereditary right. William clearly regarded hereditary succession as being part of the natural

---

[23] *WT*, xii, 3, lines 39–40; 4, line 24 (Baldwin II); xiv, 2, lines 26–30 (Fulk and Melisende); xvi, 3, lines 7–9 (Baldwin III); xix, 1, lines 21–5 (Amaury); xxi, 2, lines 10–11 (Baldwin IV); xxii, 30, lines 25–7 (Baldwin V).
[24] *WT*, xiv, 2, lines 26–30; xviii, 22, lines 40–2; xx, 1, lines 9–14.
[25] *WT*, xii, 3, lines 37–8; xiii, 24, lines 1–6; 28, lines 7–11; xiv, 2, lines 10–17.
[26] *WT*, xxii, 30, lines 24–5.

order. He mentioned it in connection with western Europe,[27] Cilician Armenia[28] and even the Muslim world, although he noted that it was not a principle employed by the Assassins.[29] He also made repeated references to the idea that landed estates and lordships in Frankish Syria were held by hereditary tenure.[30] It could well be that he projected the principle back to a time, early in the twelfth century, before it was universally adopted.[31] In the case of the principality of Antioch he claimed that Tancred (1104–12) and Roger (1112–19) were not princes in their own right, but regents for the young Bohemond II, the son and heir of the founder of the principality, Bohemond I. This interpretation of Tancred and Roger's status was perhaps William's own; certainly it finds no support in the narrative sources closer to the period or in the numismatic or diplomatic evidence.[32]

William's emphasis on hereditary rights of succession meant that election normally had only a subsidiary role in the emergence of each new ruler. Godfrey, as the originator of the line, owed his position to election; Baldwin I owed his to election and to his right to succeed as Godfrey's brother and heir. The full interplay of the two elements is brought out most clearly in the preliminaries to the accession of Baldwin II in 1118. Baldwin I had had no children. At the time of his death, his closest kinsman was his brother, Eustace of Boulogne, a man who had fought on the First Crusade and then returned to the family's lands in western Europe. Present in the East, however, was Baldwin's first cousin once removed, Baldwin of Le Bourg, count of Edessa. The assembled prelates and lay magnates were divided between those who wanted to uphold the 'most ancient law of hereditary succession' and wait for Eustace to come from the West, and those who believed that the dangers inherent in a protracted interregnum made it expedient that they should choose a new king without delay, namely Baldwin. Thanks

[27] *WT*, IX, 13, lines 10–16; XXI, 14, lines 10–12.   [28] *WT*, XX, 26, lines 15–16.

[29] *WT*, XX, 11, lines 17–19; XXII, 20, lines 17–18. For the Assassins, see XX, 29, lines 8–10.

[30] *WT*, IX, 13, lines 42–7; X, 9, lines 26–9; 24, lines 12–13; XI, 14, lines 76–7; 22, lines 72–3; XII, 17, lines 50–2; XIV, 15, lines 17–19; 19, lines 21–2; XVIII, 12, line 3; 18, lines 50–2.

[31] For the absence of hereditary succession to lordships in early twelfth-century Jerusalem, see J. Prawer, *Crusader Institutions* (Oxford, 1980), pp. 23–8 *passim*.

[32] *WT*, XI, 6, lines 43–8; 18, lines 13–19; XII, 10, lines 23–9; 14, lines 23–9; XIII, 21, lines 8–9. See also X, 9, lines 19–24. For the numismatic evidence, see D. M. Metcalf, *Coinage of the Crusades and the Latin East in the Ashmolean Museum Oxford* (London, 1983), pp. 7–8 and plates 3–4. For the charters, see *RRH*, nos. 35, 53, 76, 86.

to the influence of Joscelin of Courtenay and Patriarch Arnulf, it was the latter view that prevailed, and Baldwin was 'chosen king with general support and common consent'. William was not happy. He was doubtful about the motivation of Joscelin and Arnulf and outraged that the 'legitimate heir to the kingdom' had been 'fraudulently excluded from the rightful succession'. The election of Baldwin II was said to have been 'contrary to law, both human and divine ("contra ius et fas") and against the most ancient rule of hereditary succession'. So we are left in no doubt as to where his sympathies would have lain had he been present, and by calling in question the motivation of its two leading advocates, he was able to surround the principle of election with an element of uncertainty. But two aspects of the affair had the effect of turning what was on the face of it an injustice into something which placed Baldwin's accession beyond reproach. Baldwin's pious character, and the evident approval of God as shown by his subsequent success as king, vindicated his right to rule, and Eustace, likewise moved by piety, waived his rights to the throne when he learnt that Baldwin had been chosen king and realized that his own claim, if pursued, would lead to strife. So William had managed to persuade his readers both that Baldwin was rightfully king and that the principle of hereditary right should be applied to determine royal succession. It is a superb performance.[33]

After 1118 there were no more aberrations. William was able to depict each new king as possessing the throne by hereditary right, and so show that the principle of legitimacy was being upheld.[34] But he wanted to do more than simply insist on the legitimate succession of the members of the royal dynasty. He wanted to portray the kings as men whose heroism and achievements not only combined with their legitimacy to justify their rule, but also served to encourage the present generation. William was concerned that the men of his own day had become enervated both physically and spiritually,[35] and he clearly believed that the deeds of past

---

[33] *WT*, XII, 3, lines 10–11, 37–8, 46–7, 62–3. Cf. IX, 5, lines 29–32. It is instructive to compare William's treatment of Baldwin II's accession with his treatment of the accession of Manuel Comnenus, who in 1143 was chosen in preference to his own elder brother. Here again William emphasized rights of hereditary succession, but was nevertheless convinced that the choice of Manuel was justified, adducing the military circumstances, Manuel's ability and God's will (*WT*, XV, 23).

[34] *WT*, XIV, 2 (Fulk); XVI, 1, lines 1–7 (Baldwin III); XVIII, 34, lines 31–2; XIX, 1; 4, lines 6–8; XXI, 1, lines 5–6 (Amaury).

[35] *WT*, XXI, 7. Cf. XX, 22, lines 1–13.

generations could be held up as an example of what still might be achieved. But he was also aware that a flat recital of praiseworthy deeds by itself would bore rather than edify and might arouse suspicions about another of his concerns, his regard for truth. He was therefore prepared to record failures as well as successes, character flaws and ill-judged decisions as well as wisdom, justice and piety.

Starting with Godfrey, William provided a character sketch of each new ruler at the beginning of his reign.[36] These were literary descriptions in a classical mould owing much to the model provided by Einhard and ultimately Suetonius, and they dealt with physical appearance, ancestry, character, bearing and morals.[37] All the portraits were generally favourable, with comments on the kings' wisdom, vigour and experience. Each was physically attractive, even Baldwin IV until his leprosy took its toll and Amaury, who was obese, but William managed to avoid making his descriptions unduly repetitive. Baldwin I and Amaury come out worst. Baldwin had been destined for a career in the Church but had chosen a secular life instead, and, one instance apart, William studiously avoided commenting on his piety or lack of it.[38] By contrast, Godfrey and Baldwin II had been extremely pious, and Baldwin III's and Amaury's piety also receive favourable comment. Baldwin I and Amaury were both guilty of succumbing to the lusts of the flesh, as indeed was Baldwin III in his youth until his marriage to Theodora Comnena. Baldwin I had placed excessive reliance on the advice of the disreputable Patriarch Arnulf. None of the other kings was criticized for his choice of counsellors, although Miles of Plancy, the effective regent after the death of Amaury, was guilty of not consulting the barons in affairs of state.[39] On the other hand, William stated with apparent approval that Amaury had been exceptional in the degree of trust he placed in his servants. But he criticized him for his unapproachable manner, and in this contrasted him sharply with his brother, Baldwin III. However, it was Baldwin who was over-fond of games of chance, and William

[36] *WT*, IX, 5; 9 (Godfrey); X, 2 (Baldwin I); XII, 4 (Baldwin II); XIV, I (Fulk); XVI, 1–2 (Baldwin III); XIX, 2–3 (Amaury); XXI, I (Baldwin IV). See also *WT*, XXI, 5 (Raymond III).

[37] For Einhard's use of Suetonius and his influence on later historiography, see R. W. Southern, 'Aspects of the European Tradition of Historical Writing. 1. The Classical Tradition from Einhard to Geoffrey of Monmouth', *TRHS*, 5th ser., XX (1970), 183–5. For verbal echoes of Einhard in William's character sketches, see *WT*, XVI, 2, lines 56–7; XIX, 2, lines 29–30.

[38] See *WT*, XI, 12, lines 1–5; 13, lines 1–3.

[39] *WT*, XXI, 3, lines 9–14; 4, lines 1–40.

praised Amaury for his lack of interest in such activities. Fulk could not remember names or faces: Baldwin III had a particularly good memory for people he had met. Baldwin III was an articulate and charming conversationalist; Amaury was monosyllabic and had a slight speech impediment. Baldwin III was a respecter of the Church; Amaury – and here William was at his most censorious – was grasping for money and placed heavy demands on ecclesiastical wealth. Baldwin III, Amaury and also Raymond III of Tripoli were moderate in their eating and drinking, and were intelligent and educated, Baldwin III exceptionally so. Baldwin III, Amaury and Baldwin IV were interested in learning and history. It is difficult to know how far William supplied his readers with conventionalized portraits into which contrasts were introduced artificially to provide variety, and how far he made a genuine attempt at characterization. The absence of unalloyed obsequiousness leaves an impression of plausibility, while the prevalance of praiseworthy characteristics invariably compensates for the different failings. Whatever modern historians might think about these character sketches, William managed to portray the kings as worthy if sometimes fallible men and, above all, as wise and able monarchs who had provided the leadership their kingdom needed.[40]

The character sketches, however, form only a small part of his treatment of their careers. The general account of each reign provides information on military and diplomatic achievements, as well as adding details to corroborate and supplement the sketches. An impression of how he did this and what sort of pictures he built up can be gained by looking briefly at his treatment of four examples, Godfrey of Bouillon, Baldwin I, Amaury and Baldwin IV.

By the time William was writing, Godfrey was regarded as the hero of the First Crusade, a paragon of valour and godliness. In the character sketch William had described his distinguished ancestry, and he made it clear elsewhere in his account that Godfrey's retinue and the deeds of his brothers on the First Crusade had added to his own lustre.[41] He had also mentioned his enormous physical strength, and this he confirmed by recounting other anecdotes at appropriate points in the story.[42] More especially, he repeatedly

---

[40] William's preparedness to admit to blemishes in his subjects distinguishes him from Einhard and his followers. See Southern, 'Aspects of the European Tradition', pp. 184–5.

[41] *WT*, II, 1, lines 1–18; IV, 13, lines 31–6; V, 9, lines 21–35; VII, 4–5.

[42] *WT*, III, 10, lines 1–16; 18, lines 24–54; V, 6, lines 56–67; VIII, 18, lines 18–30; IX, 7–8; 22.

presented Godfrey as above all a vigorous and able commander.[43] Both during the Crusade (as shown by his dealings with the king of Hungary and Emperor Alexius) and while in control of Jerusalem he revealed his gift for diplomacy,[44] and he also showed himself solicitous for the needs of others, the lowly as well as the great.[45] Godfrey's piety and religious devotion were stressed: he would not allow his army to pillage at Constantinople at Christmas; he endowed churches; at the assault on Jerusalem he drew attention to the vision of a shining warrior and so restored sagging morale; his recovery from illness was a sign of God's grace; the fact that he declined the crown was a sign of his humility, and his humility was such as to impress the native population in Jerusalem.[46] In describing the siege of Arsur in 1100, William remarked that Godfrey 'fearing God and beloved of God, endeavoured at the Lord's instigation to extend the frontiers of the kingdom'.[47] In short, Godfrey was too good for this sinful world, and he died, 'a true confessor of Christ' to go to his eternal reward.[48] But even he was not given a clear record: at the time of the siege of Antioch he had quarrelled with Bohemond over the gift of a pavilion. William's comment is instructive:

We are very much surprised that a man distinguished by such modesty and conspicuous for such dignity of character claimed back with such insistence this trivial and easily forgotten thing, nor has anything occurred to me as a solution except in the words of the proverb, 'Nothing is perfect in every respect.'[49]

Two other incidents from which Godfrey does not emerge unscathed concern the Tower of David, custody of which he obtained from Raymond of Toulouse by underhand means, and his dealings with Daimbert, to whom he was reluctant to give what was due to the Church – so much so that William could have Daimbert speak of Godfrey's 'sacrilegious intent'.[50]

Baldwin I inevitably suffers by comparison with his elder brother. Early in the Crusade there are comparatively few references to him, and these normally show him as Godfrey's coadjutor.

---

[43] *WT*, I, 17, lines 10–11; III, 16, lines 1–7; v, 5, lines 4–38; 6, lines 12–17; VI, 3, lines 22–36; 17, lines 23–5; 21, lines 7–11; VII, 3–4; 10; VIII, 18; IX, 19.
[44] *WT*, II, 1–12 *passim*; 15, lines 7–19; VII, 16, lines 36–43; IX, 13, lines 39–47.
[45] *WT*, II, 4, lines 45–62; 5; III, 18, lines 24–31; VI, 22, lines 44–7; VII, 5, lines 5–7.
[46] *WT*, II, 6, lines 14–18; IV, 22, lines 28–35; VIII, 16, lines 11–20; IX, 9; 20.
[47] *WT*, IX, 19, lines 36–7.
[48] *WT*, IX, 5, lines 3–8; 23, lines 3–7.   [49] *WT*, v, 9, lines 51–5.
[50] *WT*, IX, 3; X, 4, line 16: 'impietatis . . . proposito'.

The first episode in which he featured prominently was his clash with Tancred over the control of the Cilician towns, and here Baldwin was presented in a distinctly unfavourable light. Not only had the leaders of the Crusade quarrelled, but, thanks to Baldwin, Christian warriors had needlessly been killed.[51] His achievement in securing Edessa followed immediately after these events, and so William had to make an abrupt about-turn and portray him as a hero rather than as a villain:

he recognized his guilt with all humility and promised fitting satisfaction to the noble man [Tancred] for his offence. Since he had erred out of character and at the suggestion of another rather than on his own impulse, he received the pardon, and restored himself in the esteem, of all. Otherwise he was a man praiseworthy in everything, and there was never heard again any report of this sort concerning him.[52]

The idea that he had erred at the instigation of another reappeared much later in William's account: Baldwin's bigamous marriage to Adelaide of Sicily in 1113 was Arnulf's doing, as was his hounding of Daimbert.[53] Both instances detract from Baldwin's reputation and fit in with William's remarks in the character sketch about his undue intimacy with Arnulf. Baldwin's marriage to Adelaide and his treatment of his Armenian wife might seem to add substance to the assertion that Baldwin succumbed to the 'lusts of the flesh',[54] and it is no doubt significant that at the end of his career William refrained from giving him the sort of eulogy he had for Godfrey, Baldwin II and Baldwin III.

What made Baldwin a worthy king was his prowess as a man of action and military leader. He was courageous, inspired confidence in his troops and struck fear into the enemy.[55] The history of his contribution to the First Crusade and then to the Latin kingdom as its first king is largely the history of his success in battle, in siege warfare and in other military displays. He was ever anxious to extend the frontiers of the kingdom, and to this end not only waged war but also engaged in castle-building.[56] He was concerned to

---

[51] *WT*, III, 18, lines 1–17; 20–6.   [52] *WT*, IV, 1, lines 15–20.

[53] *WT*, X, 7; 24, lines 15–23; XI, 4, lines 26–31, 39–41; 15; 21, lines 33–5.

[54] *WT*, X, 2, line 11. For his marital affairs, see XI, 1, lines 27–58; 15, lines 17–19; 21; 29, lines 13–40. Cf. H. E. Mayer, *Mélanges sur l'histoire du royaume latin du Jérusalem* (Paris, 1984), 49–72. Mayer (pp. 70–1) argues that Baldwin was a homosexual and that William's reference to 'lusts of the flesh' was a veiled allusion to this fact.

[55] *WT*, IV, 1–6; XI, 10.   [56] *WT*, X, 13; XI, 13; 26, lines 15–33; 30.

suppress brigandage,[57] and, despite their earlier differences, he twice brought aid to Tancred in Antioch.[58] His run of success was not unbroken,[59] but on only two occasions did William attribute his defeat to his own folly.[60] William's account well bears out his remarks in the character sketch:

Skilled in arms, agile on horseback, he was indefatigable and solicitous whenever the affairs of the realm called him. It seems unnecessary to praise further his magnanimity, courage, and his experience in the art of war.[61]

William's account of King Amaury is perhaps the most difficult to fathom of any of his descriptions of the kings. On one level he gave the impression that all was well; on another he left doubts in the minds of his readers as to Amaury's true worth as a ruler. In the Prologue William spoke of him as 'of illustrious memory and distinguished remembrance in the Lord', and at his death he wrote: 'he was a man of wisdom and discretion, truly fitted for the government of the kingdom'.[62] Although his military exploits, notably the Egyptian campaigns of 1168 and 1169, were not invariably crowned with success, Amaury was clearly a careful strategist and able commander. In his strong reactions to events in the Muslim world he had shown real feeling, and he had been genuinely angered by the murder of an Assassin ambassador by the Templars.[63] William also stressed the encouragement and promotion that he himself had received from the king.[64] But, for all Amaury's good qualities, there is an undercurrent of criticism in the *Historia* and a sense that things were not as they should be. Part of the trouble was that the period of Amaury's reign saw the threat to the Latin kingdom increasing, and this was reflected in the appeals to the West for aid and in Amaury's own visit to Constantinople in 1171.[65] Despite Amaury's successes, there is a growing pessimism in the account, and this detracts from the image of the king himself. In addition there are several points which serve to undermine Amaury's standing: the disputed succession and the divorce, to which we shall return shortly, as well as the defects revealed in the character sketch and the curious discussion the king had had with

[57] *WT*, x, 8, lines 11–22; 25, lines 30–6.   [58] *WT*, xi, 7; 16, lines 32–44.
[59] *WT*, iv, 4, lines 12–21; x, 8, lines 1–8, 33–7; xi, 7, lines 41–55; 17.
[60] *WT*, x, 19; xi, 19.   [61] *WT*, x, 2, lines 21–7.
[62] *WT*, Prologue, lines 81–2; xx, 31, lines 41–2.
[63] For example, *WT*, xx, 5, lines 9–11; 19, lines 24–9; 26, lines 51–2; 30, lines 14–17.
[64] *WT*, Prologue, lines 80–5; xix, 12, lines 68–79; xx, 1, lines 23–7; 31, lines 42–3.
[65] *WT*, xx, 12; 22–4.

William on Christian apologetics and belief in the after-life, in which he had shocked William by his religious scepticism.[66] This scepticism contrasts strangely with his riposte made to those who in 1171 were concerned at the possible effects on Jerusalem of being left leaderless by his absence in Constantinople: 'Let the Lord whose servant I am rule the kingdom.'[67] But William also had some direct criticism. Although he showed that there was more than one interpretation of the incident, he evidently believed that in attacking Egypt in 1168 Amaury had broken the terms of his treaty with Shāwar and so was guilty of breaking faith.[68] But, as if this was not reason enough why God should withhold His favour and deny the Christians success in their campaign, Amaury then allowed himself to be influenced by the evil Miles of Plancy, who, playing on the king's avarice, to which William had alluded in the character sketch, persuaded him to take a course of action which proved disastrous: the Egyptians were given a respite, and in the meantime Shīrkūh, Nūr al-Dīn's commander, was able to take control of Egypt and oblige the Christians to withdraw.[69] William was aware of the long-term significance of this set-back and expatiated on it, concluding:

The cupidity of one man has brought with it all these things, and his avarice, that root of all evil, has cast a shadow over the cloudless sky granted us from on high.[70]

These are strong words, but their impact is diminished by uncertainty as to whether he was attacking Amaury, whose avarice he had already mentioned, or Miles, whose character he had comprehensively blackened. In all likelihood this ambiguity was intentional.

There is no ambiguity about William's account of Baldwin IV. He left a tragic portrait of a gifted and vigorous young man contending with his own chronic illness, with growing dissent within the kingdom and with the unparalleled Muslim threat posed by Saladin, now master of both Egypt and Syria. Despite his illness, Baldwin repeatedly led his army against the Muslims. In 1175, even before he came of age, he was raiding into Syria, and he was again in action in 1177, 1178, 1179 and 1182.[71] As recorded at the very end of the *His-*

---

[66] *WT*, xix, 3.   [67] *WT*, xx, 22, lines 40–1.
[68] *WT*, xx, 5. See J. Riley-Smith, 'Peace Never Established: The Case of the Kingdom of Jerusalem', *TRHS*, 5th ser., xxviii (1978), 100.
[69] *WT*, xx, 9–10.   [70] *WT*, xx, 10, lines 52–4.
[71] *WT*, xxi, 9; 10; 19–23; 25, lines 20–69; 26–8; xxii, 15, lines 43–6; 16, lines 66–72; 18, lines 1–2, 53–7; 19, lines 1–7, 89–92; 21–3.

toria, in the closing weeks of 1183 he led his army to the relief of Kerak.[72] Yet all this time his leprosy was increasingly debilitating.[73] It may well be that in his insistence on Baldwin as a military leader William was guilty of special pleading: there is, for example, good evidence that the commander of the Christian forces in their victory at Mont Gisard in 1177 was Raynald of Châtillon, and not the king as he alleged.[74] Only once did Baldwin make a mistake: in 1180 he was panicked by fear of Raymond of Tripoli and Bohemond III of Antioch into agreeing to the marriage of his sister to Guy of Lusignan. William later explained his suspicion of Raymond as being the work of wicked people taking advantage of the king's affliction for their own ends, and he named the king's mother, Agnes of Courtenay, and her brother Joscelin in this context.[75] He then described Baldwin's quarrel with Guy, and the *Historia* ends with Baldwin trying to get the marriage dissolved.[76] William was clearly attempting to minimize Baldwin's inability to rule: until 1183 there was no question of his relinquishing control permanently:

For although he was weak and impotent in his body, he was nevertheless vigorous in his mind, and he strove beyond his strength to disguise his illness and bear the burden of royalty.[77]

What these examples of William's treatment of the kings reveal – and an examination of the other rulers would point in the same direction – is that all were able men capable of giving strong military leadership. To William, as his remarks about the origins of the Seljük dynasty or the reasons for the election of Godfrey make clear, command in war was a primary function of monarchy. On the other hand, not one of the kings was perfect, and even Godfrey, whose piety and prowess were passing into legend, had his lapses. William also regarded piety, as evidenced by both personal devotion and concern for ecclesiastical liberty, as an attribute of the ideal king, and in this respect neither Baldwin I nor Amaury fully met his requirements. It is instructive to compare Baldwin I with Tancred,

[72] *WT*, XXII, 31, lines 36–52.
[73] *WT*, XXI, 13, line 8; XXII, 1, lines 5–7; 10, lines 31–4; 26, lines 1–14.
[74] See *WT*, XXI, 19–23. See B. Hamilton, 'The Elephant of Christ: Reynald of Châtillon', in D. Baker (ed.), *Religious Motivation: Biographical and Sociological Problems for the Church Historian* (Oxford, 1978), p. 100 and note 24. For the location of the battle, see M. C. Lyons and D. E. P. Jackson, *Saladin: The Politics of the Holy War* (Cambridge, 1982), pp. 123–4.
[75] *WT*, XXII, 1, lines 1–21; 10.
[76] *WT*, XXII, 26, lines 14–57; 30, lines 1–34; XXIII, 1.
[77] *WT*, XXII, 26, lines 11–13.

whose treatment of the Church and whose private religious observance received a warm accolade.[78] In William's eyes both were heroes of the First Crusade and the years following it, but Tancred's piety made him a paragon of crusading virtue and no doubt goes some way towards explaining why it was Baldwin who was denigrated when the two came in to conflict in Cilicia.

So the picture that William gives is of a stable, godly dynasty acting responsibly and striving to the best of its very considerable ability against mounting odds to defend the achievements of the Crusade. Against its successes or creditable failures, the individual instances of foolish or unrighteous action pale into insignificance. The meaning is clear: the monarchy has been a success and is still a success. No one should question the legitimacy of the dynasty. Rather, the dynasty should evoke admiration in all who, whether in western Europe or in the East, might read what William has to say.

For the careers of Godfrey and Baldwin I, William had been dependent on the older histories and popular tradition, and, in trying to present a picture that was true, credible and at the same time edifying, he had had to penetrate a haze of adulation. It is remarkable that his accounts were not far more romanticized. To understand his critical view of Amaury and his *apologia* for Baldwin IV is less simple. It may be that William indeed saw Amaury as a mixture of good and bad, capable of both wise and unwise political decisions, and Baldwin IV as a tragic hero; but, in writing a history of the Latin East from the vantage-point of Baldwin's reign, he could well have had more specific reasons arising out of the contemporary situation for portraying them as he did. As indicated at the beginning of this chapter, the credibility of the monarchy was in question and the future of the dynasty uncertain, while at the same time the Latin East desperately needed western aid. But if it was necessary to stress the legitimacy of the dynasty and the record of the kings as leaders in war, defending the gains of the Crusade and so providing an inspiration for his contemporaries, William may also have felt it necessary to defend Baldwin IV against specific challenges to his right to rule. Was Baldwin really the rightful king? How was the papal assertion that his leprosy represented the 'just judgement of God' to be rebutted? How far was the declining military situation attributable to his chronic illness? Answering such

---

[78] *WT*, IX, 13, lines 47–65; X, 9, lines 9–15; 17, lines 41–3; 22, lines 26–32; XI, 2, lines 40–1; 18, lines 1–4.

questions entailed raking up stories which in some instances under-mined the standing of earlier kings.

One embarrassing aspect of recent history which William could not ignore was the fact that Baldwin IV's parents, Amaury and Agnes of Courtenay, were divorced. The couple had been related within the prohibited degrees of consanguinity – they were third cousins – and as the union was regarded as incestuous a question-mark hung over the legitimacy of their children, Baldwin and his sister Sibylla. It would have been impossible to have attempted to gloss over the divorce, since both Agnes and Amaury's second wife, Maria Comnena, were still alive at the time of writing, and so William cast it in as favourable a light as possible, claiming it as a victory for the patriarch and a vindication of the principles of canon law. As for the issue of legitimacy, William was careful to add that it was agreed that 'those who had been born to the couple should be regarded as legitimate and should have full right to succeed to their paternal inheritance', and the divorce, with this explicit provision, was given the added authority of being pronounced by a papal legate who conveniently happened to be in the East at the time.[79] So, despite the divorce, Baldwin's legitimate birth and hence his eligibility to succeed were safeguarded. On Amaury's death he duly ascended the throne. William made his succession appear as the natural outcome of the dynastic situation and stressed that he was the unanimous choice.[80] So he had answered the objection that the consanguinity of his parents placed Baldwin's right to rule in doubt. Indeed, he underlined the point that he was rightly king by an uncharacteristic anecdote: at his baptism Baldwin's godfather, his uncle, Baldwin III, had, so it would seem, predicted that one day the infant would be king.[81]

William also recorded that at the time of Amaury's succession in 1163 there had been a dispute among the lay magnates over the succession. The reign had thus made an inauspicious start, but William gave no indication as to the background to this dispute.

[79] *WT*, XIX, 4, lines 19–21; XXI, 1, lines 1–12. For a discussion of the political aspects of the divorce, see B. Hamilton, 'The Titular Nobility of the Latin East: The Case of Agnes of Courtenay', in P. W. Edbury (ed.), *Crusade and Settlement* (Cardiff, 1985), pp. 198–9. For the idea that doubts about the legitimacy of Baldwin and Sibylla may have remained, see J. Riley-Smith, *The Feudal Nobility and the Kingdom of Jerusalem, 1174–1277* (London, 1973), p. 108.

[80] *WT*, XXI, 2, lines 4–7. William is explicit that Baldwin was crowned four days after his father's death, but a contemporary Arabic letter suggests there may have been a delay in recognizing him. See Lyons and Jackson, *Saladin*, p. 75.

[81] *WT*, XVIII, 29, lines 47–56.

However, he made it plain that right had prevailed: Amaury had triumphed thanks to the support of the clergy, the people and some of the nobles, with the aid of 'divine clemency'.[82] Whom the opponents of Amaury's accession had wanted to place on the throne we are not told, and no obvious potential candidate comes to mind. But once the opposition had been defeated, no more is heard of this episode and his rule was unchallenged. By contrast, William gave no hint of there having been any objection to the accession of Baldwin IV. Baldwin was the legitimate king. He was also, as the only son of his father, the only possible king. Indeed, at the time of his father's death in 1174, he was the only male descendant of his grandmother, Queen Melisende, and as such stood in the direct line of succession from King Baldwin II.

Another embarrassing episode in the history of the Jerusalemite monarchy was the dispute between Queen Melisende and her son, Baldwin III, which eventually in 1152 led to a brief civil war between them.[83] In 1131 Baldwin II had been succeeded by his daughter Melisende and her husband, Fulk of Anjou. Both during Fulk's lifetime and after it, Melisende's constitutional position was ambiguous: as her father's heiress, did she or did she not have the right to exercise authority? When in 1143 Fulk died, she assumed control, but whether as regent for her young son Baldwin III or as queen in her own right is not clear. In the end Baldwin III had to stage a military 'showdown' in order to take power fully for himself. William's attitude to Melisende is interesting. Normally he disapproved of women exercising political authority. They could not provide the political leadership necessary to rule and defend their land,[84] and in any case were wayward and capricious. The careers of Melisende's sister Alice, princess of Antioch, and of Alice's daughter, Constance of Antioch, as presented by William furnished clear examples.[85] But Melisende was different. William approved of her and was at pains to portray her not merely as a worthy consort and mother, but as a woman who had inherited and

---

[82] *WT*, XIX, 1, lines 14–20. The fact that the clergy supported Amaury against his opponents would seem to indicate that this dispute was quite distinct from the clergy's insistence on Amaury's divorce, and William himself kept the two matters separate. The dispute may have been an echo of Baldwin III's quarrel with his mother a decade earlier, or it may have been connected in some way with the war with Gerard of Sidon, which led to the promulgation of the *Assise sur la ligece*. William ignored both the war against Gerard and the promulgation of the *Assise*.

[83] See Mayer, 'Melisende', pp. 129–70 *passim*.

[84] See, for example, *WT*, XVII, 10, lines 31–5; 15, lines 1–6.

[85] For Alice, see above, pp. 65–6; for Constance, see *WT*, XVII, 18; 26, lines 1–13.

had exercised regal authority. On his death-bed, Baldwin II had 'handed over the care of the kingdom and full power' to Melisende, Fulk and their infant son, Baldwin.[86] A few years afterwards there was a major contretemps between Melisende and Fulk over Fulk's treatment of Count Hugh of Jaffa; the couple were reconciled:

> The king from that day became so uxorious ('uxorius') that he calmed her wrath, which previously he had provoked, and would not attempt to do anything, not even in small matters, without her knowledge.[87]

On Fulk's death in 1143,

> power in the kingdom rested with the Lady Melisende, a queen beloved of God, to whom it fell by hereditary right.[88]

Speaking of the regency for the young Baldwin III, William wrote:

> His mother was a woman of great wisdom who had an almost total experience of all secular affairs; she had clearly overcome the status assigned to women, so much so that she put her hand to important matters and endeavoured to emulate the magnificence of the greatest princes, to whom she was in no way inferior. For she ruled the kingdom, since her son was as yet under age, with such diligence and controlled the government so well that she may rightly be said to have equalled her ancestors in that role.[89]

As late as 1157, long after Baldwin III had taken power for himself, she was credited with being largely responsible for the recovery of a Christian-held fortress lost during her son's absence in the north;[90] and recording her death in 1161 William commented:

> For thirty years and more, both during the lifetime of her husband and also in the reign of her son, the Lady Melisende, the queen, a woman who was wise and judicious beyond what is normal for a woman ('supra sexum discreta femineum'), had ruled the kingdom.[91]

The trouble with this picture is that it is contradicted by the fact that for most of the period concerned royal power was exercised by Fulk and then Baldwin III. In the *Historia* Fulk and Baldwin hold the centre of attention, and William's scheme for the division of the *Historia* into books beginning and ending with the accession and

---

[86] *WT*, xiii, 28, lines 9–10.
[87] *WT*, xiv, 18, lines 62–5. See Mayer, 'Melisende', pp. 102–10; B. Hamilton, 'Women in the Crusader States; The Queens of Jerusalem (1100–1190)', in D. Baker (ed.), *Medieval Women* (Oxford, 1978), pp. 149–51.
[88] *WT*, xv, 27, lines 42–4. Cf. xvii, 13, lines 8–15.   [89] *WT*, xvi, 3, lines 10–17.
[90] *WT*, xviii, 19, lines 11–19.
[91] *WT*, xviii, 27, lines 32–5. Cf. xviii, 32, lines 7–19.

death of these monarchs underlines this point. Of Fulk's coronation in 1131 he wrote: 'the count, with his aforesaid wife . . . was solemnly crowned and anointed ("coronatus et consecratus est") in the customary manner by the patriarch'.[92] Melisende was associated with Fulk, but, as the singular participles make clear, not as an equal. In the end Fulk and Baldwin were buried with the other kings of Jerusalem in the royal mausoleum, the church of the Holy Sepulchre; Melisende was not accorded that distinction, but was entombed in the abbey of St Mary of the Valley of Josaphat.[93] Furthermore, it is possible by reading between the lines of William's account, especially in connection with the affair of Count Hugh of Jaffa in the early 1130s and with Melisende's conflict with her son, which came to a head in the early 1150s, to obtain a portrait of the queen which was quite different from the one William intended.[94] Melisende can be seen as an ambitious, scheming woman who clung to power, and whose behaviour endangered the stability of the kingdom. In this she can be thought of as a true sister of Alice of Antioch, whose reckless ambition William had condemned. But William did not present her in that light.

It may be that he gave her favourable treatment because her memory was still held in high regard within the royal family at the time he was writing; her younger son, Amaury, had sided with her in her struggle with Baldwin III,[95] and William's account could well have been influenced by a pro-Melisende tradition which he had picked up from his informants at the court. But in addition she had a symbolic importance. It was she who had transmitted the succession from Baldwin II to the kings of William's own day and hence provided the dynastic link with the leaders of the First Crusade. He had to cast her in a positive role and emphasize her own exercise of royal authority, even to the extent that in the end it was wrested from her forcibly by her son, to stress the point that Baldwin IV and his immediate predecessors were descended from the crusaders and were not merely members of a cadet branch of the house of the counts of Anjou. It was not just a question of insisting on their legitimate inheritance, thereby denying any claim to the throne that Fulk's descendants by his earlier marriage, notably Philip of Flan-

---

[92] *WT*, XIV, 2, lines 26–30.
[93] *WT*, XV, 27, lines 35–40; XVIII, 32, lines 12–19; 34, lines 32–7.
[94] It is not our intention to re-examine the reality behind William's account of these events. In addition to Mayer, 'Melisende', see Hamilton, 'Women in the Crusader States', pp. 148–57.
[95] *WT*, XVII, 14, lines 33–5.

ders,[96] or Raymond III or Bohemond III, descendants of Melisende's sisters, might make; for Melisende also transmitted something
of the heroic aura of the First Crusade. Through her Baldwin IV
could be seen as the heir of those Christian leaders whose God-
given victories had restored the Holy Land to Christendom.

So, if Baldwin IV was legally the rightful king, he was also
morally the rightful king, inheriting the moral authority conferred
on his dynasty through its divinely granted successes. This inheritance was given visible demonstration by the fact that he continued
to enjoy God's help. Although William recorded that divine aid was
conspicuously lacking at the time of the Christian defeat suffered in
1179,[97] he noted several other instances in which Baldwin received
God-given assistance in military engagements.[98] The most notable
victory of his reign occurred in 1177 at Mont Gisard, and William
dwelt at length on the theme that this triumph was to be ascribed to
God's grace rather than to human effort.[99] Nowhere did William
suggest, as Alexander III had done in his encyclical *Cor nostrum et*,
that Baldwin's leprosy was divine punishment. Rather, the king's
illness was a matter for sadness and compassion.[100] In every sense
Baldwin was the heir of his forefathers.

William also portrayed Baldwin as a capable king. As has been
mentioned already, Baldwin regularly led his army against the
Muslims throughout his reign, and William was clearly minimizing
the adverse effects of his illness on the conduct of affairs. The

---

[96] See above, p. 63 and note 6. There is no way of knowing whether William was
aware of the belief, recounted by the *Gesta Regis Henrici Secundi* (I, 116), that
Philip had ambitions to gain the throne, or, if he was aware of it, whether he took
it seriously. There is independent evidence that Philip considered remaining
permanently in the East (Hildegard of Bingen, *Epistolarum liber*, PL, 197, cols.
187–8). See also H. Adolf, 'A Historical Background for Chrétien's *Perceval*',
Publications of the Modern Language Association of America, LVIII (1943), 597–620, for
a theory linking Chrétien's romance with Philip's supposed ambition to become
king of Jerusalem. Cf. *eadem*, *Visio Pacis: Holy City and Grail* (Pennsylvania,
1960), pp. 18ff. We are indebted to Professor A. Diverres for these references.
Philip's putative claim would presumably have been based on his descent from
King Fulk, but it might also be noted that there were historical traditions which
viewed Count Robert of Flanders as a potential king of Jerusalem following the
First Crusade and Count Charles 'the Good' of Flanders as a potential king in the
mid-1120s. See C. W. David, *Robert Curthose, Duke of Normandy* (Cambridge,
Mass., 1920), p. 198; J. Richard, *The Latin Kingdom of Jerusalem* (Amsterdam,
1970), p. 70. At the time of Philip's visit to the East the heirs of Eustace of
Boulogne, the claimant of 1118, were his nieces, the daughters of his recently
deceased younger brother. See *Gesta Regis Henrici Secundi*, I, 133, 136, 269.
[97] *WT*, XXI, 29.
[98] *WT*, XXI, 10, lines 39, 48; 27, lines 43–4; XXII, 17, lines 50–65; 22, lines 79–81.
[99] *WT*, XXI, 21–3. See below, pp. 163–4.   [100] *WT*, XXI, 1, lines 34–41.

military situation was worsening, but this was not Baldwin's fault. In large measure the growing power of Saladin was outside Christian control.[101] In one significant passage William castigated the Christians of the East for their wickedness, which had lost them divine favour, and for their apathy towards military training, which had rendered the army less effective, but his accusations were directed at the people as a whole, not at the king.[102] He was, however, well aware that Saladin's seizure of power in Egypt in 1169 was the turning-point which marked the beginning of the Muslim threat to Jerusalem, and he was explicit in his criticism of Amaury for the diplomatic and military failures in 1168 and 1169 which had in effect made Saladin's rise possible.[103] So, if anyone was to blame for Saladin's rise, it was Amaury, not Baldwin. Nevertheless the fact remained that by the early 1180s Baldwin was incapable of ruling and incapable of securing the future of the dynasty, and no amount of special pleading could disguise this truth. William, however, in the closing pages of the *Historia*, was able to demonstrate that the present difficulties were but a passing phase. There was from the latter part of 1183 a new king-designate, Baldwin's nephew (the son of his sister), whose right to succeed had been assured by a preemptive coronation. It was not just that dynastic continuity had been guaranteed; provision had also been made for effective and wise rule until the young Baldwin V should come of age. Raymond III of Tripoli was to act as regent for the remainder of Baldwin IV's life and for the minority of Baldwin V. William had already explained Raymond's close kinship to the royal family and his worthiness; now he was able to lay down his pen with these words:

the king [Baldwin IV] again called his barons together and entrusted the care and general administration of the kingdom to the count of Tripoli, having his hope in his wisdom combined with his magnanimity. In doing this he seemed to satisfy the desires of the whole population and the majority of the princes: for it was apparent to everyone that the only way of salvation lay in committing the affairs of the kingdom to the aforesaid count.[104]

[101] *WT*, xxi, 6, lines 1–18; 7, lines 37–72; 8; xxii, 8; 20; 25.
[102] *WT*, xxi, 7, lines 1–37.
[103] *WT*, xx, 10, lines 33–55. See also xx, 15, lines 49–71.
[104] *WT*, xxiii, 1, lines 50–6. See also xxi, 3, lines 14–40; 5; xxii, 30, lines 48–53.

Chapter 6

REGNUM AND *ECCLESIA*

Just as William of Tyre had views about the monarchy, so too he had views about the Church and the nature of the relationship between priest and king. Although he was well placed to write about the history of the Church in the Latin East, the *Historia* was not conceived as an ecclesiastical history, and when he did introduce material of ecclesiastical interest it was normally only incidental to his narrative. Indeed, on occasion he in effect admitted that by writing about such matters he had allowed himself to digress from his main purpose.[1] As mentioned already, it seems that William introduced much of his ecclesiastical material at the time he was making his revisions following his attendance at the Third Lateran Council and his realization that his work could be of interest to a clerical audience in western Europe. But, because much of his information on the Church had only a tangential bearing on the main thrust of his political history and may well have been added as something of an afterthought, there are many aspects of the history of its growth and organization which either escape mention altogether or receive only the briefest reference. William, for all his concern with the royal dynasty, nowhere gave any clear indication of the extent of royal control over the Church: we can search the *Historia* in vain in the hope of discovering whether the kings enjoyed rights of *spolia* and *regalia* during episcopal or abbatial vacancies; nor do we find allusions to disputes between the ecclesiastical hierarchy and the secular princes over tithes, even though other evidence survives to prove that such disputes had occurred.[2] But it is nevertheless true that the *Historia* forms a major source of information for Latin Syrian church

[1] *WT*, XIV, 14, lines 59–64; XVI, 17, lines 48–9. Cf. XIX, 12, line 79.
[2] H. E. Mayer, 'The Concordat of Nablus', *Journal of Ecclesiastical History*, XXXIII (1982), 531–43. Note *WT*, XIX, 2, lines 22–4.

history, and so for this reason, if for no other, William's attitudes are important.

The Gregorian Reform movement and the Investiture Disputes cast a long shadow over twelfth-century ecclesiastical politics. Gregorian Reform can be defined as the attempt to liberate the clergy and their churches from subjection to lay authority through the establishment of the effective jurisdiction of the papacy over the religious life and institutions of Christendom. Necessarily it brought the problem of the respective roles of *regnum* and *ecclesia* in Christian society into sharp relief. As we shall see in the next chapter, William could be critical of the papacy, but the legacy of the reforming movement did influence him in a variety of ways. Mention of Gregorian Reform in the context of the medieval West often conjures up an image of ideological strife between clergy and lay rulers, but the experience of the Latin East as recorded by William scarcely accords with this picture. A few episodes apart, notably in the immediate aftermath of the First Crusade, the impression he leaves is of co-operation and harmony, and the careers of Patriarchs Daimbert and Stephen in Jerusalem, and the fate of Patriarchs Ralph and Aimery at the hands of successive princes of Antioch, should not be allowed to obscure this fact. But, because the theme of conflict between *regnum* and *ecclesia* did not recur frequently in the *Historia*, William rarely afforded himself the opportunity to comment on the question of what he believed their proper relationship to be. Nor did he utilize contemporary events in Europe as a springboard for a discussion of the subject: thus he described the papal schism of 1159 and the murder of Archbishop Thomas Becket in 1170, but in neither instance did he dwell on their relevance to the issues surrounding the right ordering of Christian society.[3]

In the chapters setting out the background to the First Crusade, William gave a brief account of the Investiture Disputes.[4] His understanding was limited. Of the struggle to establish the primacy of the papacy within the Church and the primacy of the *sacerdotium* over the laity he says nothing. What he did know about was the practice of lay investiture by ring and staff and the idea that bishops should be canonically elected and not simply nominated by the lay ruler. He was also suitably appalled by Henry IV's actions in raising up an anti-pope and hounding those bishops who resisted his will. William's sympathies were clearly on the side of the papacy. There is no

---

[3] *WT*, XVIII, 26; XX, 21, lines 22–43. [4] *WT*, I, 13, lines 1–41; cf. XII, 8.

evidence, furnished either by the *Historia* or, so far as we are aware, by any other source, that the ritual of lay investiture was ever practised in the Latin East, and William made no explicit accusations of simony, the abuse commonly associated with lay investiture in the minds of eleventh-century reformers. But in his account of the dispute he did introduce two basic ideas which can serve as a starting-point in our enquiry: church appointments should be conducted canonically, and laymen should not oppress the Church or harass the clergy.

Writing of his own election as archbishop of Tyre, William stated that he was chosen 'by the common consent of the clergy and people, the king also adding his assent as is the custom'.[5] It is a conventional description, designed to give the impression that all had gone in accordance with the precepts of canon law, and it is matched by similar bland statements about episcopal elections elsewhere in the *Historia*.[6] Such accounts avoid giving any indication as to the lobbying and pressures which led the 'clergy and people' to elect the individual concerned, but in a few instances William was not so reticent. In 1135 Patriarch Ralph of Antioch was 'elected' by popular acclamation before the assembled bishops of the patriarchate had completed their deliberations, but William recorded nothing which might suggest that this form of irregularity was repeated in the East.[7] More commonly the formalities of the election would seem to have been conducted in the proper manner, but with outside influence brought to bear. In 1140 the Antiochene clergy elected as patriarch Aimery of Limoges 'at the instigation and suggestion of the prince [Raymond of Poitiers], and especially, so it is said, by the use of bribes', and in 1164 Frederick of la Roche became archbishop of Tyre, 'the lord king [Amaury] greatly desiring it'.[8] William indicated his disapproval by his aspersive comments on the men concerned: both were unlettered; Aimery was of dubious moral character, Frederick inordinately obsessed with warfare. The election of Amaury of Nesle as patriarch of Jerusalem in 1157 was said to have been 'contra iuris regulas' owing to the intervention of Queen Melisende, aided by her sister Hodierna and her stepdaughter Sibylla of Flanders, and William underlined his disapproval by commenting on Amaury's unsuitability and on the bribery it was claimed had been used to secure papal confirmation.[9]

5 *WT*, XXI, 8, lines 76–7.   6 *WT*, VI, 23, lines 27–42; XIII, 25, lines 8–10.
7 *WT*, XIV, 10, lines 4–19.
8 *WT*, XV, 18, lines 23–5; XIX, 6, line 5.   9 *WT*, XVIII, 20.

In two instances he recorded kings imposing candidates on sees, only to have the election quashed by the papal authorities. Ebremar was made patriarch of Jerusalem by Baldwin I in 1102, while his predecessor, Daimbert, was still alive, and six years later he was deposed by a papal legate, thanks, so William would have us believe, to the irregular circumstances of his appointment.[10] In 1146 the archbishopric of Tyre fell vacant. According to William, King Baldwin III, Queen Melisende, the patriarch of Jerusalem and the suffragan bishops of the province met to decide the appointment; there was a division of opinion with Baldwin and Melisende pressing the candidacy of the chancellor, Ralph, and the patriarch and a number of prominent ecclesiastics opposing them. The upshot was that Ralph 'obtained the church by violence and invaded its properties'. So the clergy appealed to the pope, who upheld their objection, and Ralph was removed.[11]

This series of examples could well give the impression that William was opposed to lay involvement in the appointment of bishops, allowing rulers only the right of confirmation after the event. But other examples would seem to point in the opposite direction. Writing of the events of 1096, he stated without comment that Raymond of Toulouse established Peter of Narbonne as bishop of Albara. William admired Peter, even though his activities after his appointment would appear from his account to have been as much military as spiritual.[12] In 1099 it was the princes that assembled to determine who should be patriarch of Jerusalem, and their choice fell upon Daimbert, one of William's heroes; indeed, William made two separate explicit references to lay involvement in his election.[13] In the case of the election of Archbishop William I of Tyre in 1128 he indicated that the choice had been made by the king, the patriarch and the leading men of the realm. Interestingly, a papal letter William quoted spoke of his namesake being elected canonically.[14] So in William's eyes there was nothing basically wrong with secular rulers participating in episcopal elections; it was only when the candidate chosen was unsuitable or lay involvement excessively obtrusive that he became censorious.

---

[10] *WT*, x, 25, lines 1–9; xi, 4, lines 14–31.   [11] *WT*, xvi, 17, lines 33–4.

[12] *WT*, vii, 8, lines 7–13. Cf. vii, 11, lines 11–16; 12, lines 28–35; 13, lines 5–11; 20, lines 53–5; viii, 19, lines 25–8; ix, 3, lines 51–2; 3, lines 20–6. See Hamilton, *Latin Church*, pp. 10–11. The account by Raymond of Aguilers (pp. 91–2) which William was précising at this point gives Peter's appointment a more canonical ring.

[13] *WT*, ix, 15, lines 1–4; x, 4, lines 1–6.   [14] *WT*, xiii, 23, lines 1–4, 36.

Nor was royal influence in ecclesiastical appointments confined to bishoprics. William made explicit reference to benefices in the king's gift, and he readily admitted that his own preferment had been facilitated by King Amaury's active support.[15] Earlier, Bohemond I, acting with the consent of the patriarch of Antioch, had given the exiled Daimbert a benefice at Antioch.[16] Not only did lay rulers exercise ecclesiastical patronage; they took the lead in determining ecclesiastical organization. Godfrey founded canonries in the Holy Sepulchre and the Templum Domini; Tancred organized the Church in Galilee; Baldwin I took the initiative in the creation of the see of Bethlehem. Indeed, it may be significant that it was only in connection with the creation of this diocese that William wrote with approval of Baldwin's piety.[17] But there were limits. The creation of the see of Bethlehem required papal sanction; and, a little later, the extension of patriarchal authority beyond its traditional boundaries to include all the territories under royal control also needed the pope's concurrence.[18] As with appointments, correct procedures had to be adopted, however much the course of action had been instigated by the king. Even so, the impression that William leaves is of a Church whose organization and personnel owed much to royal or princely initiative, and in which the lay rulers exercised considerable influence.

What is more, he was clearly content that it should be so. Defence of the Church and the Holy Places might be a primary function of monarchy, but William did not subscribe to the view that the lay ruler should be subservient to the *sacerdotium*. He related how, immediately after the capture of Jerusalem in 1099, a group of clergy demanded that the headship of the church should be determined before the choice of secular ruler on the basis of the superiority of the spiritual over the temporal. But, although this can be read as a definite assertion of Gregorian principles, it was an argument which William regarded as specious, and he discredited the whole idea by ascribing base motives to its supporters.[19] He then described with evident approval how the secular ruler, Godfrey, was chosen first, and how he and the other princes subsequently had a part in selecting Daimbert as patriarch.

But if William was prepared to allow a considerable measure of

---

[15] *WT*, XIX, 12, lines 68–75; XX, 1, lines 23–7. See Huygens, 'Guillaume de Tyr', p. 816.
[16] *WT*, X, 24, lines 23–30.   [17] *WT*, IX, 9, lines 4–10; 13, lines 47–52; XI, 12.
[18] *WT*, XI, 28. See below, pp. 113, 117–18.   [19] *WT*, IX, 1.

lay influence in the Church, he was not prepared to tolerate lay abuse of the clergy or lay oppression of the Church in the form of undue financial demands being made upon it. He was thus highly critical of Baldwin I for his treatment of Daimbert, and of Raynald of Châtillon and Bohemond III for their treatment of the patriarch of Antioch, Aimery of Limoges.[20] Of Raymond of Poitiers's treatment of Patriarch Ralph of Antioch, he was less critical, but then Ralph's election had been irregular, he had usurped papal prerogatives, oppressed the clergy of his patriarchate, attempted to make Raymond politically subservient to himself and apparently tried to undermine his position as prince. In other words he had been asking for trouble, and, although William had some sympathy for the patriarch, he stopped short of censuring Raymond for his determination to get rid of him.[21] But generally he was firm in his condemnation of laymen who attacked the clergy.

As for lay attempts to obtain the Church's wealth, William could be equally strident. Writing of King Baldwin III, he stated that men praised him because he did not trouble ('nec . . . vexabat') the patrimonies of churches: quite possibly the implication of this comment was that Baldwin had been the exception.[22] By contrast, King Amaury was

a violent assailant of the liberty of churches, whose patrimonies by frequent and unwarranted exactions in his time he drained to the utmost extremity, with the result that he compelled the holy places to burden themselves with debt beyond the resources of their income.[23]

But his attitude was ambiguous: in the same chapter as this denunciation, he noted with approval Amaury's insistence on the payment of tithes and showed that he appreciated that the political situation meant that the king needed a plentiful supply of cash in order to defend the kingdom's interests. Elsewhere he noted without comment – and this must surely be taken as tacit approval – that churchmen were taxed in the taxation ordinance of 1183, that King Amaury induced the clergy to contribute to the ransom of Count Raymond III of Tripoli in 1173 and that the clergy were to share in the taxes raised from 1178 onwards to pay for the repairs to

---

[20] *WT*, x, 24, lines 15–23; 25, lines 1–9; xi, 1, lines 21–6; xviii, 1.
[21] *WT*, xiv, 10; 20; xv, 12–17 *passim*. For Ralph's career, see B. Hamilton, 'Ralph of Domfront, Patriarch of Antioch (1135–40)', *Nottingham Medieval Studies*, xxviii (1984), 1–21.
[22] *WT*, xvi, 2, lines 7–8.   [23] *WT*, xix, 2, lines 46–50.

the walls of Jerusalem.[24] Perhaps William's outburst against
Amaury was not so much a protest against churchmen being
expected to contribute towards military expenses as the *cri de coeur*
of a senior bishop who believed that the general level of church
endowments in the East was insufficient to match the honour due to
the churches there.[25] One of his more serious charges against
Patriarch Arnulf had been that he had alienated Jericho from the
endowments of the Holy Sepulchre – said to be worth '5,000 pieces
of gold' annually – and writing of the creation of his own see of
Tyre he uttered an eloquent complaint that the delay of four years in
establishing an archbishop in the city after it had been captured
resulted in 'churches being alienated and the cathedral church being
shorn of its own members'.[26] We know from other evidence that in
the intervening period the former orthodox cathedral at Tyre had
been given to the Holy Sepulchre with parochial status, and it is
possible, though by no means certain, that the Venetians too were
quick to establish a church under the peculiar jurisdiction of their
own bishop in their sector of the city. Thus, when the first archbishop was installed, he found at least one and possibly two major
inroads into his jurisdiction within Tyre itself.[27]

So, although William was prepared to allow royal (or, in the case
of Antioch, princely) influence in the church, he nevertheless sympathized with many of the ideals which had developed as part of the
Gregorian Reform programme. Laymen should not harass the
clergy or impose oppressive taxes on the Church. The endowments
of the Church should be adequate to support the clergy in their
proper dignity. The rights of the laity to involve themselves in
elections should not extend to the imposition of unsuitable candi-

[24] *WT*, xx, 28, lines 37–41; xxi, 24, lines 47–54; xxii, 24. Cf. xix, 13, lines 27–9
(where taxation of the clergy is implied rather than stated).

[25] To develop the arguments for suggesting that the Church in the Latin East was
poorly endowed by comparison with many churches in the West would be to
digress from our subject. However, as pointers to the relatively low level of its
income we might note the small size of many of the cathedrals, the fact that even
after it had been refashioned by the crusaders in the middle years of the twelfth
century the Holy Sepulchre was a very modest structure by comparison with the
great shrine churches of the West, and the fact that the crusaders were prepared to
allow Emperor Manuel Comnenus to undertake and pay for the redecoration of
the church of the Nativity at Bethlehem.

[26] *WT*, xi, 15, lines 7–13; xiii, 23, lines 16–17.

[27] Mayer, *Bistümer*, pp. 98–111; Hamilton, *Latin Church*, pp. 88, 94, 104, 291.
Disputes between the Venetians and the archbishops of Tyre, including William
himself, over the parochial rights of the Venetian church in Tyre continued into
the thirteenth century. See R. Hiestand (ed.), *Vorarbeiten zum Oriens Pontificius*, iii:
Papsturkunden für Kirchen im Heiligen Lande (Göttingen, 1985), nos. 89, 161, 175.

dates into benefices, and the elections themselves should be conducted in the correct manner. He also shared the reformers' views as to how the clergy should conduct themselves. The sort of standards that William expected can be seen from his criticisms of various individuals. Aimery of Limoges was unlettered and by implication ill equipped to hold high ecclesiastical office; he also led an ignoble life. Ralph, later bishop of Bethlehem, was 'too worldly'. Archbishop Hugh of Edessa was miserly with his personal wealth when his city was under attack.[28] Archbishop Frederick of Tyre was inordinately concerned with warfare, and of another cleric who had clearly disregarded the church's ban on priests bearing arms and who had been killed in battle William quoted St Matthew: 'He who takes up the sword shall perish by the sword.'[29] But it was Arnulf, archdeacon of Jerusalem and later patriarch (1112–18), who was exposed to the greatest censure. Clergy should be of legitimate birth, but Arnulf was the son of a priest; they should be celibate, but Arnulf was notorious for his dissolute life; they should conserve the patrimony of their churches, but Arnulf alienated a choice possession to his own niece. 'An evil man', 'a fomentor of discord', he was 'careless of the sacred nature of his office'.[30]

Enough has been said to show that William was a typical, conscientious prelate of his day. Just as he expected his fellow-bishops to exhibit those qualities which befitted their office, so he expected lay rulers to show discretion in the exercise of their prerogatives in church affairs. He accepted that lay rulers did have certain rights over the Church, and he also had definite ideas about the role churchmen could play in the political life of the kingdom. It would also seem that he was less than satisfied with the state of the Church in the East at the time he was writing.

Exactly what William thought of his episcopal colleagues in the

---

28 *WT*, xv, 18, lines 26–7; xvi, 5, lines 22–31; 17, line 23.

29 For Frederick, see *WT*, xix, 6, lines 6–9; cf. xix, 28, lines 5–8; xxii, 17, lines 87–92, quoting Matt. 26:52. Clergy normally accompanied the armies, but William's only example of a bishop commanding a division in combat is Adhemar of Le Puy in battle against Kerbogha (*WT*, vi, 17, lines 14–17). Note that William (*WT*, iii, 16, lines 14–20) did not follow the *Gesta Francorum* (p. 20) in having Adhemar lead a detachment at Dorylaeum. At xiii, 25, lines 1–5 William spoke of Patriarch Gormond besieging a fortress.

30 *WT*, vii, 18, lines 9–12; ix, 1, lines 25–42; x, 2, lines 29–34; 24, lines 15–23; 25, lines 1–3; xi, 15; 26, lines 1–14; xii, 6, lines 35–6. Apropos Arnulf's niece, Hamilton (*Latin Church*, p. 63 note 2) rightly warns against the assumption that references to the nephews and nieces of the clergy are euphemisms for sons and daughters.

1170s and 1180s is largely lost beyond recall, but from what little he did say and by inference from what he did not it appears that he was not impressed. The *Historia* may be an *apologia* for the monarchy of Baldwin IV; it is certainly not an *apologia* for Baldwin's episcopate. William had a poor opinion of the patriarch of Jerusalem, Amaury of Nesle (1157–80): he was a 'very simple and pretty useless man' whose election had been irregular.[31] Even his one positive achievement, his insistence on the divorce of King Amaury and Agnes of Courtenay, had been in accordance with a policy inherited from his predecessor.[32] What William thought of Amaury's successor, Patriarch Eraclius (1180–90), he was careful not to reveal; if there was tacit approval for Eraclius' efforts at the settlement in Antioch in 1181, it is clear that William disapproved of the patriarch's support for Guy of Lusignan and of his indignation when Baldwin IV refused to restore Guy to favour at the beginning of 1184.[33] However, if indeed Eraclius had been chosen patriarch in preference to William himself thanks to the intervention of the queen-mother, if he had excommunicated him and if his private life was the public scandal other sources might seem to indicate, then William's silence has to be understood in terms of his unwillingness to publicize a state of affairs which would have detracted from the reputation of the Latin East.[34]

Aimery of Limoges, patriarch of Antioch (1140–93), was another leading churchman for whom William could evince no enthusiasm. He was unlettered and not particularly honourable; his election had smacked of corruption, and, when on one occasion he used his private wealth in the defence of his city, it was contrary to his usual habit.[35] He was a man who suffered at the hands of successive princes of Antioch, and, although William deplored their behaviour, he made no reference to any positive qualities Aimery may have had.[36] Another senior ecclesiastic of William's own day

---

[31] *WT*, XVIII, 20; XXII, 4, line 75.

[32] *WT*, XXI, 1, lines 5–9. Cf. XIX, 4. For his career, see Hamilton, *Latin Church*, pp. 75–9. But Hamilton is mistaken in saying that he did not carry the True Cross into war (*WT*, XX, 19, lines 29–30).

[33] *WT*, XXII, 7; XXIII, 1, lines 29–43.

[34] See Edbury and Rowe, 'Patriarchal Election', pp. 24–5 *et passim*. For Eraclius, see Hamilton, *Latin Church*, pp. 79–84; Kedar, 'Patriarch Eraclius', pp. 177–204.

[35] *WT*, XV, 18, lines 26–7; XVII, 10, lines 35–9.

[36] *WT*, XVIII, 1, lines 1–31; XXII, 6, lines 1–20. William omits to record that in 1165–70 Aimery was supplanted by a Greek patriarch in Antioch. For his career, with a more favourable assessment than William's, see Hamilton, *Latin Church*, pp. 38–50.

who received a distinctly unfavourable portrait in the *Historia* was his predecessor as archbishop of Tyre, Frederick of la Roche (1164–74). Insufficiently educated and, as noted already, excessively interested in warfare, he was accused of bribing the papal officials to secure the confirmation of Amaury of Nesle's election as patriarch. He and William may have been locked in some sort of dispute at one point, and William seems to have taken quiet satisfaction in recording – twice – that his diplomatic embassy to the West in the years 1169–71 achieved nothing.[37]

William had positive things to say about very few of the bishops whose periods of office overlapped with his own. Archbishop Letard of Nazareth (1158–90), who by the 1180s was the longest-serving bishop in the patriarchate of Jerusalem, was 'a very pleasant man, affable and kindly'.[38] He was only mentioned once. In 1181 William recorded the death of Raymond, bishop of Beirut (1175–81) – 'of blessed memory in the Lord, he was taken from this world to obtain for ever through the grace of God the rewards of eternal life' – and his replacement by Odo (1181–90), 'an honourable and educated man'. But it should be recalled that he himself had consecrated them both.[39] Apropos the embassy to Antioch of 1181, William described Archbishop Monachus of Caesarea (1180–97) and Bishop Albert of Bethlehem (*c.* 1177–after 1181), together with Raynald, abbot of Mount Zion, and Peter, prior of the Holy Sepulchre, as 'wise and discerning', adjectives which he avoided applying to the leader of the embassy, Patriarch Eraclius.[40] Other bishops were mentioned in passing without any qualification. There was thus no attempt to portray the episcopate as a whole as an outstanding or exemplary group of prelates; if anything, William's silence is indicative of their lack of distinction.

This point can be appreciated more readily if his treatment of his contemporaries is contrasted with his treatment of some of the bishops of the immediately previous generation. William, bishop of Acre (*c.* 1164–72), was 'prudent and discerning', and his death by murder was notable for his dying wish that the perpetrator of the deed should not be punished.[41] Elsewhere both he and Archbishop Ernesius of Caesarea (*c.* 1157–75) were described as being 'wise and endowed with eloquence'.[42] Ernesius too received

---

[37] *WT*, XVIII, 20, lines 15–21; XIX, 6; XX, 12, lines 29–38; 17, lines 32–5; 25, lines 11–15. See Hamilton, *Latin Church*, pp. 125–6.
[38] *WT*, XVIII, 22, line 6.   [39] *WT*, XXII, 7, lines 56–63. Cf. XXI, 10, lines 62–6.
[40] XXII, 7, lines 21–5.   [41] *WT*, XIX, 12, lines 63–4; XX, 25, lines 42–75.
[42] *WT*, XX, 12, lines 13–20.

favourable notice from William as one of the bishops who had appealed in vain to the pope against the election of Patriarch Amaury.[43] Others whom he mentioned with affection include Mainard of Beirut (1156–75) and Amaury of Sidon (*c.* 1153–after 1170),[44] while Ralph of Bethlehem (1156–74), whose intrusion into the see of Tyre in the 1140s William had roundly condemned, could nevertheless be described as 'a generous and very kindly man'.[45]

Not only was William unwilling to refer to his contemporary bishops with any warmth or enthusiasm; it is also clear from a careful reading of the *Historia* that the Church was labouring under a number of difficulties. Throughout most of his period in office, Patriarch Amaury of Nesle found himself confronted by King Amaury and Agnes of Courtenay, whose marriage he had insisted on dissolving, and by an archbishop of Caesarea and a bishop of Bethlehem (who was also the royal chancellor) who had made some attempt to get his election set aside by the papacy. In the previous generation the then patriarch, Fulcher of Celles, had led the episcopacy in a successful attempt to stop the king imposing this same chancellor on the see of Tyre. So relations with the crown and among the bishops themselves were not always harmonious. Furthermore, the episcopate had had to contend with the growing power and exemptions of the military Orders. William described how matters came to a head in the 1150s, when the patriarch and a powerful delegation of bishops mounted an unsuccessful appeal to Rome against the Orders' privileges.[46] Then there were financial exactions imposed by King Amaury and aggravated by additional charges, such as the burden of having a papal legate in the East for at least two years from 1161, or the expenses arising from the disputed episcopal succession at Bethlehem in the mid-1170s.[47]

So, from references scattered through the sections of the *Historia* dealing with William's own day, it is possible to obtain a picture of a province of the Church in which things were far from perfect. But William managed to avoid saying so in as many words, and it

[43] *WT*, XVIII, 20, lines 13–15. Cf. XX, 1, lines 1–8; XXI, 9, lines 22–5.
[44] *WT*, XVII, 26, lines 41–6; XXI, 8, lines 71–4.
[45] *WT*, XX, 30, line 54. Cf. XVI, 17, lines 21–40. William is inconsistent in his attitude to Ralph, accusing him of acquiring Tyre by force and Bethlehem thanks to the favour of his compatriot, Pope Adrian IV. He then records various creditable actions and concludes with the accolade quoted above (*WT*, XVIII, 1, lines 19–24; 20, lines 13–15; XIX, 25, lines 54–7; XX, 19, lines 30–2; 26, lines 55–6).
[46] *WT*, XVIII, 3; 6–8. Cf. J. Riley-Smith, *The Knights of St John in Jerusalem and Cyprus, c. 1050–1310* (London, 1967), pp. 398–400. See below, pp. 126–7.
[47] *WT*, XVIII, 29, lines 44–6 (cf. XIX, 4, lines 13–16); XX, 30, lines 55–60.

would be easy for the reader of his work to fail to appreciate this point, so dispersed are the elements which comprise it. William wanted to tell the truth but was naturally unwilling to make explicit attacks on his colleagues, and it is possible that he was reluctant to give full vent to his feelings about the Church, since to have done so would have damaged the Latin East in the eyes of the West. What he could do, however, was to hold up churchmen of an earlier age as examples to his contemporaries of the standards they should seek to emulate and, by telling something of the achievement or intentions of these men, to give an indication of what he thought his con-temporaries should be doing. Three men in particular had excited his admiration: Adhemar of Le Puy, the papal legate on the First Crusade, Peter of Barcelona, archbishop of Tyre (1151–64), and Daimbert of Pisa, patriarch of Jerusalem at the beginning of the twelfth century; by examining each in turn, it is possible to gain an idea of the qualities William respected and might hope to find in the prelates of his own day.

Adhemar of Le Puy was a papal legate, but William was not particularly concerned with his role as the interpreter of Pope Urban's intentions for the Crusade or with his function as the man who could exercise delegated papal responsibilities. In fact he made only three specific allusions to his legatine status, and it is clear that what was important about it in William's eyes was the authority in the army that it conferred:

afterwards, in discharging his duties as legate of the Apostolic See on this expedition, he ruled over the people of God both faithfully and wisely.[48]

At one point in his description of the siege of Antioch, William wrote:

by the command and on the authority of the lord bishop of Le Puy, who exercised the legation of the Apostolic See . . . it was decreed that a three-day fast be held, that by scourging their bodies they could join the more strongly in spirit for prayer.[49]

Any bishop could decree a fast within his own diocese: the sig-nificance of Adhemar's position was that as legate he could exercise ecclesiastical jurisdiction beyond the confines of his diocese and over the other clergy and the laity on the expedition. After his death at Antioch and the death soon afterwards of Bishop William of Orange, whose standing is unclear, there was no one who could

---

[48] *WT*, I, 16, lines 36–8. [49] *WT*, IV, 22, lines 10–15.

claim authority over the army as a whole or over the clergy accompanying it. As a result, so William assured his readers, the clergy fell into decadence.[50] In the army of the First Crusade there could be no established ecclesiastical hierarchy and system of jurisdiction as in a settled province of Christendom, and so he portrayed Adhemar's position as legate as making up for this deficiency. In this sense Adhemar was the precursor of the Latin patriarchs in the East. He was the senior cleric in the crusading army; they were to be the senior clerics in the new Christian society established in its wake.

Adhemar emerges from the pages of the *Historia* as a leader of the Crusade who was accepted by the secular leaders as their equal and was widely respected by the crusaders in general. Although he was frequently shown in the company of Raymond of Toulouse, the authority vested in him as legate, coupled with his evident ability, meant that he was considerably more than just a bishop in Raymond's entourage. William was careful not to show him bearing arms, but he did indicate that he had his own contingent and played a part in military engagements, carrying the Holy Lance as he led a division into battle against Kerbogha.[51] At Antioch he was active in preventing desertions from the army, on these occasions working not with Raymond, but with Bohemond and Godfrey of Bouillon.[52] His importance lay not so much in the fact that he was one of several commanders as in the fact that it fell to him to inspire the whole army. At Dorylaeum

The lord bishop of Le Puy, with other co-workers in the same office, admonished the people and encouraged the princes not to relax their efforts, but, certain of the victory to be conferred from on high, to avenge the blood of the slain: they should not allow the enemies of the faith and name of Christ to glory any longer over the destruction of the faithful. With these and similar words the men of God incited the people to battle and, so far as they were able, inspired them with courage.[53]

Before the battle with Kerbogha

The priests . . . promised the indulgence and full remission of sins to those

---

[50] *WT*, IX, 1, lines 42–52. William's statement is based on Raymond of Aguilers (p. 152), but Raymond's point is that after the deaths of Adhemar and William of Orange there was no one among the clergy who could treat with the princes on equal terms, not that the clergy became decadent.

[51] *WT*, IV, 18, lines 11–13; VI, 17, lines 14–17. See also II, 16, lines 31–3; IV, 13, lines 26–8. See above, note 29. According to Raymond of Aguilers (p. 82) he, Raymond, and not Adhemar bore the lance in this battle.

[52] *WT*, VI, 5, lines 34–42; 13, lines 38–44.   [53] *WT*, III, 16, lines 14–20.

who should fight bravely in battle . . . as defenders of the Christian faith. The bishops also exhorted the princes and leaders of the army . . . urging them on with all the eloquence granted them from on high, and, blessing the people, commended them to God. Chief among them was that servant of Christ, the lord bishop of Le Puy: ever constant in exhortations, fastings and prayers, and profuse in the generosity of his almsgiving, he was giving himself as a sacrifice ('holocaustum') to the Lord.[54]

Elsewhere William described him as the 'patronus' of the army.[55] It is not surprising that Adhemar was clothed in a variety of laudatory epithets: he was 'of revered life and immortal memory', 'venerable', 'a great and distinguished man', 'a man beloved of God', 'of pious memory in the Lord'.[56] As has been noted already, he took the lead in proclaiming a penitential fast, and this was followed by decrees tightening up the moral standards of the crusaders. His death was the occasion for mourning throughout the army.[57] What was more, he had a special role in the divine plan for the Crusade. Early in the expedition he was captured by Bulgars:

But because so great a priest was still necessary to the people of God, through His mercy he was saved from death.[58]

As final testimony to his qualities, William recorded that at the time of the capture of Jerusalem:

On that day the Lord Adhemar, bishop of Le Puy, a man of noble character and of immortal memory, who had departed this life at Antioch . . . was seen by many in the Holy City, so much so that many venerable and trustworthy men claimed that they had seen him with their own eyes as the first to ascend the city wall, inspiring others to enter.[59]

William's admiration was unqualified. Adhemar clearly lived up to his ideal of what a bishop should be: a man of godly life who was also a man of action; a man loved and respected by the great as well as the lowly, and a man who could give a lead to those in his charge and could inspire his flock to greater efforts in the Christian cause.

Peter of Barcelona held the see of Tyre from 1151 until his death in 1164. Writing of his appointment, William gave him perhaps the warmest accolade of any bishop in the East:

[54] *WT*, VI, 16, lines 52–63.   [55] *WT*, VI, 23, line 2.
[56] *WT*, I, 16, line 36; II, 17, line 1; VI, 14, line 11; VII, 1, line 31; IX, 1, line 44.
[57] *WT*, IV, 22, lines 10–30; VII, 1, lines 29–36.
[58] *WT*, II, 18, lines 27–9. Cf. Raymond, *Le "Liber"*, p. 39.
[59] *WT*, VIII, 22, lines 1–6. Cf. Raymond, *Le "Liber"*, p. 151.

a man of rare simplicity and gentleness, who feared God and shunned evil, and whose memory is held in benediction both by God and men . . . noble according to the flesh but even nobler in spirit, his life and deeds deserve longer and more careful treatment.[60]

His actions as William recorded them are indicative of a much more forceful churchman than this tribute to his personal qualities might suggest.[61] What is noteworthy is that he had several characteristics in common with Adhemar. Peter participated in the siege of Ascalon in 1153 and was numbered among the leaders of the army. William showed him debating military policy with the secular lords; together with the other higher clergy, he counselled persevering with the siege when the king and many of the lay leaders were for giving up. So, like Adhemar, he was cast in the role of a man who inspired the Christian army to victory.[62] Just as William reported Adhemar carrying the Holy Lance into battle against Kerbogha, so he reported Peter carrying the relic of the Cross in the Christian victory over Nūr al-Dīn in 1158.[63] He also noted that Peter accompanied Patriarch Fulcher on his journey to the papal court in the mid-1150s to appeal against the privileges of the Hospitallers and that he took the lead in arguing for the recognition of Pope Alexander III following the schism of 1159.[64] He was thus a pious man who was a leader of the Christians in war and peace.

There is no figure in the *Historia* more difficult to interpret than Daimbert of Pisa, patriarch of Jerusalem from 1099 until his deposition in 1101/2. To William he was an outstanding churchman. On our first encounter with him he is 'a learned and prudent man of great piety and a friend of integrity'. Elsewhere he is called 'a religious man and a lover of peace'.[65] Other evidence,[66] and indeed a close reading of the *Historia*, cast him in a different light: as a man who was ruthlessly ambitious, acquisitive and divisive. Our question is not which view is nearer the truth, but why William adopted the attitude he did. There is no reason to suppose that he had at his disposal all the documentation assembled by modern scholars; and,

---

[60] *WT*, xvi, 17, lines 42–7.
[61] Information on Peter's career as prior of the Holy Sepulchre and archbishop of Tyre gleaned from other sources also supports an impression of forcefulness. See Hamilton, *Latin Church*, pp. 119–20, 138–9.
[62] *WT*, xvii, 21, lines 33–5; 23, lines 10–15; 28, lines 1–40.
[63] *WT*, xviii, 21, lines 29–32.
[64] *WT*, xviii, 6, lines 24–7; 29, lines 21–6.
[65] *WT*, ix, 14, lines 29–30; x, 24, lines 20–1.
[66] See Hamilton, *Latin Church*, pp. 14–17, 53–7.

although to a certain extent it is possible to identify his sources of information,[67] it can never be known whether or how far he deliberately suppressed material which contradicted the portrait he wished to give. To understand William's view of Daimbert it is therefore necessary to rely on an examination of the internal evidence afforded by the *Historia*, a task made more complicated by his own apparent inconsistencies.

Perhaps the simplest answer – but not the whole answer – to the question of why William admired him lies in the fact that Daimbert was opposed by William's *bête noire*, Arnulf of Chocques, the archdeacon of Jerusalem who himself was later (1112–18) to be patriarch. In 1099 Arnulf had been named patriarch-elect, thanks to the machinations of the bishop of Martirano. In William's eyes he had 'invaded the patriarchal see'. He was soon obliged to stand down, although William did not explain the precise circumstances.[68] Then, towards the end of the year, Archbishop Daimbert of Pisa arrived in Jerusalem accompanied by a large band of pilgrims from Italy and also by Bohemond of Antioch and the then ruler of Edessa, Baldwin of Boulogne. The 'princes who were present' convoked an assembly at which he was chosen patriarch, and he was thereupon enthroned. To William, Daimbert was incontrovertibly the legitimate patriarch, and in the letter purporting to have been written by him to Bohemond William had him use the canonical formula, saying that he had been 'elected by the common consent both of clergy and people and of the princes'.[69] Arnulf does not reappear in the narrative until after the death of Godfrey of Bouillon in July 1100. William related how he attempted to undermine Daimbert's position by making accusations against him to Godfrey's successor, Baldwin I, and inciting some of the clergy to oppose him; so effective were his schemes that Daimbert retired to Mount Zion.[70] In time he and Baldwin were reconciled, thereby allowing for Baldwin's coronation as king of Jerusalem at Christmas 1100; but then Arnulf rekindled the quarrel and stirred up the clergy against the patriarch, with the result that he was obliged to flee to Antioch. Then, 'led astray by Arnulf's malice', Baldwin intruded Ebremar into the patriarchal chair.[71] Eventually, in 1105, Daimbert arrived in Rome, where he 'set forth both Arnulf's

[67] See above, pp. 49–50.
[68] *WT*, IX, 4, lines 1–13; 15, lines 6–8; X, 2, lines 32–3.
[69] *WT*, IX, 15, lines 1–13; X, 4, lines 4–5.   [70] *WT*, X, 7.
[71] *WT*, X, 9, lines 1–8; 24, lines 15–23; 25, lines 1–5.

all-too-effective wickedness and the lord king's evil intent whereby he was trying to humiliate the Church of God'.[72] Pope Paschal ruled that he had been wrongly 'expelled by royal violence', and, armed with a papal letter requiring his reinstatement, he was sent back to the East. So Daimbert was vindicated, but on the way back he died.[73] He was thus the righteous victim of the evil Arnulf and of King Baldwin I, who himself had been corrupted by Arnulf. William's attitude was consistent with his view, found elsewhere, that secular rulers ought not to harass the clergy.

But the account is far from convincing. William had to contend with two problems. First, he regarded Baldwin I as a hero whose military leadership had done much to establish the kingdom of Jerusalem, and it might seem that he introduced Arnulf in an attempt to explain away the contradiction between Baldwin the military leader fighting in defence of the Holy Places, and Baldwin the oppressor of the liberties of the Church, who hounded the patriarch into exile and illegally supplanted him with someone else. Secondly, and more importantly, William had previously described how Daimbert had strenuously attempted to prevent Baldwin's succession. But he evidently wanted to avoid giving the impression that Daimbert's own actions had precipitated the breach between the two men, and so this initial opposition on Daimbert's part is forgotten and Arnulf's evil purposes substituted as the explanation for their quarrel.

So why did Daimbert oppose Baldwin's succession? This question brings us to the second reason for William's favourable treatment of the patriarch: he admired him because he had vigorously championed the principle that the Church should be well endowed and that endowments should not be withheld by the laity. The story as told by William goes as follows. After he had become patriarch, Daimbert was given the former possessions of the Greek patriarchs of Jerusalem and more besides. He subsequently demanded that Godfrey give him the whole of Jerusalem, including its citadel, the Tower of David, and also Jaffa. In February 1100 Godfrey gave a quarter of Jaffa to the church of the Holy Sepulchre, and this grant was followed at Easter by the cession of Jerusalem, subject to the proviso that Godfrey should continue to hold it and draw revenues from it until he had enlarged the kingdom by obtaining one or two other cities. But it was also stipulated that, if in the meantime he should die without heirs, the patriarch should

[72] *WT*, XI, 1, lines 21–5.   [73] *WT*, XI, 4, lines 1–14. See below, pp. 110–11.

101

receive possession at once.[74] A few months later Godfrey did die. By the terms of the agreement Daimbert should have taken control of Jerusalem, but in fact Godfrey's retainers prevented him and summoned his brother Baldwin from Edessa. Daimbert, aware that Baldwin's arrival would put an end to any hope that the terms of the grant would be fulfilled, tried to send word to Bohemond of Antioch to stop Baldwin from coming, using force if necessary.[75] So Daimbert was prepared to use every means at his disposal to fight for what he believed to be the rightful possessions of his church, and William clearly approved his actions. To William, Garnier of Grez, the leading opponent of Daimbert on the death of Godfrey, was an 'enemy and persecutor of the church', whose death after a short illness was seen as 'a miracle ascribed to the merits of the lord patriarch'.[76] Daimbert's claims found an echo in the late 1120s, when Patriarch Stephen of Chartres appears to have revived them, and William again leaves his readers in no doubt as to his own attitude: 'For he [Stephen] was a distinguished man, firm in his intentions, of honourable character, a conscientious stickler for his rights'.[77]

William's account of Daimbert's struggle to obtain Jerusalem and Jaffa for the Holy Sepulchre raises various problems. In calling on Bohemond to prevent Baldwin from coming to Jerusalem even if it required violent action, Daimbert would seem to have been prepared to plunge the nascent Latin states in the East into civil war. Elsewhere William decried strife among the Christian leaders; here he seems not to have noticed the implications of the patriarch's request. Furthermore, in demanding Jerusalem and Jaffa – a claim reiterated in his letter to Bohemond – he was demanding the only two cities in Palestine of any significance then in Christian hands. The likely consequence for the defence of the crusaders' gains against Muslim attack if the military leadership were deprived of its only strongholds was a consideration to which William seems similarly oblivious. On the other hand, he did appreciate a more fundamental problem: by what right could Daimbert make these

---

[74] *WT*, IX, 15, lines 13–17; 16, lines 1–19.
[75] *WT*, X, 3–4. Note that in Daimbert's letter he claims that at Easter Godfrey had also promised him his remaining possessions in Jaffa, and that not only had he not received the whole of Jerusalem, but he was prevented from occupying what the Greek patriarchs had held under Muslim rule.
[76] *WT*, X, 3, lines 24–5. Cf. X, 4, lines 32–7.
[77] *WT*, XIII, 25, lines 26–7. What Stephen was claiming was Jaffa and, when Ascalon should be captured, Jerusalem.

territorial demands on Godfrey in the first place? William explicitly stated that no such requirement had been laid on Godfrey by the other leaders when he was chosen to rule in Jerusalem. He then attempted to explain Daimbert's claim by a lengthy digression on the subject of the patriarch's quarter in Jerusalem, but in fact this digression fails to provide any support for Daimbert at all. In the twelfth century, as we know from the *Historia* and other sources, the patriarch had franchisal jurisdiction in the north-western quadrant of Jerusalem in the area around the church of the Holy Sepulchre; all William succeeded in saying was that this area corresponded to the Christian quarter in Jerusalem as it had existed in the period immediately before the First Crusade.[78] His account gave no explanation of how Daimbert could claim to be entitled to the whole of Jerusalem and to Jaffa as well. So, far from explaining why he could feel justified in making his demands, William confused the issue by drawing his readers' attention away from this question to the question of the origins of the patriarchal quarter as it existed at the time he was writing.

The subject of Daimbert's territorial demands is further complicated by William's statement that immediately after his enthronement as patriarch, Godfrey and Bohemond 'humbly received from him, the one the investiture of the kingdom, the other that of the principality, showing thereby that they ascribed honour to Him whose servant and representative on earth he was believed to be'.[79] Then, according to Daimbert's letter to Bohemond, at Easter 1100 Godfrey 'as the vassal ("homo") of the Holy Sepulchre and of ourselves vowed that henceforth he would fight faithfully for God and for us'.[80] Some historians have interpreted these remarks to mean that Daimbert was attempting to inaugurate an ecclesiastical polity under patriarchal rule, with Godfrey acting as a sort of commander-in-chief, and this view has in the past been underpinned by the now discredited belief that Godfrey was styled *advocatus Sancti Sepulchri*.[81] But, although the phrase just quoted from Daimbert's letter certainly seems to support this interpretation, the idea is by no means generally accepted by modern scholars.[82] Nor is it

---

[78] *WT*, IX, 16–18. For the patriarch's quarter, see Prawer, *Crusader Institutions*, pp. 296–314.
[79] *WT*, IX, 15, lines 9–13.   [80] *WT*, X, 4, lines 20–2.
[81] See J. Riley-Smith, 'The Title of Godfrey de Bouillon', *Bulletin of the Institute of Historical research*, LII (1979), 83–6.
[82] J. G. Rowe, 'Paschal II and the Relations between the Spiritual and Temporal Powers in the Kingdom of Jerusalem', *Speculum*, XXXII (1957), 475–9;

likely that William himself would have supported patriarchal pretensions to govern. He had roundly condemned the party that had demanded that the patriarch be chosen before the lay ruler after the conquest of Jerusalem,[83] and nowhere else in the *Historia* is there any suggestion that rulers of Jerusalem did homage to the patriarchs or were subservient to them. On one occasion he called King Amaury 'defender and *advocatus* of the venerable places of the Lord's passion and resurrection', but, as has been seen, Amaury was the king whose evident mastery of the Church was demonstrated by his heavy financial demands upon it.[84] In 1136 Patriarch Ralph of Antioch induced Raymond of Poitiers to swear fealty to him for Antioch on his arrival in the East, but William leaves his readers in no doubt that this was abnormal and that Ralph was a self-seeking opportunist.[85] So, despite possible appearances to the contrary, it would seem that William was trying to convey the idea that in making his demands Daimbert was aiming at a substantial ecclesiastical lordship within the kingdom, not control of the kingdom itself.

The true significance of the investiture of Godfrey and Bohemond lay in the measure of legitimacy it gave their respective rules. Previously they could claim to govern by right of conquest and election; now they could claim divine sanction. Their homage was not an act of submission to the patriarch, but an act of submission to God, and a year later Baldwin would take this formality a stage further and receive a crown, again at the hands of the patriarch.[86] By investing Godfrey and by crowning Baldwin, Daimbert had asserted that it was the prerogative of the patriarch to inaugurate the rule of the secular princes. As in the case of the archbishop of Canterbury or the archbishop of Rheims, this was a jealously guarded right, but it no more signified the superiority of the *sacerdotium* over the *regnum* in Jerusalem than it did in England or France.

So a composite portrait of William's ideal bishop emerges. Like Daimbert, he should be a righteous man who should attempt to stand firm in the defence of ecclesiastical liberty in the face of evil oppressors of the Church. Like Adhemar of Le Puy and Peter of

H. E. Mayer, *The Crusades* (Oxford, 1972), pp. 66–7, 294 note 23; *idem, Bistümer,* chapter I *passim*. But see Hamilton, *Latin Church*, pp. 52–4; J. France, 'The Election and Title of Godfrey de Bouillon', *Canadian Journal of History*, XVIII (1983), 323–4, 328–9.

[83] *WT*, IX, I, lines 23–42; 2, lines 1–2.
[84] *WT*, XX, 22, lines 60–2. See above, pp. 72, 90.
[85] *WT*, XIV, 20, lines 36–49.   [86] *WT*, X, 9, lines 1–8.

Barcelona, his uprightness and other qualities should compel respect from the people as a whole and should earn him a position of leadership in the kingdom alongside the lay leaders. Again like Adhemar and Peter, he should inspire the Christians in their defence of Christendom and go with them (though not as a combatant) into battle. Like Daimbert and Patriarch Stephen, he should strive to conserve and expand the endowments of his church – William was apparently of the opinion that the Church in the East was inadequately endowed, and in any case he would have shared the medieval view that to allow any ecclesiastical possessions to be lost would be to dishonour the patron of the individual church concerned. Like Daimbert again, he should assert and preserve the prerogatives of his office, such as the patriarchal right to officiate at the coronation of each new king. But, however much William might have hoped that the bishops of his own day would live up to these ideals, it would be wrong to assume that he set out with the deliberate intention of persuading them through the *Historia* to improve their ways. He had his views about the sort of things a bishop should be doing. He also had views about the calibre of his contemporaries. But he did not preach at them.

An appreciation of William's presuppositions about the nature and function of episcopal office goes far to illuminate the ideas about the relationship between *regnum* and *ecclesia* in the Latin East he wished to present to his readers. In the *Historia* he made a clear distinction between clergy and laity, which reflected the polarity between the two orders of society accepted throughout western Christendom in the twelfth century. Thus, for example, we frequently find phrases such as 'the king, the patriarch and all the princes of the kingdom, both ecclesiastical and secular';[87] and on occasion William seems to distinguish *ecclesia* from *regnum*.[88] The clergy of course had their own special responsibilities: care of churches, guardianship of the faith, and preservation of moral and ecclesiastical discipline. William recorded how in 1120 a council at Nablus issued decrees dealing with public morality and church affairs. He listed those present, in all probability copying the list of witnesses attached to the decree: the patriarch, the king, a group of bishops, abbots and priors, a group of lay lords, 'and many others of each order whose

---

[87] *WT*, XXII, 16, lines 71–2. Cf. XV, 24, lines 1–2; 25, lines 18–19; XVII, 28, lines 1–4; 30, lines 37–9; XVIII, 29, lines 15–17; XIX, 13, lines 24–5; XXI, 13, line 6.
[88] *WT*, XX, 29, lines 1–3.

number and names we do not have'. The order is instructive: in spiritual matters the *sacerdotium* came before the laity. But it is also significant that in a council whose decrees William depicted as an act of penitence and propitiation the laity was nevertheless associated with the clergy.[89] Another assembly made up of both secular and ecclesiastical leaders took place in 1161 to determine whether or not to receive the legate sent to the East by Pope Alexander III. To do so would have meant recognizing Alexander as the legitimate pope after the schism of 1159, and it was thus a matter of diplomatic as well as of ecclesiastical importance. On this occasion the wishes of the king, Baldwin III, did not prevail, and it would seem that he backed down in the face of pressure from the clergy.[90]

Neither the clergy nor the laity could exist independently, and William made it clear that the lay rulers did not always have their own way. Any notorious breach of the moral law elicited a strong response from the clergy even though the *regnum* might be badly inconvenienced by clerical opposition. According to William, on the accession of King Amaury, Patriarch Amaury of Nesle had obliged the new king to divorce his wife on the grounds of consanguinity, and William portrayed this incident as a victory for the Church as the upholder of matrimonial law.[91] In the early 1180s a major crisis developed when Bohemond III of Antioch rejected his wife, a niece of Emperor Manuel Comnenus, and married a certain Sibylla. His behaviour was doubly sinful since not only was the marriage bigamous, but Sibylla was a practitioner of the black arts. The consequent excommunication by Patriarch Aimery of Antioch only enraged the prince, who subjected the patriarch and the other clergy to physical attack, driving them to take refuge in one of the patriarch's castles. Bohemond then proceeded to seize churches, carry off church treasure and confiscate ecclesiastical estates. The plight of the clergy received sympathetic support from a number of lay nobles, several of whom were forced into exile thanks to their criticism of Bohemond's conduct. A high-level delegation from Jerusalem managed to work out a temporary arrangement whereby the clergy were restored to their churches and possessions, but the

---

[89] *WT*, XII, 13, lines 25–35. Cf. Mayer, 'Concordat', pp. 531–43. Mayer shows that this assembly marked a reconciliation between the Church and the king in the matter of tithes, to the Church's advantage – a point overlooked or suppressed by William.

[90] *WT*, XVIII, 29.   [91] *WT*, XIX, 4. See above, p. 79.

central issue of Bohemond's marriage and excommunication remained unresolved. So a stand taken by the church on an issue of morality led to a serious rift within the principality, with the very real possibility that its security would thereby be endangered.[92]

But, although the clergy had their own responsibilities and sphere of activity, and although they were not simply the instruments of the lay powers, they shared in the task of working to secure the total well-being of the Christian states in the East. William accepted that unity in the face of Muslim attack was all-important and that the clergy had a role to play in defence. But under normal circumstances it was the king who bore the responsibility of leading the defence, and William more than once stressed how important it was for the safety of the kingdom that the king should avoid capture.[93] The role of the monarch as the leader of the kingdom in war no doubt goes a long way to explain why William was content that the kings should have considerable influence in the organization of the Church and in the appointment to benefices and should be able to tax the wealth of the Church. It also explains why in the East, as in the West, it was accepted that clerics should be employed by the king in secular service. Thus bishops accompanied armies on campaign and directed the construction of fortresses,[94] as well as performing traditionally clerical duties such as serving on diplomatic embassies or acting as the royal chancellor. So, although kings could make their influence felt in the affairs of the Church and prelates likewise could affect political decisions, and although disputes between *regnum* and *ecclesia* did arise, William's portrait of the Latin kingdom of Jerusalem was of a kingdom in which kings and clergy worked in partnership for their common goal of defending Christendom. To William, bishops had an important role as counsellors of the king and as leading members of society, besides being prelates of the Church. He was happiest when he could show his bishops fulfilling these roles in harmony with the crown. Contemporaries in the West reading the *Historia* would see in the Church in the East an ecclesiastical province which looked much like any other province. They would see kings in the western mould – and successful kings at that – in partnership, or, on occasion, in conflict, with a Church which was at once recognizable as being like their own. If the kingdom deserved sympathetic understanding and

---

92 *WT*, XXII, 5, lines 26–9; 6–7.
93 *WT*, XIV, 25, lines 47–51; XVI, 10, lines 50–60; XVIII, 14, lines 1–5, 26–46.
94 *WT*, XIV, 8; 22, lines 28–33; 26, lines 16–21.

assistance in its struggle against the Muslims, so too the Church in the East, as an integral part of the Christian community, merited support in time of need, all the more because of the sacred associations of its location.

Chapter 7

THE PAPACY

There is never any question that William of Tyre accepted the papacy's own claims to apostolic authority within Christendom. His respect for the importance of papal office is immediately apparent from his condemnation of Guibert of Ravenna, the anti-pope installed by Henry IV in 1080, and by his comments on the threat to Christian Europe caused by the schism of 1130. He noted with approval how the schism which had originated in 1080 was settled in the early 1120s, how the irregular election of Pope Honorius II in 1124 was rectified, and how the 1159 schism was eventually brought to an end in 1177.[1] He was also at pains to emphasize the role of Urban II in launching the First Crusade, and of Eugenius III in launching the Second. Both popes were spoken of warmly. William stressed Urban's God-given eloquence, and Eugenius too was a 'godly man'.[2] On the other hand, in recording the election of Pope Lucius III in 1181, William remarked that the new pope was 'somewhat elderly and not very ("modice") learned'.[3] It is a dismissive description which might easily be passed over were it not for the fact that Lucius was still pope at the time of writing. Of his predecessor, Pope Alexander III, whose long pontificate (1159–81) spanned almost the whole of William's public career, he was equally dismissive. Scattered through the pages of the *Historia* are a mere handful of references to him, and William avoided making any comment at all on either his personality or his achievements.[4] Yet Alexander, who is regarded by modern scholars as one of the outstanding popes of the middle ages, had worked hard to encourage western aid for the Holy Land, and William himself had visited

---

[1] *WT*, I, 13, lines 15–22; XII, 8; XIII, 15, lines 42–55; XIV, 11, lines 10–14; XVIII, 26, lines 17–22.
[2] *WT*, I, 13, lines 41–5; 14–16; XVI, 18, line 11.   [3] *WT*, XXII, 7, line 55.
[4] Alexander III is referred to in eight separate places. See *WT*, Index général, s.n.

the papal court twice (in 1169, and in 1179 for the Third Lateran Council) during his reign. The disparate treatment of these popes is arresting and suggests that William had a decidedly ambivalent attitude to the papacy. Should the almost total silence surrounding the popes of his own day be understood as coolness towards them? Or did he regard the papacy and the actions of his contemporary popes as having little relevance for the affairs of the Latin East and its struggle against its Muslim neighbours?

At first sight there seems nothing unusual about the papacy and its relations with the clergy and churches of the Latin East. The validity of the decisions of the popes is accepted; on occasion clergy have recourse to papal jurisdiction in their disputes; the pope denotes his confirmation of a new patriarch by conferring the pallium;[5] the prerogatives of the papacy are recognized; papal legates turn up from time to time to sort out disputes. Two cardinal legates accompanied the armies of the Second Crusade, and on one occasion a legate came to the East to secure adherence to Alexander III after the divided election of 1159. Alexander had sent out Cardinal John of St John and St Paul, and his arrival precipitated a debate as to whether the new pope should be recognized. In what was the closest he ever came to recording a rejection of papal authority in the kingdom of Jerusalem, William described how the king originally proposed that he should not be received but then gave way to a pro-Alexander group among the clergy.[6] The general impression, so far as the papacy was concerned, is that William and the other Latins in the East were 'sons of obedience';[7] but to understand his attitude more fully, his handling of particular instances of the exercise of papal jurisdiction in the East requires examination.

As we have seen, William's account of the early history of the Latin patriarchate of Jerusalem abounds with difficulties. According to the *Historia*, Daimbert's removal from the patriarchal see in 1101/2 was the work of King Baldwin and Archdeacon Arnulf.[8] Albert of Aachen, however, provides information about the specific charges levelled at Daimbert and informs us that he was deposed by a papal legate, reinstated on Tancred's insistence and then deposed by a second legate.[9] William, by contrast, made no mention at all of these legations, and it is likely, since the deposition of a patriarch

[5] *WT*, XVIII, 20, lines 15–21.   [6] *WT*, XVII, 1, lines 9–12, 27–9; XVIII, 29.
[7] Cf. *WT*, XIV, 14, line 58. William's phrase is reminiscent of I Peter 1:15.
[8] *WT*, X, 24, lines 15–23.
[9] Albert, 'Historia Hierosolymitana', pp. 538–41, 545–8, 598–600. See Rowe, 'Paschal II', pp. 481–3; Hamilton, *Latin Church*, pp. 55–6.

was no small matter and he is otherwise reasonably well informed on the subject, that he deliberately suppressed this information. To have admitted the serious nature of the accusations and that Daimbert's deposition had had the authority of a legatine council would have placed the patriarch in a much less favourable light than he would have wished. But by concealing the legality of his demotion he was creating problems for himself, and his narrative in consequence contains various loose ends. Thus he can offer no explanation as to why Daimbert remained in Antioch until 1104 instead of appealing immediately to the pope against his deposition, or to why Baldwin and Arnulf seem not to have thought it necessary to rebut his charges against them when, in 1105, travelling in Bohemond's entourage, he did get to Rome.[10] What seems to have happened was that the former patriarch initially realized there would be little hope for him in challenging the legatine judgements at Rome, that when he did appeal he did so with the support of Bohemond of Taranto's immense popularity and reputation behind him, and that the king assumed that the legates' decisions would stand. However, the case against Daimbert went by default, and Pope Paschal II restored him to his see. Then in June 1105, while on his return journey to the East, he died at Messina.[11]

Suppressing the legates' deposition of Daimbert also affected William's treatment of his successor. He related how the simple priest Ebremar allowed himself in his ignorance to be intruded into the patriarchal see through the scheming of Baldwin and Arnulf. But if Daimbert had been properly deposed Ebremar could in good conscience have become patriarch, and the idea that he had been somehow duped has to be rejected. William's charge of ignorance against him would seem to be designed simply to increase Baldwin's and Arnulf's culpability.[12] Pope Paschal's restoration of Daimbert, even though never actually effected, necessarily entailed Ebremar's demotion. William described how he went to the pope to assert his innocence and how Paschal committed the affair to a new legate, Archbishop Gibelin of Arles, who was to hold a council in Jerusalem to determine the case. The council upheld the pope's earlier decision that Daimbert had been unlawfully expelled and consequently pronounced Ebremar deposed. Then, according to

[10] *WT*, x, 24, lines 23–32; xi, 1, lines 6–7, 21–6; 4, lines 1–10.
[11] *WT*, xi, 4, lines 8–13. For the date of his death, see Rowe, 'Paschal II', p. 486 note 84.
[12] *WT*, x, 25, lines 1–9. Ebremar's election had been presided over by the papal legate, Robert of Paris, See Rowe, 'Paschal II', pp. 482–3, 485.

William because of his great piety, he was given the archbishopric of Caesarea.[13] What William did not say is that after Ebremar had arrived at Rome with letters from the king and clergy calling on the pope to confirm him as patriarch, Arnulf arrived with letters from the king and clergy calling for his removal and alleging irregularities in his re-election following Daimbert's death. It appears that it was then that Paschal dispatched his legate and also that it was the pope who had originally stipulated at the time of Daimbert's restoration that Ebremar was to be found another see or even in due course re-elected to the patriarchate.[14] Nor, since he gave no hint of any breach between Baldwin and Ebremar, did William explain how Ebremar, the royal protégé, could be supplanted. William's story is of how a foolish cleric, who had gained his see illegally, was duly deposed by a papal legate. A closer examination of the sources suggests that what happened was that a man who was a perfectly respectable choice was properly elected as patriarch; his position was then undermined by a legal tangle, and then, for reasons which are not at all clear, the king decided to get rid of him and was able to exploit the operation of papal jurisdiction to secure this end.

Despite the shortcomings and omissions in William's account, the papacy emerges well from the presentation of these episodes in the *Historia*. The worthy Daimbert was vindicated at the papal court, the ignorant Ebremar, the creature of Baldwin and Arnulf, deposed by the pope's legate. But when we move on to the next decade and the problems of Arnulf's own patriarchate (1112–18) a different picture appears. As we have seen, William's hostility to Arnulf was unremitting. After Arnulf had become patriarch, William accused him of alienating the estates of his church, leading an immoral life and inducing the king to contract a bigamous marriage. In 1115, as William records, Pope Paschal sent another legate to investigate these charges: Bishop Berengar of Orange, who presided over yet another legatine council, which pronounced the patriarch deposed. Arnulf promptly appealed in person to Rome, where by 'flattering words and a great profusion of gifts' he won the day and was restored. But, says William, on his return he continued in his former licentious ways.[15] So the papal court could

---

[13] *WT*, XI, 4, lines 14–34.

[14] See Paschal's letter dated 4 Dec. 1107: *Cartulaire du Saint-Sépulcre*, no. 90. William (*WT*, XI, 12, lines 37–45) mentioned Arnulf's visit to Rome in a completely different context.

[15] *WT*, XI, 15; 26, lines 1–14. See above, pp. 92, 100–1. According to Paschal's letter dated 19 July 1117, Arnulf had to answer charges of irregularities in his election,

be bribed and hoodwinked. This explanation of Arnulf's re-instatement trivializes the pope's decision to the point of disbelief. The truth is that Rome was on the fringe of William's consciousness. The right of the pope or his legate to sit in judgement on a patriarch was never in doubt, but the papal actions were considered solely from William's own point of view and evaluated in accordance with what he regarded as being good for the Church and the Latin presence in the East. Furthermore, although the pope had rights of jurisdiction over the Church in the East, William presented the papacy as having an essentially passive role. It was the Latin clergy in Jerusalem who took the initiative in appealing to Rome, not the pope who intervened on his own account.

William acknowledged that the papacy had jurisdiction over the diocesan structure of the Church in the East as well as over its personnel. This point emerges clearly from his description of the foundation of the bishopric of Bethlehem and his preservation in the *Historia* of the foundation charter of 1110. Bethlehem had never previously been a bishopric, and the charter makes it clear that the idea of creating one there had originated with the king. Arnulf had raised the matter with Pope Paschal, evidently at the same time as he had been in Rome to call for Ebremar's demotion, and the pope had committed the affair to his legate, Gibelin of Arles. Gibelin, by virtue of his legatine authority, did three things which belonged to the papacy as its prerogatives: he raised Bethlehem to a bishopric; he decreed that Ascalon, hitherto a bishopric in its own right, should be a parish in the Bethlehem diocese; and he translated Aschetinus, who had been elected bishop of Ascalon (then still in Muslim hands), to the new see. Once again papal rights of jurisdiction were recognized and made operative, but the initiative lay with the king, and it would appear from the charter that Gibelin, who by now was himself patriarch-elect of Jerusalem, had done precisely what Baldwin had asked.[16] The decisions as enshrined in the charter seem so unambiguous that it comes as something of a surprise to discover from the *Historia* that in 1153, immediately after the capture of Ascalon, Patriarch Fulcher, whom elsewhere William had described

immorality and being of illegitimate birth (*Cartulaire du Saint-Sépulchre*, no. 91). Cf. Hamilton, *Latin Church*, p. 63.

16 *WT*, XI, 12. For an exhaustive discussion, see Mayer, *Bistümer*, pp. 44–80. Notice, however, that William makes no reference to any papal sanction for the revival of the bishopric of Banyas in 1140 and the archbishopric of Petra in 1168, or for the creation of a new bishopric at Hebron also in 1168 (*WT*, XV, 11, lines 60–9; XX, 3, lines 1–18).

as 'very devoted and faithful to the Holy Roman Church' and 'magnanimous and discerning', proceeded to ordain a bishop there. The then bishop of Bethlehem objected and appealed to Rome, where his appeal was upheld and the newly consecrated bishop put aside. It is difficult to believe that Fulcher was unaware of the rights of Bethlehem, and, although William says nothing about his motives, his action could be read as suggesting that he was indifferent or defiant towards papal authority.[17]

One prelate who certainly did defy papal authority was Ralph of Domfront, patriarch of Antioch. Ralph had become patriarch in 1135. As has been seen, his election was irregular, but, more significantly, he 'immediately, without delay, and showing no respect to the Church of Rome, took the pallium for himself from the altar of St Peter (the cathedral church of Antioch)'. William's comment is particularly noteworthy: had Ralph been able to remain on good terms with his own clergy he would have got away with it.[18] In fact he was soon at odds with members of his cathedral chapter and with the new prince of Antioch, Raymond of Poitiers, and in 1138 he was obliged to go to Rome to answer charges laid against him by his adversaries. According to William, he claimed that, as each was the Church of St Peter, Antioch should not be subservient to Rome. In other words, he was asserting that the pope had no jurisdiction over him personally or within his patriarchate. It then appears that he backed down, surrendered his pallium and received a new one in the normal way before departing for the East.[19] But, although Ralph had now acknowledged Rome's supremacy and his own position had been regularized, the original charges against him (improper election, simony, fornication) remained unresolved, and it was decided that a legate be sent to try the case on the spot. The first legate died soon after his arrival in the East in 1139, and a second legate, Alberic of Ostia, was not able to convene a council in Antioch until November 1140. William described this tribunal in some detail. Ralph himself refused to answer the summons to attend; the clergy were divided; but what was significant was the attitude of Prince Raymond. William informs us that he overawed the proceedings, that it was only fear of his authority that prevented a popular uprising against the council on Ralph's behalf, and that when the legate proclaimed

---

17 *WT*, xv, 16, lines 3–6; xvii, 30, lines 45–55. See Mayer, *Bistümer*, pp. 112–71.
18 *WT*, xiv, 10, lines 19–42 (at lines 20–2).
19 *WT*, xv, 12, lines 53–8; 13, lines 1–30.

Ralph's deposition and degradation he was relying on the prince's protection. William then rounded off his account with a brief and rather unconvincing postscript: after several years in prison Ralph escaped to Rome, where he enjoyed a measure of papal favour and then died from poisoning.[20]

The latter part of the story, the legatine council, is strongly reminiscent of accounts of those other councils which had dealt with the earlier patriarchs of Jerusalem: the initiative for involving the papacy had come from the East – this despite Ralph's seizure of the pallium in defiance of Rome – and ecclesiastical justice had been meted out in effect at the behest of the prince. But there is one difference: although William condemned Ralph as clever, unscrupulous and arrogant, he also showed a certain grudging respect and sympathy for him as a man of obvious ability who had suffered indignities at the hands of a lay ruler. Ralph's defiance of Rome, however, does draw attention to the question of the status of the eastern patriarchs *vis-à-vis* the papacy. The Orthodox view had been that the five ecumenical patriarchs were peers, but William was clearly scandalized by Ralph's presumption in claiming equality with the pope. In fact the position of the Latin patriarchs of Jerusalem and Antioch was more or less equivalent to that of primates in western Europe.[21] It was a papal prerogative to confer the pallium on the patriarch, thereby confirming his appointment, but it would appear that the patriarchs normally granted the pallium to the archbishops of their provinces. Thus William noted Patriarch Bernard of Antioch conferring the pallium on Archbishop Peter of Apamea, and it would seem from his account that when the successive archbishops of Tyre, William I (1128–35) and Fulcher (1135–46), applied to Rome for their pallia it was in the face of opposition from the patriarch of Jerusalem.[22]

If William accepted that papal prerogatives, and in particular the right of the popes to try *maiores causae*, applied within the patriarchates of Jerusalem and Antioch, it is nevertheless true that the perception of papal involvement with the Latin East he conveys to his readers is limited. There is much that he left out about the

---

[20] *WT*, xv, 13–17. For Raymond's role at the time of the council, see xv, 16, lines 58–60; 17, lines 7–18. For the chronology and a discussion of the wider political implications, see Hamilton, 'Ralph of Domfront', pp. 1–21. For the legatine council, see also Hiestand, *Vorarbeiten zum Oriens Pontificius*, iii, no. 46.

[21] See Y. Katzir, 'The Patriarch of Jerusalem, Primate of the Latin Kingdom', in P. W. Edbury (ed.), *Crusade and Settlement* (Cardiff, 1985), pp. 169–72.

[22] *WT*, vii, 8, lines 15–19; xiii, 23, lines 25–31; xiv, 11, lines 38–45.

normal intercourse between the *curia* and Latin Syria. The papacy was distant and only concerned, so it would seem, when its interest was aroused by appeals from the East. Furthermore, its actions were not always above reproach. As mentioned already, Arnulf could recover his see by bribery and flattery at Rome. William also alleged that bribery was used to secure confirmation of the election of Amaury of Nesle as patriarch in 1157, and that Ralph, the chancellor of the kingdom, whose election to Tyre had rightly been quashed by Pope Eugenius III, became bishop of Bethlehem thanks to the favour of Adrian IV, 'because he was his compatriot'.[23] The legates too were open to criticism. Gibelin of Arles was 'old and decrepit', a fit candidate for the machinations of the evil Arnulf. Alberic of Ostia seems, so William implied, to have allowed his impartiality in the process against Ralph of Antioch to have been compromised by Raymond of Poitiers. John of St John and St Paul, Alexander III's legate, whose admission to the kingdom had been controversial – William's sympathy clearly lay with those who were for not receiving him – proved to be burdensome to many of the very people who had wanted him.[24]

William was typical of his age. He accepted papal claims as a part of the right ordering of Christian society; but at the same time the popes stood at the periphery of his vision and, with the equity of their judgements open to question, by no means exempt from his criticism. Indeed, two issues in particular focused his anger on the papacy: the division of his own province of Tyre, and the exemptions from episcopal jurisdiction afforded the military Orders.

The material dealing with the controversy over the province of Tyre, including the texts of a number of papal letters, was probably inserted into the *Historia* at the time of the general revision of 1181–2. It is grouped into three sections and placed in the reigns of Baldwin I, Baldwin II and Fulk. The problem originated from the fact that the Latin conquest of the coastal cities of Acre, Sidon, Beirut, Jubail, Tripoli and Tortosa predated the conquest of Tyre, and, whereas the more southerly cities (Acre, Sidon and Beirut) were conquered by the king of Jerusalem and became part of his kingdom, the others lay in the county of Tripoli beyond the reach of royal authority. Hitherto all six had been suffragan bishoprics in

---

[23] *WT*, XVI, 17, lines 33–40; XVIII, 20, lines 15–21.
[24] *WT*, XI, 4, lines 39–41; XV, 11, lines 73–8 (and see above, note 20); XVIII, 29, lines 42–6.

the province of Tyre, and Tyre itself was the premier metropolitan church within the patriarchate of Antioch. So ecclesiastical tradition demanded that the province, stretching south to include Acre and the inland city of Banyas (held by the Christians in the middle years of the twelfth century), fell under the jurisdiction of Antioch, while political realities placed the southern portion of the province in the control of Jerusalem. The kings of Jerusalem did not want ecclesiastical jurisdiction over a substantial section of their realm to be exercised from outside, and so took steps to see to it that the patriarch of Jerusalem had authority over all the bishoprics within the Latin kingdom. In this they were assisted by the Pseudo-Isidorian doctrine that *provincia* equals *regnum*; in other words, that ecclesiastical organization should be modelled on secular organization, a view held generally by canon lawyers at that time. Our enquiry, however, is concerned not with the rights and wrongs of the case, but with William's presentation of it.[25]

William's story begins with Baldwin I petitioning Pope Paschal II that all the cities and provinces he might conquer from the Muslims should fall under the ecclesiastical jurisdiction of the patriarch of Jerusalem. The pope agreed, and the texts of his two bulls, issued at the time and dated June 1111, have been preserved for us in the *Historia*. Paschal justified his concurrence on the grounds that after the long period of Muslim rule there was uncertainty over the boundaries, and he enjoined obedience to the patriarch on all bishops in the kingdom. William then reported how Patriarch Bernard of Antioch protested indignantly to the pope over the injury thereby done to his church, and provided the text of two papal replies to Bernard and a further letter addressed to King Baldwin. In his first letter to the patriarch (August 1112) Paschal stood firm, assuring him that there had been no intention to dishonour the church of Antioch and trying to fob him off with bland statements about peace and unity. But in the second letter (March 1113), he began to give ground: although boundaries were often uncertain, where they were known, and where there had been no confusion despite Muslim occupation, it was the pope's desire that individual churches should 'be subject to that church to which they are known to pertain as of ancient right'. And in his letter to the king of the same date he was more explicit: the patriarch of Antioch

---

[25] On the issues themselves, see J. G. Rowe, 'The Papacy and the Ecclesiastical Province of Tyre (1100–1187)', *Bulletin of the John Rylands Library*, XLIII (1960–1), 160–89; Katzir, 'The Patriarch of Jerusalem', pp. 169–71.

had complained that the patriarch of Jerusalem with the king's connivance has been attacking the rights of those churches over whose allegiance to Antioch there had never been any doubt; the pope now commands that such actions cease and, where there is no uncertainty about rights of jurisdiction, that the traditional position be maintained; the clergy of Jerusalem are not to try to usurp the possessions definitely known to belong to Antioch.[26]

In this passage William kept his own comments to a minimum. He made no attempt to explain the background to the original petition, except to say that Baldwin acted 'perhaps at the suggestion of the clergy', and in any case the context is obscured since he misleadingly placed the episode in his narrative for the years 1115–16.[27] At no point was the province of Tyre explicitly referred to – although the statement about the patriarch of Jerusalem attacking the rights of churches owing allegiance to Antioch must refer to Sidon, Beirut and Acre – and there is no suggestion that these exchanges marked the starting-point of a controversy which was to rumble on for years to come. Nor is anyone criticized: the letters are simply allowed to speak for themselves. What the reader is left with is a sequence of papal pronouncements in which Pope Paschal began by saying one thing and ended up by saying virtually the opposite. In his bulls of March 1113 he claimed that his policy had always been to guarantee the traditional ecclesiastical obedience of cities and regions where it was known. This claim was not strictly true and forced him into accusing Baldwin and patriarch Gibelin of misinterpreting his original concession. More importantly, the 1113 letters also left open the possibility that a city or region might owe temporal allegiance in one direction and ecclesiastical allegiance in another.[28]

When we move on to the reign of Baldwin II and the next group of documents dealing with the controversy, we find William taking a much less detached view of the affair. He began by recording that four years after the capture of the city (in other words in 1128) the king, patriarch and leading men of the realm chose an Englishman, William, prior of the Holy Sepulchre, to be archbishop of Tyre. He

---

26 *WT*, XI, 28.
27 The passage is unquestionably a later insertion: see B/K, I, 513 note 97. In 1111 Baldwin had recently acquired Beirut and Sidon, and these acquisitions could well have precipitated his original petition.
28 Note the pope's comments at *WT*, XI, 28, lines 119–21, 149–51: 'For we wish neither the Church to be damaged in the interests of the power of princes nor the power of princes to be mutilated in the interests of ecclesiastical dignity.'

then poured forth a great flood of plaintive rhetoric: because of this four-year delay 'churches had been alienated and the cathedral church shorn of its own members', damage which had lasted to William's own time.[29] An archbishop had been elected two years before Tyre was captured – this was Odo, whom William had previously mentioned as having died during the siege of Tyre – and then this delay in electing his successor had been allowed out of 'indolent and thoughtless circumspection'.[30] William's remarks are opaque. He did not make it clear who was to blame, nor was he precise about the nature of the harm done to his church, although it appears that he was alluding both to the loss of episcopal rights within the diocese of Tyre and to the break up of the province. Behind the phrase 'thoughtless circumspection' could lie the idea that the delay was caused by the fear that the patriarch of Antioch would embark on litigation if the patriarch of Jerusalem consecrated an archbishop to Tyre, but, even if correct, this interpretation is not immediately apparent.

Directly after his consecration by the patriarch of Jerusalem, Archbishop William set off for Rome to obtain the pallium. The patriarch tried to prevent him going. Exactly why is again not made clear, although the inference could be that the patriarch was claiming that he rather than the pope should confer the pallium. The new archbishop was well received by Pope Honorius II, and the text of two letters from the pope, dated July 1128, which he brought back with him on his return, are incorporated into the *Historia*. The suffragan bishops, clergy and people of Tyre are informed of the grant of the pallium and the powers symbolized by it and ordered to show William the obedience due to a metropolitan. The patriarch similarly is told of the grant of the pallium and notified that the suffragan bishops are to render obedience to their archbishop. We are then told that Archbishop William returned to the East in the company of a papal legate, Giles of Tusculum, who brought with him letters ordering the patriarch of Antioch to restore to the archbishop the suffragans of his province then under his own jurisdiction.[31]

This is the first time in the *Historia* that the fact that part of the province of Tyre was under the jurisdiction of the patriarch of

---

[29] *WT*, XIII, 23, lines 1–25. See above, p. 91.
[30] *WT*, XIII, 23, line 14: 'supina et crassa prudentia'. For Odo, see XIII, 13, lines 64–7.
[31] *WT*, XIII, 23, lines 25–69. For Giles of Tusculum's letters to Antioch, see Hiestand, *Vorarbeiten zum Oriens Pontificius*, III, nos. 29–30.

Antioch is mentioned. Read in isolation it would seem that the pope was supporting the archbishop in his campaign to get his province established on a proper footing; only when placed alongside the rulings of Pope Paschal of fifteen years before can it be seen that Honorius had reversed papal policy. He had confirmed in office an archbishop chosen and consecrated by a patriarch of Jerusalem and had commanded that the province as a whole obey him, even though it must have been well known that of old it had been subject to the patriarchate of Antioch. The papal position was now hopelessly contradictory. It was one thing to say that Tyre belonged to Jerusalem by right of conquest; it was something else to say that the northern dioceses, Tripoli, Tortosa and Jubail, belonged to Tyre and hence to Jerusalem by ancient tradition. In fact William made no reference back to his earlier material, and as roughly two books and a decade of narrative separate these episodes in the *Historia* it may be wondered how many of his readers would have understood that Honorius' intervention had not solved anything, especially since the patriarch of Antioch evidently remained deaf to papal instructions. In William's narrative there is no hint of any criticism of the papacy, or indeed of his namesake and predecessor. Furthermore, the insufficiently explained questions of the delay in William's election, the harm done to the church of Tyre and the dispute over the pallium could easily have distracted attention. We are left wondering whether William himself understood the relevance or the significance of the material he had presented: in what is tantamount to a confession that his treatment had not been adequate he concluded by announcing that he would explain later how it was that the patriarch of Jerusalem could consecrate an archbishop of Tyre when historically the province had been subject to Antioch.

He resumed his story with the death of Archbishop William and the election of Fulcher of Celles (later patriarch of Jerusalem, 1146–57) as his successor in about 1134. Like his predecessor, Fulcher was consecrated by the patriarch of Jerusalem and then came into conflict with him over applying to Rome for his pallium. William incorporated in the *Historia* a letter from Pope Innocent II to the patriarch upbraiding him for dealing harshly with Fulcher after his return and ordering that he do justice to him on pain of having the province of Tyre withdrawn from his obedience and made directly subject to the Holy See.[32] Once again the papacy appears to be coming to the aid of an archbishop of Tyre. But there

[32] *WT*, XIV, 11, lines 17–80. The letter has been dated Jan. 1139.

was another side to the controversy. What Fulcher and his predecessor, William I, had done by going to the pope for the pallium
was to assert their independence of patriarchal jurisdiction. Hence
the patriarchs' opposition to their going. What William did not
mention, though whether through ignorance or through deliberate
suppression we cannot know, were earlier letters from Innocent II
ordering Archbishop Fulcher and his suffragans to submit themselves to the patriarch of Jerusalem as their primate.[33] Maybe
Fulcher had wanted his province to be made directly subject to
Rome as a way around the conflict over allegiance between the
patriarchs. William continued by reporting that on his return the
pope had ruled that Fulcher should be subject to the patriarch of
Jerusalem pending a decision as to which patriarch he should obey
in perpetuity. He then went on to explain that the archbishops of
Tyre had previously ranked first among the metropolitans of the
patriarchate of Antioch, and that the pope now decreed that they
should hold first place among the suffragans of Jerusalem. But the
papal letter he quotes does not actually say this and seems to be no
more than an exhortation to the patriarch to treat Fulcher kindly
and show him the honour due to him.[34]

William then quotes three more papal letters dealing with the
obedience of the suffragan bishops to Tyre. Here he manages to
combine and so to confuse two distinct issues. It would seem that,
in the course of Fulcher's dispute with the patriarch of Jerusalem,
the patriarch had ordered the bishops of Acre, Sidon and Beirut to
render their obedience directly to himself and that, caught in the
middle of the conflict, they had been unwilling to accept the archbishop's authority after his return. Hence Innocent had to give firm
instructions that they should obey their metropolitan.[35] The other
two letters are concerned with Antioch. William explained that the
dioceses of Tripoli, Tortosa and Jubail were retained by the patriarch of Antioch illegally ('violenter') and gave the text of a letter to
the bishops of these dioceses ordering that they obey Archbishop
Fulcher and freeing them from their oaths to the patriarch of
Antioch, together with a letter to the patriarch of Antioch of a

[33] *Cartulaire du Saint-Sépulcre*, nos. 104–5 (July 1137 and Mar. 1138).
[34] *WT*, xiv, 12. This letter is dated July 1138. It contains (at lines 41–3) the sentence,
'Indignum est enim ut honor qui sibi, si ei obediret, ab Antiochia exhiberetur, a te
vel tuis successoribus subtrahatur' (cf. *WT*, xiv, 11, lines 66–8, for the same
phraseology in the letter of Jan. 1139), but this would seem to be no more than a
pointed reminder that the pope could still transfer Tyre back to Antioch.
[35] *WT*, xiv, 13, lines 1–3, 54–84.

similar purport.[36] So Innocent gave Fulcher his support and in so doing adopted the same policy as had Honorius.

William could now move on to explain how the situation with Antioch had come about. Bishops had been consecrated to Tripoli, Tortosa and Jubail by the patriarch of Antioch and held under his own jurisdiction in the expectation that when Tyre was recovered he would then institute a Latin archbishop and make these dioceses subject to him. As they lay in the county of Tripoli, where the king could not interfere, the patriarch had a free hand. But in Acre, Beirut and Sidon the patriarch of Jerusalem had consecrated bishops with a similar view in mind, relying on the original grant of Pope Paschal that all bishoprics within the kingdom of Jerusalem should be under the patriarch's authority. Hence the province was divided between the two patriarchates before Tyre itself was captured. But in the immediate aftermath of its capture and before the appointment of Archbishop William I, the churches within the diocese of Tyre were alienated. Thus it was that the archbishops found they had a divided province and a mutilated archepiscopal see, a situation which continued throughout the twelfth century and indeed beyond. William concludes:

But we impute the reason for this great evil not undeservedly to the church of Rome, since while she commands us to obey Jerusalem she allows us to be unjustly maimed by Antioch. But we, if our unity were restored to us, would be prepared to subject ourselves without any argument or protest to either one with a ready will inasmuch as we are sons of obedience.[37]

So the papacy was to blame! This conclusion comes as something of a surprise, since all the letters of Honorius II and Innocent II were presented by William as showing the papacy supporting the archbishops and their claims. On no other issue had William incorporated the texts of papal letters into the *Historia*, yet they neither evoke sympathy for the plight of his church nor prepare the reader for this verdict. Paschal, it is true, had made contradictory statements which had contributed to the origins of the problem, but what incensed William was that the papacy, so it would seem, had lacked the will to enforce its own decisions and compel the northern suffragans into obedience to Tyre. As it happened, the papacy had an ideal opportunity to unite the province when in 1140 the patriarch of Antioch was deposed by a legatine council. Archbishop Fulcher was present on that occasion, yet Alberic of Ostia, the papal

[36] *WT*, xiv, 13, lines 3–53.   [37] *WT*, xiv, 14, lines 54–9.

legate, is not known to have made any attempt to enforce Innocent's bulls ordering the northern bishops to accept him as their metropolitan. William, however, despite a certain coolness towards Alberic, made no allusion to the question of Tyre in his discussion of that episode.

In his conclusion William left open the possibility that Tyre could yet be placed under the authority of the patriarchate of Antioch. He had omitted all reference to Pope Innocent II's bull of July 1138, which formally transferred the obedience of Tyre to Jerusalem,[38] and perhaps managed, deliberately or not, to leave the impression that this question had never been settled. On the other hand, the absence of any reference in the *Historia* to the plight of the province of Tyre after the time of Innocent II and Archbishop Fulcher would lead one to suppose that the issue had burnt itself out. In fact there is evidence to show that the dispute lingered on well into the thirteenth century.[39] In many respects therefore, William's handling of his materials and his treatment of the controversy are unsatisfactory. But what do they tell us about his attitude to the papacy? The popes respond to petitions from the East and normally tell their petitioners what they want to hear. Thus King Baldwin I and Patriarch Bernard of Antioch had what they wanted from Paschal, and Honorius and Innocent were responsive to Archbishops William I and Fulcher. But the papacy let the archbishops down by not pushing their decisions through into practice. In one sense William's verdict is unfair, since the whole subject was much more complex than he indicates, with political implications extending far beyond the question of the structure of the ecclesiastical hierarchy. Circumstances would not admit the simple solution he seems to have believed possible. In another sense William was able to illustrate an important truth about the papacy. For all its claims and prerogatives, its effectiveness in dealing with the affairs of the East, and indeed of other parts of Christendom, was limited; the popes had had to accept that they could not always solve problems in a way which either they or the parties concerned might wish.

Into his narrative of the early part of the reign of King Baldwin II William inserted a description of the origins of the Templars. It is an idealized and sketchy account, outlining their saintly and heroic

---

[38] *Cartulaire du Saint-Sépulcre*, no. 106.
[39] See Rowe, 'The Papacy and Tyre', pp. 186–8. See also Hiestand, *Vorarbeiten zum Oriens Pontificius*, III, nos. 69, 128, for evidence that in the time of Eugenius III the

beginnings and commenting on their large accumulation of possessions, both in the Holy Land and in western Europe. According to
William, after a good beginning they had lost their early humility,
had withdrawn from their obedience to the patriarch of Jerusalem,
who had first established them, and had refused tithes and first
fruits to other churches.[40] These remarks are vague, and in particular there is no reference to the point that their actions had been
sanctioned by a series of papal bulls which exempted the Order
from episcopal jurisdiction.

With the Hospitallers, however, he was much more specific. He
introduced his discussion of the Knights of St John in connection
with the appeal against their exemptions made by the bishops of
the Latin East in the mid-1150s. The Hospitallers had been making
difficulties over parochial rights and tithes, and William enumer-
ated specific charges against them, all of which illustrated their
independence from the secular Church. All bishops had reason to
be aggrieved, the patriarch of Jerusalem especially, since of late the
Hospitallers' behaviour towards him had been insupportable,
insulting and violent. After describing various outrageous
examples of the Order's contumacy, William concluded:

The Roman Church, although perhaps not realizing nor fully weighing
the consequences of what was being sought from her, seems to those who
have considered the matter carefully to have been responsible for the
origin of this great evil. For without due reason it freed the aforesaid place
[the Hospitaller convent in Jerusalem] from the jurisdiction of the lord
patriarch of Jerusalem, to whom for a long time it had properly been subject.[41]

William then says that, to explain how the Order had grown so
powerful and could continue to act unjustly against the churches of
God until the present day, he will give an account of its origins. In
fact his information on the Hospitallers' early history sheds no
light at all on their exemptions from episcopal control,[42] and at the
end he simply reiterated that as their wealth grew they were freed
by the Roman Church from the authority of the patriarch. Furnished with this 'pernicious freedom' ('perniciosa libertate'), they
ceased showing respect for the bishops and refused to pay tithes.

obedience of Beirut and Sidon to Tyre was in doubt and that in the 1180s Patriarch
Eraclius raised the question of Tyre with Lucius III on his visit to the West of
1184–5.
[40] *WT*, XII, 7.   [41] *WT*, XVIII, 3, lines 56–61.   [42] *WT*, XVIII, 4–5.

Other religious institutions then followed their example in gaining similar exemptions.[43]

William had concentrated on bewailing the losses of authority and revenue incurred by the Latin hierarchy. At no point did he discuss the motivation of the papacy in granting these privileges to either Order; nor did he show any particular knowledge of the bulls themselves. He was content to lay the blame on the papacy's lack of consideration, which he saw as giving rise to the destitution of the secular church. He was in a dilemma, for in common with all other informed observers in the 1180s he was conscious of the importance of the military Orders in the defence of the Latin East. So far as the Hospitallers were concerned, almost his only criticisms of them were concentrated in the passages discussed in the previous paragraph; otherwise they were normally spoken of with respect.[44] The Templars too were shown taking a significant share in the military activities of the kingdom of Jerusalem, but in their case there are a number of anecdotes scattered through the later books of the *Historia* which are clearly designed to detract from their reputation, and which demonstrate William's hostility towards them.[45]

One story in particular is of interest. Towards the end of King Amaury's reign the ruler of the Ismāʾīlī sect of the Assassins, which held a group of strongholds to the north of the county of Tripoli, sent an embassy to the king offering to embrace Christianity if the Templars would remit the tribute of 2,000 pieces of gold they paid them annually. On the way home the envoy, who was travelling under the king's safe conduct, was killed by some brothers of the Order. The king was greatly angered and demanded that the perpetrators of this deed should be handed over to him for punishment. Odo of St Amand, the master of the Templars, replied that he had enjoined a penance on the brother responsible, and, since as a part of his penance he was sending him to the pope, he forbade anyone, in the name of the pope, to lay violent hands upon him. But the king seized the individual concerned and put him in prison. William

---

[43] *WT*, XVIII, 6, lines 1–9. For the papal exemptions granted the Templars and Hospitallers, see Hiestand, *Vorarbeiten zum Oriens Pontificius*, I–II. For exemptions to other religious foundations, see Mayer, *Bistümer*, part II *passim*.

[44] An exception is Gilbert d'Assailly's role in promoting the Egyptian campaign of 1168 (*WT*, XX, 5). For an example of a favourable notice of the Hospitallers, see *WT*, XIV, 22, lines 46–50.

[45] For positive notices, see *WT*, XIII, 26, lines 1–7; XV, 6, lines 48–56, 81–3; XVII, 12, lines 28–38; XVIII, 14, lines 17–18; XIX, 8, lines 18–21; XXI, 29, lines 19–22. For the critical anecdotes, see XVII, 27, lines 42–6; XVIII, 9, lines 48–64; XIX, 11, lines 56–64; XXI, 28, lines 40–6.

rounded off the story by stating that, had he recovered from his last illness, Amaury had intended to raise the matter with the 'kings and princes of the world'.[46] The issue was one of 'benefit of clergy', a familiar source of friction between secular and ecclesiastical authorities throughout twelfth-century Latin Christendom. As an exempt Order of the Church, the Templars could invoke papal authority in an attempt to place the guilty man beyond the reach of royal justice. In fact Amaury, who early in his reign had hanged some Templars who had surrendered a fortress without making what he considered a sufficient attempt at resistance,[47] was too tough a king to allow Odo of St Amand's assertion to stand. However, a rather opaque remark near the end of his account to the effect that Amaury behaved with moderation – so much so that the matter remained unresolved at the time of his death – suggests that perhaps after all he had been inhibited by the Templars' privileges and that Odo's attempt to place the culprit in papal hands had had the effect of saving him from the gallows.[48] But, whatever the truth, the incident does show that the papal grants to the military Orders could sour their relations with the crown as well as with the bishops.

The most important section in the *Historia* on the theme of the papacy, the military Orders and the Latin East concerns the appeal of the hierarchy to the pope in the mid-1150s, in the vain attempt to persuade him to rescind the exemptions from episcopal authority accorded the Hospitallers. Having explained the baleful effect of the Order's privileges and given an account of their early history, William went on to record how the aged Patriarch Fulcher, together with the archbishops of Tyre and Caesarea and the bishops of Acre, Sidon, Lydda, Sebastea and Tiberias, set off for Italy in the spring of 1155. The narrative brilliantly conveys the difficulties of their journey to the papal court. A civil war was raging against King William I of Sicily. Pope Adrian IV and Manuel Comnenus were active participants, with Frederick Barbarossa an interested observer. After much hardship the patriarch and his bishops arrived before the pope in the first week of October. From the start things went badly. It was being said that the pope was deliberately avoiding the patriarch and so wearing him down and increasing his expenses, and that the Hospitallers had already won his goodwill through bribery:

[46] *WT*, xx, 29–30.   [47] *WT*, xix, 11, lines 56–64.
[48] *WT*, xx, 30, lines 46–8.

It was certainly evident that he and his entourage had shown their favour to the Hospitallers too intimately, while he had repelled the lord patriarch and his party with a certain contempt and disdain as if they were illegitimate and unworthy sons.[49]

Despite his frosty reception, Fulcher persisted with his suit until eventually convinced he had no chance of success. There were only two cardinals who 'as followers of Christ' were prepared to support his cause; the others had all been bribed. The patriarch's efforts had been counter-productive. William's account of Fulcher's appeal is thus marked by a deep hostility to the papacy, which is also a feature of his account of the civil war in Sicily with which his narrative of the appeal is intertwined. On the one hand the Hospitallers' victory was due to bribery; on the other the papacy, having instigated the war, faithlessly abandoned its allies.[50]

William, as we have seen, had accused the papal court of being open to bribery on other occasions as well. It is a facile explanation for Fulcher's failure, although William may have been voicing a widely held view.[51] But he shows no appreciation of the potential implications of the patriarch's demands. The sight of the patriarch of Jerusalem accompanied by almost his entire episcopate appearing in person to petition the pope must have been striking. Yet Fulcher was demanding a reversal of papal policy, which would in itself have been seen as a costly climb-down for the papacy, with possible consequences for all exempt Orders and monasteries throughout western Christendom. Furthermore, William seems oblivious to the point that in the aftermath of the Second Crusade many people in Europe had lost confidence in the zeal and effectiveness of the Latins settled in the East, and that the papacy, partly through the granting of privileges of exemption, had been encouraging the growth in importance of the military Orders, whose international character equipped them to make an effective contribution to the defence of the Christian possessions there. In all probability Rome saw Fulcher as a selfish prelate who put his own welfare before the welfare of the Holy Places. So here again William's criticisms of the papacy reveal his own narrow perspective: the interests of the secular Church in the East have been damaged, and it is all the papacy's fault.

After the pontificate of Adrian IV, the papacy appears but rarely in the *Historia*. Alexander III receives only a few passing references,

[49] *WT*, xviii, 7, lines 55–9.   [50] *WT*, xviii, 2; 6, lines 21–35; 7–8.
[51] See Riley-Smith, *Knights of St John*, pp. 385, 400.

Lucius III only one. William could well have had some sympathy for the rival pope, Victor IV, elected in opposition to Alexander in 1159. As Cardinal Octavian he had been one of the two cardinals, the 'followers of Christ', who had supported Patriarch Fulcher's appeal in the mid-1150s. The other was John of St Martin, a former archdeacon of Tyre, who was to remain an adherent of the anti-pope.[52] As we have seen, William regretted that Alexander's legate was received in Jerusalem, and he noted that there were at least some members of the hierarchy who favoured Victor on the grounds that 'he had always been a friend and protector of the kingdom'.[53] But it is also likely that the support the military Orders received from both Alexander and Lucius rankled. At the Third Lateran Council a powerful condemnation of the Orders was approved, curtailing several of their privileges. The absence of any detailed accounts of what transpired during the discussions at that Council means that we do not know whether William himself and the Latin Syrian delegation took the lead in proposing this decree, but there can be no doubt that he would have given it his whole-hearted support. The papacy, however, was evidently out of sympathy with this move, and both Alexander and Lucius issued bulls restricting the decree's effectiveness.[54] To cap it all, in 1181 Alexander issued his encyclical *Cor nostrum et* calling on the faithful to come to the aid of the Holy Land; in it he spoke of the king of Jerusalem, Baldwin IV, as being 'scourged by the just judgement of God'.[55]

In all likelihood, therefore, the paucity of references to the popes of his own day is a sign of William's disenchantment. The province of Tyre remained divided. Only the pope could repair the damage, but evidently he chose not to. We may assume that the papacy adopted the view that to upset the compromise which had evolved would create more problems than it solved, but William gave no indication that he could appreciate this point. Similarly the military Orders prospered at the expense of the secular Church and with the active support of the papacy. Here again William made no attempt to see the issue from the papal point of view. Indeed, this lack of perception runs through his entire treatment of papal dealings with

---

[52] *WT*, XVIII, 8, lines 15–20.   [53] *WT*, XVIII, 29, lines 26–8.

[54] See Riley-Smith, *Knights of St John*, pp. 387–9. For the decree, see J. Alberigo *et al.* (eds.), *Conciliorum Oecumenicorum Decreta*, 2nd edn (Freiburg im Breisgau, 1962), pp. 191–3. For the papal bulls, see also Hiestand, *Vorarbeiten zum Oriens Pontificius*, I, nos. 104, 105, 107, 110, 111, 124.

[55] See above, p. 63.

the Latin East. The popes were judged by the standard of whether their actions conformed to William's own preferences. In effect he was a spokesman for both the monarchy and the Latin clergy in the East. He evidently believed that the papacy ought to be supporting the kings in their defence of the Holy Places and the clergy in their quest for adequate endowments, due respect and their proper role in society. So when popes would not do what he might have expected of them, he saw this as a betrayal and condemned them as corrupt or insufficiently motivated. It is a one-sided view and, to modern historians, a serious distortion of papal efforts on behalf of the Holy Land. William acknowledged the importance of the papacy in Christendom, the doctrinal orthodoxy of the Roman Church,[56] the significance of the papacy in preaching the Crusades, and the right of the pope to exercise jurisdiction over the eastern patriarchates, but for all that it was Jerusalem that stood at the centre of his affection, while Rome lay at the periphery. The popes were distant, and the popes, all too often, had failed the Latin East.

[56] *WT*, xxii, 9, lines 11–13; 11, lines 29–35.

Chapter 8

THE BYZANTINE EMPIRE

The relationship of the crusaders and their successors in Latin Syria with the Greeks of the Byzantine empire is a subject which deservedly has occupied the attention of historians. Without doubt the crusading movement made a major contribution to the growing estrangement between the Catholic West and the Orthodox East in the course of the twelfth century. At the time of the First Crusade the Greeks and the westerners had each benefited from the other's assistance, but soon mutual incomprehension and conflicting political ambitions in the East gave rise to disputes and bitter recrimination. However, relations were not uniformly sour throughout the period, and many contemporaries continued to envisage cooperation. In the twelfth century, as in later periods, Byzantium and its rulers had both detractors and apologists, and William of Tyre was among those who had much to say in this connection.[1]

A considerable amount of material dealing with Byzantine affairs is included in the *Historia*, and it is important to understand William's attitudes towards the Greeks in order to evaluate his perception of their relations with the Latins. He was well placed to provide an appraisal of the empire and its emperors. Twice, in 1168 and in 1179–80, he had been engaged in diplomatic activities in Byzantium, and he had also had dealings with the Byzantine envoys to Jerusalem in 1177. Moreover, as archbishop and chancellor he would have had frequent contact with the queen, Maria Comnena, as well as with Greek Christians of less exalted standing. But even a

---

[1] There is a large literature on Byzantine relations with the West and the crusading movement. Two invaluable studies, each with a full bibliography, are C. M. Brand, *Byzantium Confronts the West, 1180–1204* (Cambridge, Mass., 1968), and R-J. Lilie, *Byzanz und die Kreuzfahrerstaaten. Studien zur Politik des Byzantinischen Palästina bis zum vierten Kreüzzug (1096–1204)* (Munich, 1981). But see the review of Lilie by H. Möhring in *Historische Zeitschrift*, CCXXXIV (1982), 601–8, and also H. Möhring, 'Byzanz zwischen Sarazenen und Kreuzfahrern', in W. Fischer and J. Schneider (eds.), *Das Heilige Land im Mittelalter* (Neustadt an der Aisch, 1982), pp. 45–75.

cursory reading of the *Historia* reveals that he had widely differing approaches to the Byzantine empire and its subjects. On the one hand he could be overtly hostile, verging on the xenophobic, and display a marked lack of objectivity and insight. Then again he could show a friendly appreciation of the efforts of the Byzantines to aid the western enterprise in the East; while on other occasions he could be dispassionate in providing a lucid account of Byzantine policy, its effectiveness, limitations and weaknesses. Often these attitudes were closely intertwined with one another, so much so that his real opinion is obscure or ambiguous.[2]

The opening chapters of Book I of the *Historia*, with their emphasis on the sufferings and degradations inflicted on the Christians in Jerusalem prior to the First Crusade, provide an admirable illustration of William's dispassionate objectivity. After describing Emperor Heraclius' recovery of the True Cross and restoration of the Church in Jerusalem in the seventh century, he related how the emperor abandoned Syria and Palestine to their fate in the face of Muslim expansion. But, instead of criticizing the emperor, he simply noted that he lacked the strength to defend these provinces. However, he made it clear that the Christians in Jerusalem had looked to Heraclius for protection and that this habit of mind persisted, so that after the destruction of the Holy Sepulchre by Hakim early in the eleventh century they turned for aid to the emperors Romanus III and Constantine Monomachus. But later in the eleventh century, with the Byzantine defeat at Manzikert and the loss of almost all Asia Minor, the Church in Jerusalem was plunged into despair, since it was now clear that no help could come from Byzantium.[3] In these early chapters William was never derogatory. Greek Christians, whether in Jerusalem or in the Byzantine empire, were part of a unified Christendom; the tragedy of the Church in Jerusalem was a tragedy to be felt by all Christians. Through no fault of their own, the Greeks could no longer do anything to defend their co-religionists in Jerusalem. The point he was working up to was that the failure or the weakness of the Byzantine empire was to be the occasion for Latin intervention. Charlemagne's benefactions, which (following Einhard) he had recorded in these chapters, were a foretaste of what was to come.[4] The crucial incident was the meeting of Peter the Hermit and the patriarch of Jerusalem. According to William, the patriarch spoke

[2] See Lilie, *Byzanz*, pp. 284–301.   [3] *WT*, I, 1, 6, lines 1–34; 9, lines 65–76.
[4] *WT*, I, 3, lines 15–47.

of both Frankish strength and the weakness of the Greeks, from whom nothing could now be expected. The implication was obvious. Interestingly, Albert of Aachen, who had made this supposed encounter the starting-point of his narrative of the Crusade, did not record the patriarch talking about Byzantine inability to intervene on behalf of his Church. This element was William's own and is indicative of his originality: henceforth the Latins would take over the historic role of the Byzantines in defending the eastern Christians.[5]

The *Historia* therefore opens with the theme of Byzantine weakness and inadequacy – but in the context of setting the stage for Latin involvement in the East. The absence of vilification continues in the earlier parts of the account of the First Crusade. The emperor Alexius is shown treating the unruly bands of Walter Sansavoir and Peter the Hermit with great moderation and kindness, and when disaster befell these groups William placed the blame squarely on the pilgrims, not on the Greeks.[6] But all this changes with the arrival of the main armies on Byzantine soil. The wild uncultivated terrain through which Godfrey of Bouillon and his men had to travel was a sign of Byzantine weakness which William attributed to the end of Latin rule and, as the result of sin, to the passing of the empire to the Greeks.[7] So for the first time Byzantine weakness was coupled with hostile criticism. But then, as the armies approached Constantinople, even this theme was submerged under a barrage of invective, hatred and contempt. The Greeks were enemies; Alexius was a perfidious traitor, a wicked and crafty man; his words were outwardly kind and generous, but in reality full of poison; his actions showed his treacherous intent. On the march to Constantinople and at the capital, Alexius and the crusaders were playing a cat and mouse game which ultimately makes for tedious reading. The moves had a distinct sameness: tension built up between the crusaders and the imperial officials; the westerners grew restive under the silken cords thrown around them; the Greeks were concerned at the threat thus posed to their empire; bloodshed became frequent, with the crusaders resorting to violence to stem Alexius' machi-

---

[5] *WT*, I, 11, lines 36–49. Cf. Albert, 'Historia Hierosolymitana', pp. 272–3.
[6] *WT*, I, 18–26.
[7] *WT*, II, 4, lines 1–39. William placed the transfer from Latin to Greek rule in the time of Nicephorus I (802–11). This date is of course much too late but may be an echo of the idea that the imperial title had been transferred from East to West at the time of Charlemagne's coronation – thereby, in western eyes, invalidating Byzantine imperial pretensions.

nations.[8] At Constantinople each crusade leader was seen individually by the emperor, so that by a show of courtesy and munificence he could extract oaths of allegiance and fidelity. Almost all complied with this Byzantine manoeuvre, and then, still full of trickery, Alexius managed to get the armies across the Bosphorus and into Asia Minor.[9]

Once William had taken the crusaders beyond Constantinople and away from the emperor's presence, his anti-Greek outbursts began to diminish. In his description of the siege of Nicaea he made the first of several references to the existence of a treaty between the Byzantines and the crusaders. Although he had described how most of the leaders had sworn oaths to Alexius at Constantinople, there was no reference to any formal agreement at that point in his narrative. However, from a series of later allusions it is clear that a treaty had been made in which the crusaders undertook to restore to the emperor the cities they recovered and Alexius promised to allow them to keep their booty, to supply them with provisions and to follow them in person at the head of a Byzantine army.[10] This somewhat tardy interest in the treaty was largely due to William's determination to show Alexius as its violator. Its breach was to be the justification for the crusaders' retention of Antioch, a city which had been in Byzantine hands as recently as 1084. Thus at the surrender of Nicaea the crusaders were denied their rightful spoils as prescribed in the treaty, and then, more importantly, in the summer of 1098 Alexius turned back at Philomelium (Akshehir) instead of fulfilling his obligations and pressing on to succour the Latin armies at Antioch.[11]

But a significant change has come over the portrayal of Alexius. The emperor's withdrawal, although a violation of the treaty, did not elicit a torrent of anti-Byzantine abuse. Instead it was Stephen of Blois, whose report had encouraged his action, who was condemned. In fact William was pleased that Alexius had not come to Antioch; had he done so, he would rightly have taken for himself the glory of capturing the city, but, as it was, those who had suffered the hardships of the siege had the rewards of their labours. After the capture of Antioch the leaders sent a high-ranking delegation to ask Alexius to follow them on the road to Jerusalem. If he

[8] *WT*, II, 4–16; 19–20; 24 *passim*.
[9] *WT*, II, 15–16; 19–23. For the oath, see Lilie, *Byzanz*, pp. 10–25.
[10] *WT*, III, 12, lines 30–4; 13, lines 9–26; VI, 10, lines 18–21; VII, 1, lines 1–7; 20, lines 1–28. Cf. Lilie, *Byzanz*, pp. 10–13, 17–20, 21–3.
[11] *WT*, III, 13, lines 9–26; VI, 10–12.

refused (which he did, although William did not actually say so), they would regard him as having broken his side of the treaty and so be free from their own obligations towards him. Once again it was not Alexius but Hugh of Vermandois, who had failed to rejoin the Crusade after delivering this message, who was censured.[12] Then early in 1099, as the crusaders began to move south, Byzantine ambassadors caught up with them and reproved them for giving Antioch to Bohemond and not restoring it to Alexius. William justified the crusaders' decision on the grounds that the emperor had broken his understanding by not following their army or furnishing supplies. The ambassadors then promised that he would come and distribute gifts on a lavish scale. Some took the ambassadors at their word, but most did not and pointed to the emperor's record for trickery.[13] This episode too afforded the opportunity to heap abuse on Alexius, but instead William showed considerable restraint.

But there is more to William's attitude to the Byzantine empire than shrill denunciations of treachery as the crusaders passed through Constantinople, moderating to a less emotively articulated story of Alexius' failure to honour his promises during the campaigning that followed. Much of William's hostility is to be explained by the tone of his sources. Even the earliest, such as the *Gesta Francorum*, have stories of Byzantine duplicity and Alexius' hatred, and it is likely that this historiographical tradition had been stimulated by the anti-Byzantine propaganda disseminated by Bohemond before his crusade of 1107–8.[14] It is, however, also true that in simplifying and rationalizing his materials William if anything heightened their anti-Greek sentiments, and it may be suspected that he also knew of oral traditions which consistently vilified Alexius. But at the same time there are other more complex, and contradictory, threads running through his narrative. His repeated allegations of mendacity seem to be belied by the reactions of the leaders who at Constantinople accepted Alexius' generosity at face value and, outwardly at least, were prepared to be reconciled with him. Thus, when at one point Alexius overplayed his hand in a brutal attack on Raymond of Toulouse's army and Raymond felt quite properly betrayed, the crusaders maintained their equanimity, remarking that this was no time for revenge; directly afterwards we

---

[12] *WT*, VII, 1, lines 1–24.   [13] *WT*, VII, 20, lines 1–47.
[14] See, for example, *Gesta Francorum*, pp. 5–6, 9–13, 17. See J. Riley-Smith, *The First Crusade and the Idea of Crusading* (London, 1986), pp. 136–7, 145.

find the crusaders, the count of Toulouse chief among them, entertaining the notion that Alexius should act as commander-in-chief of
the armies.[15] After their departure from the capital it is clear from
the *Historia* that many crusaders continued to believe in Alexius'
goodwill. As we have already noted, they sent to him for aid after
their victory at Antioch, and it would seem that when the Byzantine
envoys reached their army in 1099 there were some at least of the
Latins who regarded the emperor as a friend.

Furthermore it seems that William recognized that in Alexius'
eyes the crusading armies posed a major threat to the empire and its
capital. In the midst of his invectives he expressly stated that the
emperor regarded the advent of the Crusade with misgivings and
feared the concentration of armies in and around Constantinople. In
particular he was apprehensive at the presence of Bohemond among
the crusaders, an understandable sentiment in view of the attacks on
Byzantium he and his father, Robert Guiscard, had made in the
past. Alexius' treacherous behaviour and his munificence both proceeded from fear and mistrust and were directed to moving the
crusaders across the Bosphorus, thus preventing their armies
uniting outside his city.[16] Here William's interpretation is in line
with the construction placed on these events by most modern
historians. Yet, despite his appreciation of the situation, he was
unable to break away from the idea that Alexius was the inveterate
opponent of the Latins. When the crusaders gave him the opportunity to lead the Crusade and he declined on the grounds that his
empire was threatened by attacks from beyond its borders,
William, who had already described the weakness of the empire and
so should have realized that the emperor's excuse was valid,
denounced him for falsely seeking a pretext to hinder the expedition.[17] The tradition of the evil Alexius pitted against the heroic
integrity of the crusaders was just too strong. No doubt the viru-
lence of William's attacks on Alexius in the passages dealing with
the crusaders at Constantinople reflected an ingrained antipathy
arising from the earlier histories at his disposal, but it also served as
a literary device to emphasize the virtues of the crusaders, especially
Godfrey and Bohemond. This consideration may also help explain
why William refrained from heaping abuse on Alexius after the
armies had set out across Asia Minor. The Crusade was now facing

---

[15] *WT*, II, 19–21; 22, lines 17–22.   [16] *WT*, II, 13, lines 36–8; 19, lines 24–30.
[17] *WT*, II, 22, lines 14–33.

its real enemy, the Muslims, and so the emperor had been super-seded in his function as the foil for its leaders.

So William spoke with two voices when he described the relations of the crusaders with the Byzantines during the First Crusade. The first voice, more strident than the second, told of the Greeks as the perfidious opponents of the Latins. The second, more muted, often completely obscured but always more sophisticated, recalled that in his anxiety for the security of his empire the emperor feared the coming of the crusaders but did, within limits, aid the expedition as far as he was able; for their part the crusaders looked to him for material assistance and, largely in vain, for leadership and military support. The first voice reflected the historical traditions to which William had access and served to underline the integrity and godliness of the crusade leadership. The second, on the other hand, was more in keeping with the tone and attitude displayed in the opening chapters of the *Historia*: Byzantium is too weak to defend eastern Christendom.

The intensely anti-Byzantine tone reappeared briefly when Alexius was confronted by the Crusade of 1101. The crusaders had a reasonably kind reception, but then the emperor, jealous of their success, stirred up the Turks to attack them. This calumny, which during the First Crusade had made only a passing appearance, now has pride of place. But William went on to explain the disasters which befell the crusaders as the result of their own indiscipline rather than as the consequence of Byzantine duplicity.[18] The emperor's alleged collusion with the Turks was subsequently given as the principal pretext for Bohemond's crusade against Byzantium in 1107–8; Alexius' kindly words and splendid gifts for the crusaders in 1096–7 and 1101 had been simply a screen for his treachery. William, who here was dependent on Fulcher of Chartres, evidently knew little about this expedition and the Treaty of Devol of 1108 which concluded it. All he could say was that Alexius promised to stop hindering the pilgrims and that Bohemond swore fealty to him. Behind this last statement lay Bohemond's recognition of Alexius' suzerainty over Antioch, but it is open to question whether William saw it that way. Although he knew that Byzantium had a claim to Antioch, he was evidently of the opinion that it

[18] *WT*, x, 11, lines 25–42; 12, lines 1–25. The charges against Alexius are not to be found in Fulcher of Chartres, the one extant historical source William was using for his information on this expedition. See Fulcher, *Historia Hierosolymitana*, pp. 428–33. For a suggestion of Byzantine connivance with the Turks against the armies of the First Crusade, see *WT*, iii, 13, lines 44–6.

was nullified by the emperor's failure to fulfil his part of the agreement with the original crusaders; and the information at his disposal would not necessarily convey the idea that Bohemond recognized Byzantine overlordship at Devol.[19]

Except for a note recording the death of Alexius, 'the greatest persecutor of the Latins', in 1118 and the accession of his 'more acceptable' son John, Byzantium recedes from view until the 1130s.[20] In 1137–8 and 1142–3 John II Comnenus led two expeditions to Cilicia and northern Syria. In William's narrative of these campaigns the emperor occupied the centre of attention and was enveloped in a cloud of adulation: adjectives would not suffice to describe the splendours of his army, the incalculable imperial treasure and John's position as the foremost prince in the world. But even when William puts his own rhetorical flourishes aside, the emperor emerges as a truly commanding figure. His courage, his mastery of the art of war and his brilliant generalship all demanded William's admiration. He was a monarch with a fitting sense of the dignity of his position. Faced with certain death, this dignity did not desert him. If his self-control carried him through in the face of fierce opposition from the Latins, his courage and good judgement effected the transition of power to his son Manuel. At times his self-control, especially when confronted by the disgraceful behaviour of Raymond of Antioch and Joscelin of Edessa, seems almost superhuman. Even when his ambitions were checked, his prudence and far-seeing counsel won the praise of all.[21]

But, although William admired John, he had less reason to be enthusiastic about his actions. In 1137 the emperor began his campaign by seizing the Cilician cities captured during the First Crusade by Baldwin of Boulogne and Tancred, and in undisputed possession of the princes of Antioch for forty years. William was outraged; his wording indicates his acute sense of injustice. John's goal was the recovery of Antioch, which according to William he was claiming by virtue of the agreements sworn by the leaders of the First Crusade. Conquest was therefore his aim, and William went

---

[19] *WT*, XI, 6. Cf. Fulcher, *Historia Hierosolymitana*, pp. 518–25. For William's view of Byzantine claims to suzerainty, see *WT*, XIV, 24, lines 24–34. Lilie (p. 299) has argued that here and elsewhere William has suppressed the suggestion that the Latin principalities were in any way dependent on the empire.

[20] *WT*, XII, 5, lines 1–6.

[21] For John, see *WT*, XIV, 24; 30; XV, 1–5; 19–23. Cf. Lilie, *Byzanz*, chapter 3.

on to relate how he embarked on a siege of Antioch itself.[22] But diplomacy soon replaced open warfare. Prince Raymond agreed to surrender the citadel on demand and allow John and his army free access to the city. For his part the emperor promised to attempt the conquest of four major Muslim-held cities in Syria, Aleppo, Shaizar, Hamah and Hims, which if captured would be given to Raymond as hereditary fiefs in exchange for relinquishing Antioch. In reporting this agreement William passed no judgement. Although he had denied the validity of Byzantine claims to Antioch on the grounds that Alexius had failed to honour his obligations at the time of the First Crusade, and although he condemned John's conquest of Latin-held Cilicia, he accepted the 1137 compact without comment.[23]

After wintering in Cilicia the emperor returned with his army to Syria in the spring of 1138. He summoned Raymond and also Count Joscelin II of Edessa to join him in besieging Shaizar. John performed nobly; Raymond and Joscelin played the fool, thereby earning William's ashamed disapproval. In disgust the emperor allowed the citizens of Shaizar to buy him off, raised the siege and withdrew to Antioch.[24] He now demanded occupation of the citadel and free entry into the city for his troops in accordance with the 1137 agreement; the conquest of the adjacent Muslim-controlled region would take longer than anticipated, and Antioch would have to serve as the base for operations. Apparently a campaign against Aleppo was now envisaged. According to William, Joscelin and Raymond and their barons were stunned. In their hearts they could not tolerate the notion that Antioch, whose conquest had cost the blood of so many princes, should be surrendered to the 'effeminate people of the Greeks'; without Antioch, the entire province would be lost. Thus, expressed here as the private thoughts of the Latins, William's own belief that the Byzantines were militarily weak and ineffective reasserted itself. In a particularly dishonest speech Joscelin now asked for time for reflection; then, by circulating extravagant rumours, he was able to raise a riot in Antioch and contrive to drive John from the city. The emperor, vowing to return yet preserving his equanimity and dissembling his indignation, soon departed with his army for Constantinople. William seems to preserve a strict neutrality. He probably agreed with the hidden senti-

---

[22] *WT*, XIV, 24. For the siege, see also XIV, 25, lines 18–21; 26, lines 32–5; 30, lines 1–17.
[23] *WT*, XIV, 30, lines 17–58.   [24] *WT*, XV, 1–2.

ments of the Latins, while being unhappy at their devious behaviour and unwillingness to abide by their agreement. On the other hand, John's withdrawal from Antioch may have served as an illustration of the weakness of Byzantine arms.[25]

The emperor returned to Antioch in September 1142. He had come partly in response to appeals for help from Raymond of Antioch, but he also came demanding fulfilment of his agreement with the prince: possession of the citadel and the use of Antioch as his military base. Raymond was now in a serious quandary. He and his advisers did not trust the Greeks, whose 'indolence' (a variant on weakness and ineffectiveness) would lose Antioch and the entire province to the Muslims. Yet he was honour-bound to keep his side of the 1137 agreement. Once again the people of Antioch came to his aid. A solemn delegation of prominent nobles, denying that Raymond had any legitimate obligation to him, bluntly told John to cease and desist. So the imperial claims were rejected out of hand. That St Peter and the patriarch were invoked to justify this defiance suggests that there were ecclesiastical as well as political dimensions to the confrontation, but William did not enlarge on this point. Once again, it is hard to discern his attitude to these events.

John, rebuffed at Antioch, withdrew his armies to Cilicia for the winter but continued to harbour designs upon the city. However, in concealing his intentions he turned to Jerusalem and King Fulk. He proposed bringing his army to the kingdom, where he would pray at the Holy Places and assist the king in his military operations against the Muslims. Fulk refused the offer on the grounds that his lands lacked the resources to support the imperial army and invited him to come with a following of 10,000 men. John was incensed by this response, as emperors did not travel with such a small retinue, yet again he dissembled his anger and was generous to Fulk's embassy. William insisted, however, that he still had the intention of achieving something notable in Syria the following summer. It was not to be. In April 1143, following a hunting accident in Cilicia, John died. William's description of the emperor in his last days is both favourable and memorable.[26]

Taking the account of John's campaigns in Syria as a whole, the absence of anti-Byzantine invective is notable. In his attitude to imperial ambitions to take control of Antioch, William was remarkably restrained, especially in the light of the city's historical and political significance for the Latins. His narration of the Byzantine

[25] *WT*, xv, 3–5.   [26] *WT*, xv, 19–23.

efforts to subject northern Syria to their dominion is for the most part dispassionate. He clearly believed that the Latins were entitled to rule there, and he also believed that the Greeks, effeminate and indolent as they were, would not be able to defend Antioch against the Muslims. So, while he admired John's courage and strength, he could not rid himself of his conviction that Byzantium was too weak to defend the East. As for John himself, William allowed his admiration to be tempered by accusations of duplicity only after he had described his rebuff in 1142.[27] All in all it was the Latin leaders who appeared in a bad light. The story was of three successive attempts which failed in their object of subjecting Antioch to Byzantium, a failure which would appear to have resulted from the emperor's inability or unwillingness to reduce the city through military action. The probability that a Byzantine administration in Antioch would have meant the end of the Latin patriarchate, and the fact – which William could have known since the letter concerned was preserved in the archives of the Holy Sepulchre – that apparently in 1138 Pope Innocent II had forbidden Latin Christians serving in John's armies to participate in the capture of Antioch, passed unmentioned.[28]

So why was William so restrained here when he had been so hostile earlier and could very easily have indulged in further anti-Byzantine outbursts? Part of the answer must lie in John's other ambition: the subjugation of Muslim cities and the defence of Antioch against Muslim encroachments. In 1138 he had led the Christians in a campaign against Shaizar and was said to have been contemplating a siege of Aleppo. Although in the light of William's narrative this may seem surprising, John's arrival in 1142 had been in response to Raymond's appeals for aid, presumably against Zangī. William recognized the sincerity of the emperor's intentions and saw too that co-operation between Latins and Byzantines against the Muslims ought to have been possible, even though on this occasion it had proved abortive. Faults on both sides had prevented them from working together, and so his account contained both a warning and a promise of hope. He was conscious of the limitations of what the Greeks could do for the Latins, but in writing appreciatively of John he was indicating his own awareness that a new era in relations between them had begun. This positive mood is continued in his description of the accession of the emperor

---

[27] *WT*, xv, 21, lines 1–8. Cf. xii, 5, lines 3–6.
[28] *Cartulaire du Saint-Sépulcre*, no. 10.

Manuel. Despite the tragic circumstances of his father's death and the questionable expedient of passing over his elder brother, Manuel's elevation to the imperial dignity brought satisfaction to many, especially to the Latins serving under John. In his first portrayal of the new emperor, William, who had met him and had experienced his courtesy and generosity at first hand, showed no reservations.[29]

But this positive approach to Byzantium was soon nipped in the bud. With the advent of the Second Crusade William's hostility returned in full force. The malice inherent in the Greek race, and its customary hatred for western pilgrims, meant that the Greek guides treacherously connived with the Turks to annihilate the German army under Conrad III: they had either been ordered to do this by their lord or had been bribed by the Turks.[30] Yet William had already made it clear that the sultan of Iconium had been anxiously preparing for the crusaders' arrival, without, it would seem, any encouragement from Manuel, and he later recorded how well Conrad and Manuel, who were related by marriage, got on together when Conrad returned to Constantinople.[31] So the accusations do not altogether ring true. William was not alone in blaming the Greeks for the disasters which overtook the Crusade in Asia Minor – Odo of Deuil, a participant in the expedition whose account of these events he seems not to have known, was unremitting in his hostility – but it is apparent that his attack on the Byzantines was drawn from a body of historical stereotypes which he carried within himself and found corroborated in the memories of others. He could not shake himself free of these animosities. The disastrous outcome of the Second Crusade was sufficient to release his xenophobic prejudices once more.

As William himself noted, the aftermath of the Second Crusade saw a visible deterioration in the condition of the Latin East. With the death of Raymond of Antioch in battle in 1149 and the imprisonment and subsequent death of Joscelin II, northern Syria was left without adequate leadership.[32] Writing in his voice of dispassionate detachment, William related how Manuel now proposed to pension off Joscelin's widow in exchange for the fortresses still in her possession in what remained of the county of Edessa. The imperial offer was discussed at Antioch by the nobility and King

---

[29] *WT*, xv, 23.   [30] *WT*, xvi, 20, lines 28–49; 21.
[31] *WT*, xvi, 19, lines 35–49; 20, lines 14–28; 23, lines 51–9.
[32] *WT*, xvii, 9; 11.

Baldwin III. There was considerable disagreement as to whether such an exchange was necessary, but the king took the line that the region was vulnerable and that he himself could not undertake its defence; he doubted whether the Byzantines would be able to hold the area either, but he would prefer that they should bear the obloquy for its loss than that he should. So the emperor's proposal was approved. The fortresses were delivered to the Greeks, who within a year lost them to Nūr al-Dīn. Baldwin's ruthless practicality, which had taken account of the weakness ('mollicia') of the Greeks, was fully justified. We sense that William agreed with Baldwin but restrained himself from indulging in recriminations. In fact he obscured his perception of Greek inadequacy by concluding that the region was lost 'because of our sins'.[33]

Raynald of Châtillon's raid on the Byzantine island of Cyprus in 1155 provided the opportunity for voicing friendlier opinions with regard to Manuel and his empire. When Thoros of Armenia attacked the imperial lands in Cilicia, William sympathized with the Byzantines. When Manuel ordered Raynald, the new prince of Antioch, to campaign against Thoros, promising to reimburse his expenses, William seems to have accepted that this was normal, a natural illustration of the client relationship of Antioch to the empire. But when Raynald, who had carried out the emperor's command and had then grown impatient over the delays with his recompense, conducted a savage raid on Cyprus by way of reprisal, William was appalled. His sympathy for the Greeks mirrored his contempt for Raynald, and he was to restate this position when he came to record how in 1158 Manuel was able to deal with him in person.[34]

The raid was not allowed to reverse the improving relations between Byzantium and the Latin East, and it may even have had the effect of drawing Jerusalem and Constantinople closer. In 1157 Baldwin III and his counsellors decided on an embassy to Manuel to seek a member of the imperial house as Baldwin's consort. William evidently approved of this move, commenting that the union would open the way for Byzantine subsidies to relieve the kingdom's hardships. Eventually, 'after innumerable delays and evasive replies of the sort that the Greeks, ever ones for making captious

---

[33] *WT*, XVII, 16; 17, lines 77–88. William's conclusion is a good example of his penchant for moralizing at the expense of historical analysis. Cf. Lilie, *Byzanz*, pp. 284–8.
[34] *WT*, XVIII, 10.

objections with intricate convolutions, are wont to use', agreement was reached: Baldwin was to marry Theodora, a daughter of Manuel's elder brother. William's description of the negotiations highlights the cultural gap between Greek and Latin, but his account is nevertheless straightforward. He was in favour of the marriage, which took place in September 1158, and in his narrative he was able to display his friendly appreciation of the Greeks more strongly than before.[35]

With the Armenians once more overrunning Cilicia and Raynald still unpunished for his raid on Cyprus, Manuel resolved to lead an expedition to the East in person. The account of this campaign, which took place in 1158–9, is one of the most notable passages in the *Historia*. The emperor's impending arrival struck terror into the heart of Raynald, who appeared before him at Mamistra in Cilicia and by an act of prostrate self-abasement secured a reconciliation. William's self-evident contempt for the prince was perhaps tempered by a hint that his humiliation was shared more generally by the Latin community in the East, but his primary concern was to give a favourable impression of the emperor and portray relations between the Franks and the Byzantines in the best possible light.[36] Baldwin III now presented himself at the imperial court, and this afforded William the opportunity to illustrate the unity of faith and purpose existing between the Greeks and the Latins: the king, assisted by the Templars, reconciled the emperor and Thoros of Armenia; gifts were showered on Baldwin and his companions; the emperor entered Antioch in solemn procession; when Baldwin broke his arm in a hunting accident, Manuel attended him personally. What in fact William was describing was the high-water mark of relations between Byzantium and the Latin East, and his enthusiasm is obvious. However, it all really amounted to very little. The combined forces of the empire and the kingdom of Jerusalem moved against Aleppo, but, instead of besieging this centre of Muslim power, Manuel was content to arrange with Nūr al-Dīn for the release of certain prisoners. This done, he and his army took their leave. Once again a Byzantine intervention in northern Syria had proved abortive; for the second time an emperor had acted as commander-in-chief of a combined force of Latins and Greeks and nothing had come of it. William offered no comment about Manuel's withdrawal. There is no word of either reproach or disappointment.[37]

[35] *WT*, XVIII, 16, lines 15–32; 22.   [36] *WT*, XVIII, 23.   [37] *WT*, XVIII, 24–5.

The descriptions of the expeditions of John and Manuel Comnenus to northern Syria, and the intervening incidents concerning Byzantium, reveal a variety of nuances in William's attitudes. At one extreme the Greeks are hostile and treacherous. More frequently they are not strong enough to resist the Muslims or make inroads against them. At other times William can enthuse over the disposition of the emperors and the prospects for Franco-Byzantine military co-operation. His perception of these events has to be understood in the light of the situation at the time he was writing. In 1167 the marriage alliance between Jerusalem and Constantinople had been renewed with the wedding of King Amaury and Maria Comnena; in 1168 William himself had gone to Manuel to negotiate a treaty for a joint attack on Egypt; in 1169 the combined expedition had taken place, although it achieved nothing and ended in mutual recriminations; in 1171 Amaury had gone to Constantinople, and as late as 1177 a Byzantine embassy was in Jerusalem trying to see if further combined operations could be organized. The idea of co-operation with Byzantium was clearly prominent in people's minds, and it is to be suspected that William, who was directly involved in promoting it, genuinely believed in the possibilities that such co-operation promised. It is likely, therefore, that his account of John's and Manuel's expeditions to the East, with their appreciative view of Byzantine endeavours, was written at a time when such thoughts were still prominent. William wanted co-operation to succeed, and so he described these previous Byzantine efforts, which he hoped had prefigured what was to come, in a positive fashion.

He was of course in difficulties. Not only had the Byzantines lost the Edessan fortresses, but the expeditions led by the emperors, magnificent though they had seemed, had not achieved anything. To set against the prospects of an anti-Muslim alliance were the facts that the Greeks had seized Latin-controlled Cilicia for themselves, that they had designs on Antioch and that, more recently, they had humiliated its prince. Except in his description of the Second Crusade, where his anti-Byzantine outburst has to be seen as a throw-back to the xenophobia of his account of the First Crusade and its aftermath, William evidently tried to keep his criticisms to a minimum. The terms imposed on Prince Raynald in 1158, the ecclesiastical implications of John's designs on Antioch, and indeed the whole question of the extent of Byzantine suzerainty over the Latin East that these developments entailed, were studiously avoided.

Sooner or later William's perception of the Byzantine empire as the potential ally of the Latins in the East had to make way for a radically different understanding. The empire of the late 1160s and early 1170s – an empire ruled by a pro-western emperor which would, so it was thought, come to the aid of the kingdom of Jerusalem – was a far cry from the empire of the mid-1180s. In March 1171, shortly before Amaury's visit to Constantinople, Manuel had terminated his trading agreements with Venice by ordering the arrest of all Venetians in his empire and the confiscation of their property; it was an incident which boded ill for the future and demonstrated the fragility of his pro-western stance.[38] Then in September 1176 the emperor was defeated by the Turks in battle at Myriokephalon. William appreciated the gravity of the defeat but explained it in personal rather than strategic terms.[39] In fact it signified that henceforth Byzantium would not be able to intervene in the East: by the early 1180s the Greeks had lost control of Cilicia to the Armenians, and their fleet had been run down to the extent that it could no longer operate effectively.[40] In 1180 Manuel died; his successor was a child, and the empire moved into a dynastic crisis which was to last until after the overthrow of the Comnenan dynasty in 1185. In 1182, in what was the last episode relating to Byzantium to be recorded by William, the violently anti-Latin Andronicus Comnenus seized power.[41] William, it will be remembered, was at work on the *Historia* from the late 1160s until 1184, precisely the period in which both the ability and the willingness of the empire to aid the Latin East were coming to an end.

After his account of the 1159 meeting of Manuel and Baldwin III, William's optimism in his descriptions of Byzantine involvement in the East seems to diminish, and it may be that his writing was reflecting his growing awareness that nothing was going to come of the rapprochement between Greeks and Latins. In other words, it may be that the significance of Myriokephalon for the kingdom of Jerusalem was beginning to affect his outlook. However, in trying

---

[38] See M. Angold, *The Byzantine Empire, 1025–1204* (London, 1984), pp. 199–202. The arrests were ordered on 12 March; Amaury set out for Constantinople on 10 March (*WT*, xx, 22, lines 47–50).

[39] *WT*, xxi, 11.

[40] H. Ahrweiler, *Byzance et la mer: La marine de guerre, la politique et les institutions maritimes de Byzance aux VIIe–XVe siècles* (Paris, 1966), pp. 269–70, 280–92 *passim*.

[41] *WT*, xxii, 11–14; Brand, *Byzantium Confronts the West*, chapters 2–3 *passim*.

to relate the influence of contemporary developments on his perception of the past, our inability to date his composition of the various sections of the *Historia* with any exactitude is a major drawback. Nevertheless, the contrast between his description of the events of 1159 and of what happened next is striking. In 1161 Manuel married Maria, the daughter of Prince Raymond of Antioch, in preference to Count Raymond III of Tripoli's sister. But, instead of being delighted that the emperor had chosen his bride from among the Latins, William concentrated on explaining how Manuel's decision constituted a profound insult to the king, whose advice he had requested and then rejected, and came as a major blow to the count's pride. Raymond had prepared his sister's trousseau at vast personal expense, and he retaliated by sending the twelve galleys he had made ready to bear her to Constantinople on a raiding expedition against Byzantine possessions. William was sparing in his remarks, but he clearly regarded the whole episode as another instance of Byzantine trickery and evasion. Although he disapproved of Raymond's reaction, he was clearly sympathetic towards him, and Raymond escaped the condemnation meted out to Raynald of Châtillon for his raid on Cyprus a few years earlier.[42]

Thereafter Byzantine intervention in the East normally failed to excite William's enthusiasm. The combined efforts of Bohemond III of Antioch, Thoros of Armenia and the Byzantine governor of Cilicia to raise the siege of Harim in 1164 ended with Bohemond and the governor captive. True, Manuel helped pay the prince's ransom, but William rejected the idea that Nūr al-Dīn's decision to let Bohemond go resulted from fear of Byzantine arms.[43] Then in 1167 King Amaury married Maria Comnena. William's account of this event shows that he seems to have approved of the marriage, but he made no allusions to any hopes for the future that it might bring. Instead he immediately went on to describe the scandalous and treacherous behaviour of another member of the Greek imperial family, Andronicus Comnenus, who, having been given Beirut, absconded to Damascus and then Persia with his kinswoman, Theodora Comnena, the widow of Baldwin III.[44] William himself then went to Manuel to negotiate joint action against Egypt, and in the autumn of 1169 the Byzantine fleet duly arrived in the East. Manuel had kept to his undertaking: the fleet was impress-

---

[42] *WT*, xviii, 30, lines 22–51; 31; 33.   [43] *WT*, xix, 9; 11, lines 9–42.
[44] *WT*, xx, 1–2.

ive, its commanders illustrious, and the troops subsequently fought hard. But the Greeks were insufficiently provisioned, and for this and other reasons the campaign failed in its purpose. In his concluding remarks William laid the main responsibility for this failure on the inadequate funding of the Greek forces.[45] So during the 1160s Byzantium and the Latin East were working together: there were marriage alliances; a Byzantine nobleman was given Beirut; combined operations had taken place. But there was no disguising the fact that there was not much to show for it.

In 1171, with his policy of trying to conquer Egypt in ruins, Amaury set sail for Constantinople. The state visit which followed is one of the glittering episodes in the *Historia*. Manuel prepared the age-old Byzantine display designed to impress less civilized visitors: opulence, magnificence, ceremonial, protocol, generosity, visits to historic sites and, above all, the exhibition of those sacred relics which were the very soul of the city. William described the emperor's hospitality at length but, except to mention that they discussed a joint conquest of Egypt, recorded nothing about the treaty agreed at that time. The king and his retinue, laden with gifts, returned to Jerusalem evidently regarding their mission as having been a great success.[46] William's account is of dazzling munificence. But what he does not say is also of interest. It has been argued that what was happening in 1171 was that Amaury was acknowledging Manuel's suzerainty over his kingdom and that William, anxious to avoid any suggestion that Jerusalem was less than fully autonomous, deliberately concealed this point. What is certainly true, however, is that nothing came of it. There was no combined expedition, and, although he later mentioned that the treaty was renewed by Baldwin IV and that the idea of a campaign against Egypt was still being discussed in 1177, even after the defeat at Myriokephalon, William made no direct allusion to the fact that Amaury's visit lacked any tangible consequence.[47]

During the winter of 1179–80 William was again in Constantinople. He evidently had an appreciable amount of direct contact with the emperor and his court, since Manuel entrusted him with an errand to the prince and patriarch of Antioch and also seems to have given him a subvention for his cathedral church. So he was well placed to size up the situation, and his experiences must have alerted

---

[45] *WT*, xx, 4; 13; 16; 17, lines 39–47.   [46] *WT*, xx, 22–4.
[47] See Runciman, 'The Visit of King Amalric', pp. 153–8. For the renewal of the treaty, see *WT*, xxi, 15, lines 8–12.

him to the problems which beset the empire at that time. In particular, it must by now have been clear to William that there was little chance of Byzantine military aid against the growing menace posed by Saladin.[48] Nevertheless, he continued to treat Manuel sympathetically in the pages of the *Historia*. He described with sensitivity the effect on him of the defeat at Myriokephalon, and when in 1180 the emperor died he dwelt on his generosity to churches and took it for granted that 'he had rendered his soul to heaven'. Indeed he continued to avoid any criticism of the Greeks. There is no hint of blame attached to the reverse at Myriokephalon. When Byzantine ambassadors came to Jerusalem in 1177 it was the obstructive behaviour of the count of Flanders that, much to William's embarrassment, brought about the abandonment of their proposed expedition. Of the splendours of the weddings of Manuel's son, the future Alexius II, and of his sister, which took place during his stay in Constantinople, he could write with appropriate admiration.[49]

So as the *Historia* drew to a close William could still comment with affection on the emperor whose rule had spanned almost all his adult life, and he could do so despite, or perhaps because of, what happened after Manuel's death. He was reasonably well informed about the events in Constantinople between 1180 and Andronicus' seizure of power in 1182, and his account is of course almost contemporary. At first the queen-mother, Maria of Antioch, and her lover, the *protosebastos* Alexius Comnenus, led a pro-Latin regime. But family rivalries soon led to plots. Maria's opponents, exploiting the xenophobia prevalent in ecclesiastical circles as well as among the populace as a whole, paved the way for Andronicus, the same man who in the 1160s had been lord of Beirut and lover of Theodora Comnena, to seize control. During his coup he unleashed a massacre of the Latins resident in the capital.[50] Faced with these developments, William could no longer treat the Byzantines dis-

[48] It may be that despite their awareness of the diminishing ability of the Byzantines to offer military aid, the Christians in the East still hoped for financial aid. William's later references to Manuel emphasize his largesse. See *WT*, xx, 23, lines 51–3; 24, lines 29–34; xxii, 4, lines 51–4; 5, lines 23–4.

[49] For Myriokephalon, see *WT*, xxi, 11. For the embassy of 1177, see xxi, 15–17. For William's visit of 1179–80, see xxii, 4. For Manuel's obituary, see xxii, 5, lines 19–25.

[50] *WT*, xxii, 5, lines 30–57; 11–14. At this point William's narrative stops, although the penultimate sentence of chapter 14 suggests that he may have been aware of Andronicus' assumption of the imperial title in September 1183 and the murder of the young Alexius II two months later.

passionately. 'Deceitful and treacherous Greece' had brought forth iniquity. Manuel, that 'emperor beloved of God', had relied on Latins, passing over the Greeks as being 'soft and unmanly',[51] with the result that anti-Latin feeling had increased. This hostility was increased by religious differences, and here, for the first and only time in the *Historia*, William accused the Greeks of heresy and schism; later in describing the westerners' retaliation he underlined this charge by referring to Greek 'pseudo-monks and sacrilegious priests'. His description of the massacre of the Latins, which told of the atrocities in considerable detail, emphasized the butchery of their clergy.

William's treatment of the Byzantine empire in the *Historia* thus ended in a welter of hatred and animosity directed at Greek perfidy and faithlessness. What was new was the accusation of heresy. Otherwise it is as if he had come to realize that the received view of the habitually treacherous Greeks who had done so much to undermine the western crusading efforts in 1096–9, 1101 and 1147 was correct after all. Until he came to record the events of 1182 he had offset this stereotyped image against his own quite different concepts. He had subscribed to two views: first, that, since Christian Byzantium was no longer able to defend the Holy Places, this role had now fallen to the Latins; secondly, that, since Byzantium was prepared to be well disposed towards the western regimes in Syria and Palestine, the Latins could profit from Greek assistance and so good relations were worth fostering. But after 1182 he realized that for most of his life he had been wrong about Byzantium, and in his denunciations at the end he spoke with the anger of someone whose illusions had been shattered. But there was a religious dimension as well. Hitherto the Greeks had been Christians: thus, for example, the defeat at Manzikert had been a defeat inflicted on a Christian army; the population of Cyprus was numbered among the faithful; Manuel had gone to his heavenly reward.[52] William had steered clear of discussing the growing divisions between eastern and western Christianity and had avoided references to the Byzantine ambition, which had for a few years in the 1160s been realized, of

---

[51] The adjectives 'effeminate' or 'unmanly' (*effeminati*) and 'soft' or 'weak' (*molles*) are used sparingly of the Byzantines. Apart from this passage (at *WT*, XXII, 11, lines 16–17) they only appear together once, in the context of the loss of the Edessan fortresses (*WT*, XVII, 17, line 3). Note also II, 4, line 25 (Byzantine weakness as a reason for devastation in the Balkans) and XV, 3, line 45 (Byzantine effeminacy as a reason for not letting the Greeks have Antioch in 1138).

[52] *WT*, I, 9, lines 29–31; XVIII, 10, lines 3–4; XXII, 5, lines 2–22.

restoring a Greek patriarch to Antioch.[53] Perhaps his awareness of Greek heterodoxy had hardened as a result of his attendance at the Lateran Council; more likely he had previously been prepared to overlook religious divisions, just as he had been prepared to convince himself that Byzantium would serve the interests of the Latin East. Now he knew better.

[53] For the Greek patriarch, see Hamilton, *Latin Church*, pp. 45–6, 174–7. William's failure to record the installation of the Greek patriarch in Antioch is generally seen as showing his reluctance to acknowledge a major humiliation inflicted on the Latin hierarchy. But it is also possible that his generally pro-Greek stance when writing of the events of the 1160s made him reluctant to harp on denominational differences, and that, wishing to stress the good relations that existed, he suppressed references to this and other sources of friction.

Chapter 9

THE WAR AGAINST THE INFIDEL

If there is one unifying thread which runs right through the *Historia*, it is the waging of war against the Muslims. The First Crusade, with its triumphant successes in capturing Antioch and Jerusalem, occupies the first eight books. Thereafter the story of the extension of the territory under Christian rule and of its defence dominates the narrative. William's account of the royal dynasty of Jerusalem is largely an account of the kings as leaders in war. But it is not simply the story of the crusaders and the Christians settled in the East winning and defending a particular tract of land. The Crusade was a holy war, God's war, and concerned the holiest shrines in Christendom. So, when the Christian enterprise faltered, questions of a theological or moral nature were bound to be asked. By the time William was writing there had been too many set-backs for comfort: the expeditions into Egypt had failed; the kingdom was encircled by Saladin's armies. Earlier Edessa had been lost and the Second Crusade had come to nought. People would want to know why, and explanations solely in terms of Muslim military capabilities would not do. Why should God allow the unbelievers to triumph? Was the present generation of Christians unworthy? If God had ceased to favour the Christian cause in the East, was there any point in His people trying to defend the Holy Land?

These problems, however, did not arise with the story of the First Crusade. William presented this expedition as a war fought at the behest and under the guidance of God.[1] God had summoned the Christian warriors, who are repeatedly referred to as 'God's people' or 'God's army'.[2] Over and over again their victories, whether in

---

[1] For examples, *WT*, Prologue, lines 92–5; I, 16, lines 1–6, 43–4; III, 12, lines 50–1; V, 1, lines 31–2; VIII, 23, lines 10–14; 24, lines 58–9.
[2] For examples, *WT*, I, 16, lines 37–8; 18, line 56; II, 22, lines 17 and 20; III, 6, line 38; IV, 7, line 8; V, 5, lines 6 and 26; 12, lines 15–16.

minor skirmishes or in the great battles and sieges, were God-given.[3] He had protected and prospered His people, especially their leaders, and was responsive to their prayers.[4] For their part, the crusaders were pilgrims,[5] vowed in Christ's service to combat the infidel and win back the Holy Sepulchre.[6] They wore the badge of the Cross[7] and were travelling on the 'way of the Lord'.[8] Their efforts were for the sake of Christ,[9] and they had full remission of their sins.[10] Hardships, therefore, were only to be expected,[11] and those who died were martyrs and assured of salvation.[12] Their purpose was the liberation both of a locality – Jerusalem – and of a people – the oppressed Christians who lived there.[13] In his crusade sermon at Clermont, William had Pope Urban II emphasize the special place of Jerusalem in God's affection and Christian history, before going on to mention the sufferings of the Christian popu-lation,[14] and in his account of the siege of Jerusalem he could assert: 'All had one and the same intention: either they would lay down their lives for Christ or they would restore the city to Christian liberty'.[15] As pilgrims the crusaders were striving for the Promised Land.[16] Their hope of victory was through faith,[17] their unity the fruit of love.[18] In fighting the Muslims they were seeking to

[3] For examples, *WT*, III, 5, lines 21–3; 12, lines 41–4; 16, line 46; 21, lines 34–5; 22, lines 7–9; IV, 24, lines 39–43; V, 16, lines 11–14; VI, 21, lines 33–44; 22, lines 21–5, 30–3; VII, 10, lines 16–18; VIII, 9, lines 44–5.

[4] For examples, *WT*, II, 18, lines 24–33; 23, lines 19–21; III, 17, lines 45–7; 19, lines 1–15; 26, lines 22–3; V, 9, lines 21–7; VI, 12, lines 35–8; 19, lines 1–19, 35–41.

[5] For examples, *WT*, Prologue, line 106; II, 14, lines 6–7; III, 18, lines 26–7; VI, 12, line 30; VIII, 21, lines 54–5. Note *WT*, III, 19, line 12: 'ab universa illa peregrinante ecclesia'.

[6] *WT*, II, 10, line 23; VI, 14, lines 30–7; VIII, 6, lines 64–6.

[7] *WT*, I, 16, lines 54–65.

[8] *WT*, VII, 11, line 38; 16, lines 9–10, 21.

[9] *WT*, III, 12, lines 42–3; VI, 7, line 50.

[10] *WT*, I, 15, lines 96, 109–15; VI, 16, lines 52–7. Cf. Riley-Smith, *The First Crusade*, pp. 27–9.

[11] *WT*, I, 16, lines 50–4; II, 17, lines 11–12.

[12] *WT*, III, 7, lines 16–26; 10, lines 40–7.

[13] *WT*, Prologue, lines 99–106; I, 10, lines 56–9; VII, 23; VIII, 8; 23.

[14] *WT*, I, 15. The sermon is of course William's own imaginative reconstruction. In structure it parallels the later crusade encyclicals, with its exposition of the atrocities which had prompted it followed by an announcement of the indul-gences and the other privileges. William frequently speaks of Jerusalem as 'beloved of God' or as the 'worshipper of God'. For examples, *WT*, I, 2, lines 24–5; 3, lines 1 and 49; VIII, 1, line 1. Cf. V, 11, line 1, where Antioch is a 'city beloved of God'.

[15] *WT*, VIII, 13, lines 2–4. [16] *WT*, Prologue, line 94; I, 15, line 4.

[17] *WT*, V, 5, lines 33–5; VIII, 14, lines 5–9.

[18] *WT*, VI, 16, lines 35–41; VIII, 11, lines 14–17.

avenge 'the great injury done to our Lord Jesus Christ' whenever Christian blood was shed, and were carrying out the 'righteous judgement of God' on those who had 'profaned the sanctuary of the Lord' by occupying Jerusalem.[19] At intervals the expedition was encouraged by visions and signs from God, notably the discovery of the Holy Lance at Antioch,[20] and the narrative is suffused with a religious intensity in part created by the application of biblical quotations and prophecies to the progress of events.[21]

William was saying nothing new. To a greater or lesser extent his interpretation was present in the earlier histories of the First Crusade. The larger-than-life traits of the leaders, the constant interplay of divine power and human confidence, the commonplace occurrence of Christian heroism, and the whole expedition portrayed as a divine drama, were elements in a literary tradition of the Crusade already long established by the time he was writing. Even so, his conviction about the Crusade was deeply held. It was a holy work in which God was the chief, though hidden, actor, and the crusaders, by their faith, prayer, courage and obedience, were privileged to participate in the unfolding of the divine triumph. Although the level of religious feeling is not maintained consistently throughout these first eight books, they do nevertheless possess an organic unity. More importantly, they set the tone for the rest of the *Historia*: upwards of seventy years before William was writing, God had wrought a great miracle through the participants in the Crusade; the history of the intervening period would have to be the history of how that miracle – God's gift of Jerusalem to His people, the Latins – had fared in the days of their successors.

In fact the period since the First Crusade had witnessed a mixture of success and failure, victory and defeat. The rapid territorial expansion during the first two decades of the century had given way to the steady erosion of Christian-held territory in the north by Zangī and his son, Nūr al-Dīn, while the attempts to conquer Egypt in the 1160s had in turn led to the growing threat to the security of the kingdom of Jerusalem posed by Saladin in the 1170s and 1180s. In describing these developments William made no attempt to sustain

---

[19] *WT*, III, 16, lines 16–18; V, 5, lines 21–7; VIII, 20, lines 14–18. But William will not have the crusaders take vengeance on the Christian Hungarians or Greeks (*WT*, I, 18, lines 25–33; II, 10, lines 20–4; 21; III, 13, lines 26–33).
[20] *WT*, I, 12, lines 17–31; VI, 14; 19, lines 1–19; VIII, 16, lines 7–15; 22.
[21] For prophecy, see *WT*, I, 16, lines 29–33; VIII, 22, lines 26–30.

the *Gesta Dei per Francos* theme of his narrative of the First Crusade. Although, as will be seen, in many places the interaction of divine providence and human faith and sin is reiterated, and references to God-given success or defeat as the consequence of sin are commonplace, there are also passages in which a more secular ethos predominates. William was heir to the traditional Augustinian doctrine of man's dependence on God's grace and also to the humanistic thinking developing in the Schools of the West, and in his writing he gave recognition both to the strength of God and to the activity of men. He was not interested in investigating how divine grace and human confidence coalesce; rather, he was prepared to allow historical interpretations in terms of God's providence and human endeavour to stand side by side.

Although it would be wrong to see the first eight books as 'religious' and the remainder as 'secular', after the capture of Jerusalem there is a certain shift in emphasis away from the heroic and theological to the matter-of-fact and empirical. In view of the tone set by William's treatment of the First Crusade, the number of places where subsequently he made no attempt to offer a theological explanation is striking. For example, he began his account of the Crusade of 1101 with a resounding statement of crusading ideology, but he did not go on to explain its outcome in terms of divine disfavour or human sin. Towards the end he recorded that the survivors joined forces with Raymond of Toulouse and captured Tortosa – 'with the help of the Lord' – a conventional expression which provides the sole pale echo of the grand sentiments at the head of this episode. No doubt the failure of the Crusade prevented it from being transformed into a sacred event in historical tradition, but, coming so soon after the First Crusade, the exclusively secular explanation of its failure is noteworthy.[22] Equally noteworthy are the long, detailed narratives recounting the siege and capture of Tyre in 1124 and the expedition of 1167 into Egypt. Both were major triumphs and yet were described in secular terms. Victory was not attributed to God.[23] At the conclusion of the account of the capture of Tyre, William informed his readers that this great victory was achieved largely through the efforts and expense of the common people of the kingdom.[24] In view of the numerous other

---

[22] *WT*, x, 11–12. Conversely, the failure of the 1101 expedition may well have made the success of the First Crusade seem all the more miraculous. See Riley-Smith, *The First Crusade*, pp. 132–4.

[23] See above, p. 42.   [24] *WT*, XIII, 14, lines 17–21.

places in which he made reference to divine favour or disfavour attending the military exploits of the Latins in the East, it is difficult to believe that he deliberately set out to exclude God from these episodes. More probably his narrative unwittingly reflects the growth of the kind of thinking that saw such achievements in purely human terms.

It was in the context of Saladin's rise to power in Syria that William posed the question 'Why has it happened that the enemy is prevailing ever more commonly over our own people?' He offered three answers: first, that the present generation lacked the faith of its predecessors, and because of its sins God in His anger had withdrawn His favour; secondly, that, without their predecessors' religious zeal, the present generation had become slack in its military training; and, thirdly, that the Muslims were now much more united than previously.[25] So, in explaining the current lack of success in religious, military and strategic terms, William again showed his simultaneous appreciation of both theological and secular factors. Of the importance of the disunity of the Muslims during the First Crusade and its aftermath, and the significance of later developments which strengthened their military might, there is no doubt, and William's third answer wins general approval from modern scholars. His second answer is more problematical: had standards of training slipped, or was he simply playing the part of the clerical moralist who in castigating modern youth harked back nostalgically to the illusory standards of a bygone age? It is, however, his first answer that, in the light of his account of the First Crusade, deserves attention, and it is significant that he gave it pride of place: sin has invited God's wrath; therefore divine favour has been withdrawn; therefore the Christians are being defeated.

Given that the First Crusade was a work of God, that its triumphs were *Gesta Dei per Francos*, how were the set-backs along the way to be explained? William, who at the outset had noted that not all had set out for the right motives, described the destruction of Peter the Hermit's forces in purely secular terms – their defeat had been brought about by their arrogant indiscipline – while the similarly undisciplined bands associated with Emich of Leiningen, which had sinned in turning aside to massacre the Rhineland Jews, broke up in Hungary for no visible reason, but because 'by their many sins they had provoked the Lord to wrath'.[26] So even here the two strands in

---

[25] *WT*, xxi, 7, quoting from the rubric.
[26] *WT*, I, 16, lines 19–25; 26, lines 27–31; 29, lines 6–20; 30, lines 21–8.

William's historical interpretation – the theological and the secular – are juxtaposed. But the theological is predominant. At the siege of Antioch famine and pestilence had come as a result of sin, but contrition and the prohibition of fornication and other evils had the effect of turning away God's anger. Later, confession, contrition and the putting away of enmity preceded the defeat of Kerhogha, and before the final assault on Jerusalem discord had to be set aside through fasting and a penitential procession so that mutual love could be restored and the crusaders could call on divine aid.[27] Penitence and faith gave rise to the restoration of divine grace and were the prerequisites of success.

Many of these ideas reappear later in the *Historia*. In 1105 the Egyptians invaded the kingdom of Jerusalem and were met in battle by King Baldwin I and his army. Before the battle the patriarch, bearing the relic of the Cross, exhorted the Christian forces to remember Christ's work of salvation and promised remission of sins; inspired by his words, and calling on God's aid, they repulsed their enemies and, thanks to divine goodness, despoiled their camp.[28] But increasingly things did not go right. In 1120 it was decided that the injuries inflicted by the Muslims, together with plagues of locusts and mice, 'signs from heaven' and earthquakes, were evidence of God's anger as the consequence of sin, and, as at the time of the siege of Antioch, moral legislation was imposed so that 'through works of piety they might reconcile the Lord to themselves'. But William recorded no direct consequences of this act of propitiation, although in the following chapter he did record how the 'hand of the Lord' struck down Il-Ghāzī, whose forces had in 1119 destroyed the Antiochene army, just as King Baldwin II was about to engage him in battle.[29]

All too often, however, sin gave rise to defeat. In 1129 the combined military strength of the Latin East, heavily reinforced by westerners in what was probably one of the largest Latin armies seen in the East between 1099 and 1187, embarked on a campaign against Damascus and suffered a serious reverse. In 1126 a similar expedition had been rewarded with a God-given victory. Then the Christian forces had consisted solely of the resources of the kingdom of Jerusalem and had fought 'with the fervour of their faith' in seeking to avenge the 'injuries committed against God'.

[27] *WT*, IV, 22; V, 5–6; VI, 16, lines 32–49; VIII, 10, lines 38–44; 11, lines 1–20.
[28] *WT*, XI, 3.
[29] *WT*, XII, 13–14.

But in 1129 their efforts were thwarted by the 'hidden though just judgement' of divine providence. At the end of his account William dilated on the reasons behind this lack of success. The Christians, instead of trusting in God to aid them as in the past, had put their faith in their own numbers, and divine favour had been withdrawn in the face of this sinful presumption.[30] Contrast this with the defeat of Kerbogha at Antioch: then the Christians were in a greatly weakened condition, but their penitence, prayer and faith resulted in God reinvigorating His people with a heavenly dew, giving them a renewed strength and courage and making their numbers appear far greater to the enemy than indeed they were.[31]

In 1157 Baldwin III broke his treaty with some Arab and Turkoman pastoralists by leading a raid against them near Banyas. William emphasized that he had been led astray by evil counsel, but the oath-breaking and the betrayal of the trust that these people had had in the king soon brought retribution from God. Baldwin had to relieve Banyas, which was being besieged by Nūr al-Dīn, and then when he was withdrawing to Tiberias he was ambushed by the Muslims. His army had been proceeding without due caution and suffered an ignominious defeat with many men taken captive. William was explicit that this reverse was God's penalty for the raid earlier that year but noted that in His mercy He had allowed the king to escape, thereby avoiding a much greater calamity.[32] Rather similar was his explanation of the failure of the 1168 expedition into Egypt – a failure which was to give rise to Saladin's seizure of power. In this instance there was doubt as to whether it was King Amaury or the vizier Shāwar who was the first to break the treaty of the previous year. However, William appears to have given credence to the idea that Amaury's lack of faithfulness had forfeited God's favour in this expedition, although subsequently he emphasized the king's avarice as the cause of its undoing.[33] The sin of avarice had previously come to the fore at the siege of Damascus in 1148 and had contributed directly to its break-up.[34]

In these examples William linked particular sins to the with-holding of divine assistance and the consequent defeat. Frequently, however, he was content to ascribe individual disasters or defeats to

[30] *WT*, XIII, 18; 26.   [31] *WT*, VI, 16; 19; 21, lines 33–44.
[32] *WT*, XVIII, 11–14.
[33] *WT*, XX, 5–10.   [34] *WT*, XVII, 5, lines 14–35.

sin in general.[35] On other occasions he ascribed set-backs to sin and at the same time provided mundane explanations. Thus in 1113 Baldwin I's defeat was attributed to sin and to the king's failure to wait for reinforcements. In 1157 the siege of Shaizar foundered because of sin and disputes among the Christian leaders. In 1177 it was lack of serious application on the part of the leaders that contributed to the failure of the siege of Harim, and in 1179 at Marj 'Uyūn the Christians were outnumbered and a relief column turned back.[36] In such places William's use of sin to explain defeat, with his employment of phrases such as 'peccatis exigentibus', has perhaps to be understood not as a considered theological statement, but as the repetition of an already well-worn cliché. It should be stressed again that he was doing nothing new. The attribution of reverses to the sin of Christian people already had a long history, and its application to set-backs on the First Crusade, as well as to major defeats such as those during the Crusade of 1101, were common-place in the earlier narratives.[37]

Indeed William was so used to employing punishment for sins as his stock reaction to untoward events that in some instances it would seem that he did not mean what he was saying. Nowhere is this more evident than in his discussion of the disasters which befell the armies of the Second Crusade in Asia Minor. The preaching of the Crusade and the motivation of the crusaders had been beyond reproach. William described how Louis VII and Conrad III took charge of those who 'having conceived the same fervent desire were held bound by the life-giving vows' and set off on their pilgrimage with God's approval. He then abruptly changed his tune: they had set off in the face of God's anger and achieved nothing because of our sins. Had God been favourable they would have subjugated not only the sultan but all the provinces of the East in the name of Christianity. 'But God, by his hidden though just judgement, rejected their service . . . perhaps because they had offered it with unworthy hands.'[38] William repeated his phrase 'by the hidden though just judgement of God' when he came to account for the defeat of Conrad's army at the hands of the Turks. There was no rational explanation: God's unfathomable will defied human under-

---

[35] *WT*, IX, 21, lines 15–16; X, 29, line 47; XII, 9, lines 53–4; XIV, 3, lines 47–50; XVII, 11, lines 31–3; 17, lines 83–8; XVIII, 28, lines 38–40; XIX, 11, lines 64–7; XX, 18, lines 35–49; XXIII, preface, lines 26–9. Cf. XII, 25, lines 15–18.

[36] *WT*, XI, 19, lines 14–49; XVIII, 18, lines 44–69; XXI, 24; 28, lines 10–40.

[37] See E. Siberry, *Criticism of Crusading, 1095–1274* (Oxford, 1985), pp. 69–77.

[38] *WT*, XVI, 18; 19, lines 1–8, 55–61.

standing. Although he had already invoked his clichéd response 'peccatis exigentibus' once and was to do so again when he came to record the French defeat shortly afterwards, he evidently recognized that blaming these disasters on sin was totally inappropriate. At least with the French he could give a non-theological explanation – their army had allowed itself to be split – but at the end he apostrophized Christ, confessing his bewilderment and his inability to comprehend why the crusaders with their sincere devotion had been brought to ruin.[39]

So in the Second Crusade God had allowed the French and German pilgrims to suffer disaster despite their genuine faith. For a moment William's belief that God would use and reward His faithful people in the outworking of His triumphs, or conversely that defeat could be directly attributed to sin, had wavered. But as the Crusade drew to its close at Damascus the idea that the sinfulness of the crusaders precluded God's favour and so precipitated their failure reasserted itself.[40] It was nevertheless true that even without the difficulties raised by this particular episode William had to face some unpalatable problems. If the First Crusade had been God's victory, then every subsequent defeat which served to undermine that victory could be regarded as evidence that God no longer favoured the Latins in their defence of the Holy Places. Since it was axiomatic that He would want the Holy Places to remain in Christian hands, the simplest theological explanation for the run of defeats had to be that by their sinfulness the Latins were unworthy. However much both he and his readers may have thought of this rationalization of defeat in religious terms as a cliché, in using sin as a stock explanation to account for set-backs William was contributing to the idea that the Latins in the East were failing to live up to the expectations of the rest of Christendom. Yet paradoxically this was the last thing he wanted to do.

William dearly wanted to see the Latin East enjoying success. Part of his reason for writing the *Historia* was the hope that, encouraged by victories in the past, his fellow-Latins in the East might be inspired to renewed efforts against the Muslims. But he also aimed

[39] *WT*, XVI, 22, line 29; 25, lines 45, 56–62.
[40] *WT*, XVII, 5, lines 14–35; 6, lines 22–6; 7, lines 54–5. Cf. Siberry, *Criticism*, pp. 77–81, 190–2. The only other reference to the 'hidden though just judgement' of God occurs, as mentioned already, in the account of the 1129 expedition to Damascus (*WT*, XIII, 26, lines 16–17). But there William was able to make out a coherent case for the nature of the sin that precipitated that failure.

to inspire sympathetic attitudes in the West. This was more difficult. He had to convince people not only that the East was threatened – the dismal catalogue of defeats and set-backs would leave no
doubt on this point – but also that the Latins settled in the kingdom
of Jerusalem deserved support and possessed the potential for over-
coming their difficulties. There were various ways of achieving this
purpose. He could stress the sacred associations of the lands and
shrines under Latin rule through biblical and historical allusions; he
could show that the royal dynasty was both legitimate and effective;
and he could demonstrate that God could still favour His people in
the East and could still use them in His struggle against the infidel.
But it was not easy. The First Crusade was a distant memory, and
the experiences of the Second Crusade had acted as a deterrent to
many in the West. More recent pilgrims could well have brought
back the impression that the defence of the Holy Land was a lost
cause. To give an adequate and truthful narrative with a realistic
appraisal of the situation in the East, and at the same time claim that
God had not deserted His people, required skill. What in fact
William did was to take a handful of episodes spread across the forty
or so years before the time he was writing, to point the moral that
the Latins in the East still enjoyed God's aid, could still participate in
God-given triumphs, and *ipso facto* were still worthy in God's sight
as the custodians of the Holy Land.

In 1147 Baldwin III led an expedition to Bostra, a Muslim-held
city well to the east of his kingdom. The governor had fallen foul of
the ruler of Damascus and had offered to hand the place over to the
king if suitably rewarded. Before he set off Baldwin went to
unusual lengths to satisfy his conscience that he was not in breach of
the treaty with Damascus then in force – thereby, incidentally,
losing any element of surprise his expedition might otherwise have
had. His march was opposed by Muslim forces, and then shortly
before his arrival he learnt that the governor had lost control of his
city. There was no choice but to return home. The Muslims, now
led by Nūr al-Dīn, were on hand to harass his progress, and the
royal army had to contend with thirst as well as with enemy attacks.
In these straits the Christians now experienced a series of miraculous interventions. The Muslims lit brush-fires to exacerbate their
discomfiture, but the prayers of the archbishop of Nazareth, who
was carrying the relic of the Cross, were answered when the wind
changed and blew the smoke and heat in the direction of the enemy.
Then a perjured messenger to the Muslims was struck down by the

judgement of God. After this the Christians were guided on their march by an unknown knight riding on a white horse and carrying a red banner who mysteriously disappeared each time they pitched camp. And so the army regained the safety of the kingdom.[41]

Reduced to its essentials, the story is of an expedition which failed to achieve its goal and which extricated itself with difficulty. The miraculous answer to prayer, the efficacy of the relic of the Cross, the direct intervention of divine retribution and the mysterious guide, whose description tallies with other examples of heaven-sent warrior-saints, make this episode unique in William's account of Christian warfare after the First Crusade. Normally he avoided miracle stories.[42] But here he recorded how in a most direct fashion God had intervened to rescue His people. The virtue of the youthful king, who had sought to avoid breaking his treaty and who refused to abandon his army, perhaps goes some way to explaining this extraordinary sequence. But more significant is the wider context. The expedition is sandwiched between William's accounts of the fall of Edessa to Zangī in 1144 and the disasters which befell the French and German armies in Asia Minor in 1147 during the Second Crusade. The loss of Edessa and the failure of the Second Crusade probably did more harm to the reputation of the western undertaking in the Holy Land than anything else before 1187. So William's account of the Bostra expedition can be read as a reminder that, even in the face of this political and spiritual crisis, God had not abandoned His people.

Towards the end of 1152 a Turkish attack on Jerusalem ended with the Christians inflicting heavy losses and winning much booty. William portrayed their victory as God-given and related that, guided by God, they now received inspiration for taking the offensive against the people of Ascalon. Originally their plan was to damage the surrounding orchards; but 'divine mercy wonderfully attended them', and, when the citizens shut themselves inside their walls, 'directed by divine grace' the Christians decided to besiege the city. They then summoned the rest of their forces to join them in this undertaking, 'as God had inspired them'. So it was with a tremendous emphasis on God's grace and guidance that William

---

[41] *WT*, XVI, 8–13.
[42] See above, pp. 41–2. For earlier reports of visions of warrior-saints aiding Christian armies, see C. Erdmann, *The Origin of the Idea of Crusade*, trans. M. W. Baldwin and W. Goffart (Princeton, 1977), pp. 134–5, 274–5, 279–80; Riley-Smith, *The First Crusade*, p. 105.

began his account of the siege and capture of Ascalon in 1153.[43] The campaign went well, with the pilgrims and sailors who arrived on the spring sailing pressed into helping in this 'siege and work so acceptable to God'. Eventually, after much fighting, a breach was made in the walls, but the advantage was squandered by the cupidity of the Templars, and this reverse, brought about as the consequence of their sin, had the effect of demoralizing the whole army. A council of war was held in the presence of the relic of the Cross; some advised giving up; others, arguing that 'they should trust in the mercy of God, who is not wont to abandon those who trust in Him', were for persevering. Opinions were divided, but 'divine mercy' saw to it that the latter view prevailed, and it was agreed to pray for God's aid in their undertaking. A fresh assault had the immediate effect of bringing the defenders to ask terms for surrender. The Christian leaders then gave praise to God, 'who had deigned to bestow on His unworthy people the abundance of His gifts'.[44]

In this episode there are no miraculous interventions. Instead God guides; God gives victory; God responds to the renewed faith and prayer of the besiegers. Unlike the siege of Tyre of 1124, which William had described in non-theological terms, his portrayal of the capture of Ascalon was a reaffirmation of the struggle against the infidel as the *Gesta Dei per Francos*. There can be little doubt that he deliberately presented his account as he did to offset the recent disasters of the Second Crusade. The siege of Ascalon occupies the concluding chapters of Book XVII; the abortive siege of Damascus is the subject of the opening chapters of the same book. There God's guidance and grace had been strangely absent; here they are all-pervading. The siege of Damascus had ended in accusations of treachery, that of Ascalon in a renewal of faith and praise. What is more, the capture of Ascalon had been primarily the achievement of the forces of the kingdom of Jerusalem. God had used the Latins settled in the East. As if to underline this point, William in one place referred to God giving the Christians the Promised Land.[45] This then was his riposte to those who would fasten the blame for the failure at Damascus on the venality of the Latin Syrian Franks,[46] or

---

[43] *WT*, XVII, 20–1.
[44] *WT*, XVII, 23–5; 27–30. For the quotations, see XVII, 24, line 6; 28, lines 15–16; 30, lines 13–14.
[45] *WT*, XVII, 23, lines 1–3. For other allusions to the Latins possessing the Promised Land, see *WT*, Prologue, lines 94–5; X, 11, lines 4–5; XX, 3, lines 3–4.
[46] See Siberry, *Criticism*, pp. 77, 200.

who would conclude from that failure that God no longer willed that Christian armies should be victorious in battle with the Muslims.

Much more recent than either the Bostra expedition or the capture of Ascalon was the victory over Saladin at Mont Gisard in 1177. Taking advantage of the absence of a substantial proportion of the Christian forces in northern Syria, the Muslims had invaded the kingdom of Jerusalem from Egypt. Baldwin IV brought the limited resources at his disposal to Ascalon, where, realizing his numerical inferiority, he declined to give battle. Saladin thereupon resorted to the well-tried tactic of devastating the countryside. He burnt the town of Ramla and attacked Lydda. The citizens of Jerusalem feared that he would assault the Holy City itself. At this point William paused in his narrative to inform his readers that in these dire straits God showed mercy and pity. Baldwin now led his forces out from Ascalon, barely 375 men. Invoking aid from on high, and with the bishop of Bethlehem carrying the relic of the Cross, they advanced against the much larger Muslim army: 'If the Lord, who does not fail those who put their trust in Him, had not mercifully aroused our men with a certain inner inspiration, they would have been forced to despair not only of victory but also of safety and freedom.' In the battle the Christians, 'endowed with heavenly grace which rendered them braver than usual', put their enemy to flight with only minimal losses. The slaughter of the Muslims was considerable and the booty great. William concluded with some thoughts on this God-given victory: had the count of Flanders, the prince of Antioch and the count of Tripoli been present with their men, the Christians would have ascribed victory to their own prowess and not to God; but in using so few to destroy so large an army, God had repeated the miracle of Gideon's victory over the Midianites (Judges 7:2–23). It was God's triumph, not man's.[47]

There is no doubt that the victory at Mont Gisard was impressive.[48] It showed that Saladin could be defeated and the kingdom defended. But what was significant was that in William's own day God had continued to grant the Latins success in war, at the same

---

[47] *WT*, XXI, 19–23. The quotations are at XXI, 21, lines 35–8; 22, lines 3–4. William's comments in chapter 23 form a direct contrast to the concluding remarks to the account of the 1129 Damascus expedition (XIII, 26). Note that in both passages he quotes Isaiah 42:8.

[48] For a reconstruction putting William's narrative alongside the Arabic accounts, see Lyons and Jackson, *Saladin*, pp. 121–6.

time vindicating the kingship of Baldwin the Leper. Divine support was not just a thing of the past. God's mercy and the faith of the Christians who trusted in the Lord rather than in their own strength could still combine to ward off infidel attacks. More specifically, the victory served as a foil to the futility of the expedition to the Holy Land led by Count Philip of Flanders. Earlier in 1177 Philip had arrived in the East; he had declined the offer to take command of the Christian forces in a combined operation with the Byzantines against Egypt, and then managed to obstruct plans for the campaign to take place without him; he tried to meddle in the internal dynastic problems of the kingdom, and then, travelling north to Antioch, joined the prince in the siege of Harim, a frontier fortress towards Aleppo. William commented sourly: 'For it was fitting that he from whom the Lord had withdrawn His grace should prosper in nothing since "God opposes the proud but gives grace to the humble" (I Peter 5:5).'[49] He then broke off his account of this siege to record the Mont Gisard campaign, and only after its triumphant conclusion did he continue describing events in the north. The Christians were lazy and half-hearted; because of their sins, courage and wisdom had deserted them; God's anger blinded their minds. Eventually the prince of Antioch allowed himself to be bought off by the defenders, and the count of Flanders departed for the West 'leaving behind him a memory in no way blessed'.[50] So what could have turned into one of the most significant instances of western aid for the East since the Second Crusade came to nothing through the arrogance of its leader, while at the same time God wrought a major triumph with the reduced and unaided forces of the kingdom.

Nor was the victory at Mont Gisard a unique instance of God's continuing aid. In 1182 the Christians again met a much larger force of Muslims under Saladin in battle, this time at Forbelet (Taiyiba). The outcome was not so decisive, but William gave the impression that the Latins had the upper hand. On this occasion 'the clemency of the merciful God' went before them; there is a further reminder that it is not difficult for God 'to overcome the greater multitude with a few'; and those who were killed 'obtained the fellowship of the saints'.[51] The triumphalism of the First Crusade could still find echoes.

---

[49] *WT*, XXI, 13–18. The quotation is at XXI, 17, lines 34–6.   [50] *WT*, XXI, 24.
[51] *WT*, XXII, 17. The rubric speaks of an 'uncertain' ('anceps') victory; the text of the chapter seems more positive. For the battle, see Lyons and Jackson, *Saladin*, pp. 168–9.

Despite these successes Baldwin IV's kingdom was on the defensive, and the strain on his military resources was intense. The elation of the victory of Mont Gisard was soon effaced by defeat at Marj 'Uyūn. The failure of the Latins to establish their fortress at Jacob's Ford in 1178–9, the indecisiveness of Guy of Lusignan during Saladin's invasion of 1183, even the fact that a visiting nobleman such as Philip of Flanders could behave so arrogantly and could thereby affect policy, were all indicative of the Latins' vulnerability.[52] As the *Historia* came to be a record of contemporary events, so of necessity it was becoming more annalistic in tone,[53] and this in itself heightened the sense that the kingdom of Jerusalem was living from year to year, managing with varying success to keep the Muslims at bay. Thus 1177 and 1182 were good years, 1179 and 1183 were not. As the kingdom's fortunes varied, so William seems to have wavered in his attitude to divine providence. If the events at Mont Gisard and Forbelet afforded him the opportunity to restate his faith that God would grant His people success in their military engagements, elsewhere he was not so certain. Early in his account of the reign of Baldwin IV he had written: 'so powerfully has he [Saladin] risen against us on land and sea that unless the Dayspring from on high mercifully visits us there can be no hope of resisting'.[54] He realized that only God could save His people. But would He? Commenting on the loss of the fortress at Jacob's Ford in 1179, he agonized over the inscrutability of divine judgement. Why had God allowed His faithful people to suffer so? Maybe it was because they would only take the credit for themselves rather than ascribe it to Him – but William really did not know. He could only affirm his conviction that God was in control of the affairs of men – 'Thou art just O Lord, and thy judgement is righteous' (Psalm 118 (119):137) – and in so doing confess to a lack of certainty that He would invariably reward faith with victory. It was the same uncertainty as had appeared in his account of the destruction of the armies of the Second Crusade in Asia Minor.[55] But not all was lost, and in 1184 he ended the preface to Book XXIII with a prayer that with God's help future events might turn out happily.[56]

But in these closing books theological commentary on events

[52] For the events of 1178–9 and 1183, see *WT*, XXI, 25, lines 20–34; 28–9; XXII, 27–8.
[53] Near the end of the *Historia* William refers to himself as a writer of annals (*WT*, XXIII, preface, lines 45–6).
[54] *WT*, XXI, 6, lines 37–9.   [55] *WT*, XXI, 29, lines 32–47. See above, pp. 158–9.
[56] *WT*, XXIII, preface, line 51: 'utinam fausta feliciaque, auctore domino'.

only appears sporadically. Frequently the narrative is conceived in purely human terms, with references to divine aid or its absence due to sin brought in, if at all, simply as stereotyped expressions which contribute nothing to our understanding of William's attitudes. For example, not long after the engagement at Forbelet in 1182, the Christians regained a cave-fortress to the east of the Sea of Galilee; but, except for the conventional statement that 'at the instigation of God and through His superabundant grace' the threat posed by the Muslim occupation of this place was removed, the account of this success is entirely secular in tone, with the emphasis on the military operations.[57] William's theological explanations were sincerely held – they were certainly not just pious verbiage – but it may be that increasingly he was having to make a conscious effort to jerk himself out of thinking simply in terms of human endeavour to recover the thought-patterns of his account of the First Crusade.

But, whether conceived in theological or humanistic terms, the events of the late 1170s and early 1180s could only give rise to an air of growing despondency. William's pessimism found its fullest exposition in the preface to Book XXIII. But there is an artificiality about the sentiments expressed there. The literary allusions serve to remind the reader that it is after all an exercise in the art of persuasion: the kingdom has sunk to its nadir. The tone of despair, moreover, does not match the tone of those other passages in the *Historia* – the Prologue to the whole work or the one chapter which comprises Book XXIII – which he is known to have written at the same time. In the face of adversity, William, like many before and since, needed to believe that things would get better. So far as he was concerned, there were two distinct approaches to the problem of how the kingdom might win through. One was to look to God – and, as just mentioned, he ended the preface to his final book with a prayer; the other was to pin hope on human agencies. In a previous chapter we have seen how the kings of Jerusalem had a fine record in warfare. Just as tracing divine involvement in the East might instil faith in God's aid for the future, so tracing the history of the dynasty might build up confidence in the capacity of the rulers to lead their people to victory. As if to offset the pessimism of the preface to Book XXIII, William ended the *Historia*, in the chapter that followed, on a more optimistic note; Raymond of Tripoli, the most capable figure in the East, had now taken charge as regent.[58]

[57] *WT*, XXII, 22.   [58] See above, pp. 29–30, 84.

CONCLUSION

The sheer bulk of the *Historia* has meant that all too often it has been regarded as a mine of information rather than appreciated as a treasure of historical literature. But its size and the scope of its subject-matter should not be allowed to obscure its literary form or the unity of its message. While inevitably the historical value of its contents varies, its structure and dynamic achieve an impressive level of attainment. This said, it remains true that the work took at least fourteen years to write and that its author was prey to a multitude of distractions and conflicting influences. Hence he was in no position to provide each page with an equal consistency of purpose or standard of execution. Only in the story of the First Crusade did his narrative achieve a genuine homogeneity. Here the natural flow of events and a well-defined interpretation bring the diplomatic exchanges, the battle scenes and the long and terrible marches together to sustain a unified conception on a scale unparalleled elsewhere. Thereafter the *Historia* consists of a succession of reports, episodes and vignettes through which William's theme of warfare against the unbelievers continues to run. Only occasionally did he digress to consider extraneous events in western Europe or the Byzantine empire or to include material on Latin Syrian ecclesiastical history, most notably on the misfortunes of his province of Tyre.

Scattered through the text and standing out from the surrounding material are some impressive pieces of narrative writing. Leaving aside the First Crusade, the sections devoted to John Comnenus' expeditions to the East, the story of Patriarch Ralph of Antioch and the account of the 1167 campaign in Egypt furnish some of the best examples. Equally admirable are the accounts of the appeal by Patriarch Fulcher against the pretensions of the Hospitallers, of the quarrel between Queen Melisende and her son, Baldwin III, and of the Mont Gisard campaign of 1177. These episodes have a degree of unity and coherence which underlies their vivid sense of reality. More importantly, they add both richness and moral seriousness to the *Historia*. The blend of historical interpretation and factual information, together with William's ability to select his materials and mould his narrative, exhibit to the full the power of his capacity to convince his readers of the validity of his own point of view. It is passages such as these that constitute his strongest claim to greatness as a medieval historian.

Frequently, however, William was not operating on such an exalted plane but was content to take on the role of the competent chronicler. In this he was concerned to present a string of events and facts held together by threads of chronology and causation. While his language remains rich and flexible, his tone is matter-of-fact and his rhetoric and partisanship are muted. Much of the account of the reigns of Baldwin I and Baldwin II can be viewed in this way: the skein of chronology remains taut; the grasp of the essentials of the art of historical writing does not falter. William's remarks in his Prologue about tracing the sequence of events are well taken.[1] But it is a short step from the function of the chronicler to that of the annalist. There are other places, especially towards the end, where William simply entered incidents in his narrative without much attempt to explain how they related to each other or why. We have noted that in the preface to Book XXIII he described himself as a writer of annals; and, although his prefaces are a catena of topoi and stereotyped expressions – self-depreciation among them – this description of himself has a certain validity. William the annalist believed he should include whatever seemed of interest: hence the odds and ends of information which appear from time to time, and especially in the closing books.

Several years ago the author of a monograph on twelfth-century English historiography entitled her study *Serious Entertainments*.[2] We find this phrase both suggestive and helpful. There is much in the *Historia* which its audience in the late twelfth century would have found entertaining. Indeed, despite its length, the *Historia* rarely bores, and after so many centuries it still retains its appeal. The narrative of the First Crusade is at once aesthetically pleasing and religiously satisfying, while the topographical descriptions and

---

[1] *WT*, Prologue, lines 91–2.
[2] N. F. Partner, *Serious Entertainments: The Writing of History in Twelfth-Century England* (Chicago, 1977).

the character sketches gather much information into an effective whole. Such material is telling in its power to illustrate and convince, and can leave a lasting impression on the reader. But perhaps the most compelling passages would have been the accounts of warfare which make up so much of the *Historia*. William's contemporaries, especially those in the East, would have found the campaigns of the heroes of the First Crusade and the subsequent kings of Jerusalem fascinating. Nowhere is his genius more likely to have captivated his audience than in his accounts of military conflict – accounts which are credible, edifying, entertaining and, so far as he was concerned, true.

As entertainment, the *Historia* is literature. As serious entertainment, it acquires purpose. From a literary point of view, the accounts of the siege of Ascalon and of the 1167 Egyptian expedition, to take just two examples, are hard to fault. William clearly took great pains in his presentation of these events – and rightly so, since they ought to have elicited both a sense of optimism about the East and admiration for the achievements of the Latin settlers. The writing is elegant, closely focused and persuasive. Above all, its vitality matches the daring and courage of the Christians, who had performed great deeds of arms in the service and under the guidance of God, and who had ventured far into the realms of the heathen, even to the caliph's throne-room, in search of riches and glory. On the other hand, there is a darker, more philosophical side to the *Historia*. The account of the 1168 Egyptian campaign turns on the flaws of certain individuals which brought this expedition to disaster. Both King Amaury and Miles of Plancy were implicated, and, although William was tactfully opaque, he still managed to show his feelings of grief and outrage at the greed which thwarted the original aims of this invasion.[3] Then again there is the example of Patriarch Ralph of Antioch. William made no attempt to hide his shortcomings and controversial behaviour, yet he fully appreciated the inhumanity and humiliation of his final days as patriarch and compared him to Marius, that ancient worthy who like him had endured every turn of fortune.[4] The intrinsic seriousness of the *Historia* is reinforced by the apparent absence of humour. The explanation of why Nūr al-Dīn should release Bohemond III – he was afraid a wiser and abler prince might take charge in Antioch – is plainly charged with sardonic irony;[5] but it is hard to think of other

---

[3] *WT*, xx, 10.   [4] *WT*, xv, 17, lines 32–7.   [5] *WT*, xix, 11, lines 26–42.

examples, and as the fortunes of the Latin East declined in William's own day so his tone became ever more sombre.

Besides his straightforward desire to record the history of the crusading movement from its inception until his own day with fitting intellectual seriousness, William clearly intended that in general terms the *Historia* should edify, inform and instruct. With the defence of Christendom and the protection of the places associated with the life of Christ as the *raison d'être* of the events described, it comes as no surprise to find the Christian schema of sin, repentance, grace and redemption present on many pages. God's control of the affairs of men, and the relationship of the faith and prayers of the Latins, and also of their sin, to God's will, are a recurrent theme. One of the admirable features of the *Historia* is its balance between divine providence and human activity, with the latter rarely denigrated in favour of the former. The multiplicity of human activities is gathered under the all-embracing unity of divine protection, a point well illustrated by the doxology at the end of Book VIII, following the description of the capture of Jerusalem in 1099.[6] The twelfth-century Christian humanism of the Schools has left its mark. But, if the demonstration of the ways of divine providence is present in the *Historia*, it was not a theme that William felt compelled to develop. Rather, it was an essential part of his general presuppositions being clearly present in a narrative which from time to time explained the struggle against the infidel as both a human and a divine activity. Christian conviction has therefore a fundamental place in the making of the *Historia*.

William was not writing history for history's sake. Behind the attractive story-telling and the theological or secular interpretations of past events lies a didactic purpose. If after his return from the Third Lateran Council he made extensive revisions to take account of the interests of the readership he now hoped to acquire in the West, it was still true that his first audience had been, and perhaps remained, his contemporaries and their posterity in the East. It was with them in mind that he set out to recount the glories of the First Crusade and the subsequent achievements of the royal dynasty of Jerusalem. For their benefit he would explain how the problems they now faced had come about and the reasons for their present weakness. In an important passage, to which we have referred more than once, he attributed the failures of the Christians in the East to

[6] *WT*, VIII, 24, lines 51–60.

their lack of spirituality, their loss of faith, as well as to the dereliction of their military vocation at a time when the Muslim world was being united by Saladin.[7] The remedy apparently lay in the recovery of devotion to duty and an appropriate confidence in God. But little of this conviction is expressed in theological language or tricked out in rhetorical devices. William believed that if the history of the Latin East were presented in all its aspects, with all these themes explicitly or implicitly present, and told in a pleasing yet straightforward manner, the story would of itself persuade its audience. The *Historia* was thus intended by its author to contribute to the reinvigoration of the Latin East. It would point the way towards recovery by reminding the Latin settlers of what they had been in the past and of what they should be now.

But in the course of time William came to appreciate the possibilities of having a wider audience. In October 1178 he set off to attend the Third Lateran Council. We know little of his doings in the West, although we do know that on his way home he spent several months in Constantinople and briefly visited Antioch. He had been away for the best part of two years and would have learnt much of how Byzantium and the West each viewed the kingdom of Jerusalem. His experiences during his travels resulted in a decision to make revisions to his work designed to interest and instruct those people in the West he now hoped would read it. The *Historia* was to be an *apologia*, addressed to the prelates of the Church and through them to all the faithful in Christ, explaining and justifying the Latin East to a western readership which he knew to be either ill informed or sceptical. William was now seeking to convince his audience in both East and West that the Latins not only needed assistance, but deserved it. Jerusalem could be saved; it was worth saving.

The fact was that there were many reasons why people in the West might be indifferent to the fate of the Holy Land or might be unwilling to contribute to its support. Pilgrims and crusaders had gone East in the past and had failed to make any impact. Worse, they had gone home blaming the Latin Syrians for having obstructed their efforts. The Second Crusade was the classic example. William's version of what went wrong at Damascus was carefully written: he was able to reassure people in the East that their forefathers were not to blame, be complimentary about the western monarchs, and at the same time subtly point the accusing finger at Count Thierry of Flanders.[8] He could then construct his account of

[7] *WT*, xxi, 7.   [8] *WT*, xvii, 6–8.

the siege of Ascalon, with its stylized insistence on divine initiative and control, as a conscious attempt to offset the memory of the earlier disaster. More recently there had been the pilgrimage of Count Philip of Flanders. An important magnate and kinsman of the royal dynasty, he had come to the East at what must have been considerable personal expense and achieved nothing. What tales would he have told on his return? With the king of Jerusalem a chronic invalid, the future of the dynasty uncertain and the court divided, the prospects for the kingdom would have seemed worse than ever and the chances of any future visits by western aristocrats having any positive effect even more remote. William needed to remind people in the West as well as in the East that great things had happened in the past and were still happening. More especially he was concerned to provide an *apologia* for King Baldwin IV, reiterating his right to rule and insisting on the effectiveness of his kingship. But, as we noted in our discussion of the monarchy, in trying to convince people that the kingdom deserved and could utilize support he had to engage in special pleading and gloss over or suppress embarrassing details.

William, therefore, was aiming to persuade western Christendom, in particular the clergy of western Christendom, that the Latins in the East had a fine record. Sympathetic understanding was his immediate goal, and if as a result help were forthcoming it could be used to good effect. To stimulate further the westerners' goodwill, he would show that the churches of the Latin East had many of the same attributes and problems as those in the West and so demanded fraternal support. Much of the material on the ecclesiastical affairs of the East seems to have been added in the revisions of the early 1180s. By including the details and correspondence concerning the province of Tyre, William may have been self-indulgent, and he certainly had an axe to grind; but he doubtless realized that a generous helping of ecclesiastical history would create a sense of fellow-feeling with his western readers. The dismemberment of his province, his hostility to the military Orders and his grouses about the papacy touched on issues familiar in the West.

One thing that William was not doing was making a direct appeal for either a new crusade or for smaller expeditions like that led by Philip of Flanders. It may well be that he felt that there had been too many appeals for help. Since the Second Crusade there had been a steady stream of letters and embassies, but William hardly mentioned them, and when he did he was disparaging about their effectiveness.[9] Nor was he especially enthusiastic about western nobles who came on pilgrimage to the East and brought temporary military aid. Indeed he was harshly critical of both Stephen of Sancerre and Philip of Flanders, who journeyed East in the 1170s, and omitted all mention of the visit of Henry the Lion, duke of Saxony, who was in the East in 1172.[10] The East needed help, but William never indicated what sort of help he himself would prefer. There was a shortage of man-power, but William was critical by turn of pilgrims, the military Orders and immigrants such as Raynald of Châtillon or Miles of Plancy. Elsewhere he would repeat his belief in the idea that God favoured the Latins in war when they put their trust in Him rather than in weight of numbers.

But, although the *Historia* is not overtly an exercise in crusade *excitatoria*, it is nevertheless a work of propaganda. William was hoping to educate people in both East and West and instil a proper understanding – his understanding – of the importance of the Latin East. He wanted to chronicle its significance in the outworking of divine providence, its past glories, the dangers which threatened it and the many virtues by which it merited continued succour. The glory of the kingdom of Jerusalem had resided in its lay leadership. Anyone who wanted to bring aid should, in William's eyes, work with the secular authorities – not against them, as had Philip of Flanders – and, by implication, not with the military Orders, as the papacy increasingly seemed to be directing. As he came to the end of his work, he realized too that people in the West ought to have it explained to them that the Latins could no longer turn for aid to Byzantium. A few years earlier there had been an alliance. Now the Latins alone would have to shoulder the defence of the East. Jerusalem was a part of Christendom – to William, who had been brought up there, it was the centre of the world in more than just a metaphorical sense – and, while the chief responsibility lay on those already settled in the East, Jerusalem was the common inheritance and the common responsibility of all Christians.

Few people can have read the *Historia*, at least in its final form, before disaster overwhelmed the Latins at Hattin. Despite the gloom-laden closing books, which could well have prepared the readers for the tragedy that followed, William's had been an optimistic and edifying message, emphasizing past glories and implying

---

[9] *WT*, xx, 12; 25, lines 11–15. See Smail, 'Latin Syria and the West' *passim*.
[10] For Stephen of Sancerre, see *WT*, xx, 25, lines 15–33.

hope for the future. But now all was lost. Raymond of Tripoli, on whose wise government William had seemed to pin his hopes, had been ousted in a *coup d'état* in 1186. Then in 1187 the army of the kingdom had been destroyed, Jerusalem and the other cities and strongholds had fallen and the relic of the Cross had been captured. William himself was spared the agony of having to witness these events, but the events themselves had the effect of rendering his message obsolete. As a record the *Historia* would remain interesting and entertaining, but its function as an *apologia* or guide to a sympathetic understanding of the Latin East was eclipsed. Henceforth it would only be read by people who knew what happened afterwards. As a result, William's judicious comments and humane perceptions, his sense of proportion and of causation, and his originality in drawing his disparate material together to form an organic and artistic whole, would not be fully appreciated. But his narrative possesses an intellectual integrity whose grandeur is not to be belittled, and he is thus entitled to his place among the foremost historians of the middle ages. He had succeeded in his self-appointed task of recording the works of God and man in the crusading enterprise. As someone in the sixteenth century wrote on the endpaper of one of the manuscripts of the *Historia*, 'in my mynde it is a story both of wisdome and lernyng and of good devotion'.[11]

[11] *WT*, p. 21 (from Magdalene College, Cambridge, MS F.4.22).

BIBLIOGRAPHY

(A) DOCUMENTS AND COLLECTIONS OF MATERIALS

Alberigo, J. *et al*. *Conciliorum Oecumenicorum Decreta*. 2nd edn. Freiburg im Breisgau, 1962.

Alexander III. *Opera Omnia*. PL, 200.

Bresc-Bautier, G. *Le Cartulaire du chapitre du Saint-Sépulcre de Jérusalem*. Documents relatifs à l'histoire des croisades, 15. Paris, 1984.

Hiestand, R. *Vorarbeiten zum Oriens Pontificius I–II: Papsturkunden für Templer und Johanniter*. 2 vols. Abhandlungen der Akademie der Wissenschaften in Göttingen. Philologisch–historische Klasse. Dritte Folge, 77, 135. Göttingen, 1972, 1984.

Vorarbeiten zum Oriens Pontificius III: Papsturkunden für Kirchen im Heiligen Lande. Abhandlungen der Akademie der Wissenschaften in Göttingen. Philologisch–historische Klasse. Dritte Folge, 136. Göttingen, 1985.

Röhricht, R. *Regesta Regni Hierosolymitani (1097–1291)*. Innsbruck, 1893. *Additamentum*. 1904.

Tafel, G. L. F., and Thomas, G. M. *Urkunden zur älteren Handels- und Staatsgeschichte der Republik Venedig mit besonderer Beziehung auf Byzanz und die Levante*. 3 vols. Fontes Rerum Austriacarum. Sectio 2, 12–14. Vienna, 1856–7.

(B) NARRATIVE SOURCES AND LEGAL TEXTS

Abū Shāma. *Le livre des deux jardins*. RHC Or, 4.

Albert of Aachen. 'Historia Hierosolymitana'. *RHC Occ*, 4.

Chronique d'Amadi. Ed. R. de Mas Latrie. *Chroniques d'Amadi et de Strambaldi*. 2 vols. Collection des documents inédits sur l'histoire de France. Paris, 1891–3.

L'Estoire de Eracles empereur et la conqueste de la terre d'Outremer. RHC Occ, 1–2.

Fulcher of Chartres. *Historia Hierosolymitana*. Ed. H. Hagenmeyer. Heidelberg, 1913.

Gesta Francorum et Aliorum Hierosolimitanorum. Ed. and trans. R. Hill. London, 1962.

Gesta Regis Henrici Secundi. Ed. W. Stubbs. 2 vols. Rolls Series, 49. London, 1867.

Bibliography

Les Gestes des Chiprois. RHC Arm, 2.

La Gran Conquista de Ultramar. Ed. Pascalis de Goyangos. Biblioteca de Autores Españoles, 44. Madrid, 1858.

Hayton of Gorhigos. La Flor des estoires de la terre d'orient. RHC Arm, 2.

Hildegard of Bingen. Epistolarum Liber. PL, 197.

Isidore of Seville. Etymologiae. PL, 82.

John of Ibelin. Livre des assises de la haute cour. RHC Lois, 1.

Raymond of Aguilers. Le "Liber" de Raymond d'Aguilers. Ed. J. H. and L. L. Hill. Documents relatifs à l'histoire des croisades, 9. Paris, 1969.

William of Tyre. Willelmi Tyrensis Archiepiscopi Chronicon. Ed. R. B. C. Huygens. Identification des sources historiques et détermination des dates par H. E. Mayer et G. Rösch. 2 vols. Corpus Christianorum Continuatio Mediaevalis, 63–63A. Turnhout, 1986.

   A History of Deeds Done Beyond the Sea. Trans. and annotated E. A. Babcock and A. C. Krey. 2 vols. Records of Civilization and Studies, 35. New York, 1943.

(C) SECONDARY WORKS

Adolf, H. 'A Historical Background for Chrétien's Perceval', Publications of the Modern Language Association of America, LVIII (1943), 597–620.

   Visio Pacis: Holy City and Grail. Pennsylvania, 1960.

Ahrweiler, H. Byzance et la mer: La marine de guerre, la politique et les institutions maritimes de Byzance aux VIIe–XVe siècles. Paris, 1966.

Angold, M. The Byzantine Empire, 1025–1204: A Political History. London, 1984.

Archer, T. A. 'On the Accession Dates of the Early Kings of Jerusalem', EHR, IV (1889), 89–105.

Beddie, J. S. 'Some Notices of Books in the East in the Period of the Crusades', Speculum, VIII (1933), 240–2.

Blake, E. O., and Morris, C. 'A Hermit Goes to War: Peter and the Origins of the First Crusade', in W. J. Sheils (ed.), Monks, Hermits and the Ascetic Tradition. Studies in Church History, 22. Oxford, 1985, pp. 79–107.

Brand, C. M. Byzantium Confronts the West, 1180–1204. Cambridge, Mass., 1968.

Chibnall, M. The World of Orderic Vitalis. Oxford, 1984.

David, C. W. Robert Curthose, Duke of Normandy. Cambridge, Mass., 1920.

Davis, R. H. C. 'William of Tyre', in D. Baker (ed.), Relations between East and West in the Middle Ages. Edinburgh, 1973, pp. 64–76.

Edbury, P. W., and Rowe, J. G. 'William of Tyre and the Patriarchal Election of 1180', EHR, XCIII (1978), 1–25.

Erdmann, C. The Origin of the Idea of Crusade. Trans. M. W. Baldwin and W. Goffart. Princeton, 1977.

Folda, J. 'Manuscripts of the History of Outremer by William of Tyre: a Hand-list', Scriptorium, XXVII (1973), 90–5.

Forey, A. J. 'The Failure of the Siege of Damascus in 1148', Journal of Medieval History, X (1984), 13–23.

Bibliography

France, J. 'The Election and Title of Godfrey de Bouillon', *Canadian Journal of History*, XVIII (1983), 321–9.

Giese, W. 'Stadt- und Herrscherbeschreibungen bei Wilhelm von Tyrus', *Deutsches Archiv*, XXXIV (1978), 381–409.

Gillingham, J. B. 'Roger of Howden on Crusade', in D. O. Morgan (ed.), *Medieval Historical Writing in the Christian and Islamic Worlds*. London, 1982, pp. 60–75.

Grousset, R. 'Sur un passage obscur de Guillaume de Tyr', in *Mélanges syriens offerts à M. René Dussaud*. 2 vols. Bibliothèque archéologique et historique, 30. Paris, 1939, II, 937–9.

Guenée, B. *Histoire et culture historique dans l'Occident médiéval*. Paris, 1980.

Hamilton, B. 'The Elephant of Christ: Reynald of Châtillon', in D. Baker (ed.), *Religious Motivation: Biographical and Sociological Problems for the Church Historian*. Studies in Church History, 15. Oxford, 1978, pp. 97–108.

'Women in the Crusader States: the Queens of Jerusalem (1100–1190)', in D. Baker (ed.), *Medieval Women*. Studies in Church History. Subsidia, 1. Oxford, 1978, pp. 143–73.

The Latin Church in the Crusader States: The Secular Church. London, 1980.

'Ralph of Domfront, Patriarch of Antioch (1135–40)', *Nottingham Medieval Studies*, XXVIII (1984), 1–21.

'The Titular Nobility of the Latin East: The Case of Agnes of Courtenay', in P. W. Edbury (ed.), *Crusade and Settlement*. Cardiff, 1985, pp. 197–203.

Hay, D. *Annalists and Historians: Western Historiography from the Eighth to the Eighteenth Century*. London, 1977.

Hiestand, R. 'Zum Leben und zur Laufbahn Wilhelms von Tyrus', *Deutsches Archiv*, XXXIV (1978), 345–80.

Hill, G. *A History of Cyprus*. 4 vols. Cambridge, 1940–52.

Huygens, R. B. C. 'Guillaume de Tyr étudiant. Un chapitre (XIX, 12) de son "Histoire" retrouvé', *Latomus*, XXI (1962), 811–29.

'La tradition manuscrite de Guillaume de Tyr', *Studi medievali*, 3rd ser., V (1964), 281–373.

'Pontigny et l'*Histoire* de Guillaume de Tyr', *Latomus*, XXV (1966), 139–42.

'Editing William of Tyre', *Sacris erudiri*, XXVII (1984), 461–73.

Katzir, Y. 'The Patriarch of Jerusalem, Primate of the Latin Kingdom', in P. W. Edbury (ed.), *Crusade and Settlement*. Cardiff, 1985, pp. 169–75.

Kedar, B. Z. 'The Patriarch Eraclius', in B. Z. Kedar, H. E. Mayer and R. C. Smail (eds.), *Outremer: Studies in the History of the Crusading Kingdom of Jerusalem*. Jerusalem, 1982, pp. 177–204.

'Gerard of Nazareth, a Neglected Twelfth-Century Writer in the Latin East', *Dumbarton Oaks Papers*, XXXVII (1983), 55–77.

Kletler, P. 'Die Gestaltung des geographischen Weltbildes unter dem Einfluß der Kreuzzüge', *Mitteilungen des österreichischen Instituts für Geschichtsforschung*, LXX (1962), 294–322.

Knoch, P. *Studien zu Albert von Aachen. Der erste Kreuzzug in der deutschen Chronistik*. Stuttgart Beiträge zur Geschichte und Politik, 1. Stuttgart, 1966.

Bibliography

Krey, A. C. 'William of Tyre: The Making of an Historian in the Middle Ages', *Speculum*, XVI (1941), 149–66.

Lacroix, B. 'Guillaume de Tyr: Unité et diversité dans la tradition latine', *Études d'histoire littéraire et doctrinale*, IV (1968), 201–15.

Lilie, R-J. *Byzanz und die Kreuzfahrerstaaten. Studien zur Politik des Byzantinischen Palästina bis zum vierten Kreuzzug (1096–1204)*. Freie Universität Berlin. Byzantinisch–Neugriechisches Seminar: ΠOIKIΛA BYZANTINA, 1. Munich, 1981.

Lundgreen, F. *Wilhelm von Tyrus und der Templerorden*. Historische Studien, 97. Berlin, 1911.

Lyons, M. C., and Jackson, D. E. P. *Saladin: The Politics of the Holy War*. Cambridge, 1982.

Mayer, H. E. 'Zum Tode Wilhelms von Tyrus', *Archiv für Diplomatik*, V–VI (1959–60), 182–201.

'Das Pontifikale von Tyrus und die Krönung der lateinischen Könige von Jerusalem', *Dumbarton Oaks Papers*, XXI (1967), 141–232.

The Crusades. Trans. J. Gillingham. Oxford, 1972.

'Kaiserrecht und Heiliges Land', in H. Fuhrmann, H. E. Mayer and K. Wriedt (eds.), *Aus Reichsgeschichte und Nordischer Geschichte*. Kieler Historische Studien, 16. Stuttgart, 1972, pp. 193–208.

'Studies in the History of Queen Melisende of Jerusalem', *Dumbarton Oaks Papers*, XXVI (1972), 93–182.

Bistümer, Klöster und Stifte im Königreich Jerusalem. Schriften der Monumenta Germaniae Historica, 26. Stuttgart, 1977.

'The Concordat of Nablus', *Journal of Ecclesiastical History*, XXXIII (1982), 531–43.

'Henry II of England and the Holy Land', *EHR*, XCVII (1982), 722–39.

Mélanges sur l'histoire de royaume latin de Jérusalem. Mémoires de l'Académie des inscriptions et belles-lettres, n.s. 5. Paris, 1984.

Metcalf, D. M. *Coinage of the Crusades and the Latin East in the Ashmolean Museum Oxford*. London, 1983.

Möhring, H. 'Byzanz zwischen Sarazenen und Kreuzfahrern', in W. Fischer and J. Schneider (eds.), *Das Heilige Land im Mittelalter*. Schriftenreihe des Zentralinstituts für fränkische Landeskunde und allgemeine Regionalforschung an der Universität Erlangen-Nürnberg, 22. Neustadt an der Aisch, 1982, pp. 45–75.

'Zu der Geschichte der orientalischen Herrscher des Wilhelm von Tyrus', *Mittellateinisches Jahrbuch*, XIX (1984), 170–83.

Morgan, M. R. *The Chronicle of Ernoul and the Continuations of William of Tyre*. Oxford, 1973.

Partner, N. F. *Serious Entertainments: The Writing of History in Twelfth-Century England*. Chicago, 1977.

Prawer, J. 'Colonization Activities in the Latin Kingdom of Jerusalem', *Revue belge de philologie et d'histoire*, XXIX (1951), 1063–1118.

Crusader Institutions. Oxford, 1980.

Propst, H. 'Die geographischen Verhältnisse Syriens und Palästinas nach

Bibliography

Wilhelm von Tyrus, Geschichte der Kreuzzüge', *Das Land der Bible*, IV, Heft 5/6 (1927), 1–83; continued in V, Heft 1 (1927), 1–40.

Prutz, H. *Kulturgeschichte der Kreuzzüge*. Berlin, 1883.

'Studien über Wilhelm von Tyrus', *Neues Archiv der Gesellschaft für ältere deutsche Geschichtskunde*, VIII (1883), 91–132.

Richard, J. *The Latin Kingdom of Jerusalem*. Trans. J. Shirley. 2 vols. Europe in the Middle Ages: Selected Studies, 11. Amsterdam, 1979.

Riley-Smith, J. *The Knights of St John in Jerusalem and Cyprus c. 1050–1310*. London, 1967.

The Feudal Nobility and the Kingdom of Jerusalem, 1174–1277. London, 1973.

'Peace Never Established: The Case of the Kingdom of Jerusalem', *TRHS*, 5th ser., XXVIII (1978), 87–102.

'The Title of Godfrey de Bouillon', *Bulletin of the Institute of Historical Research*, LII (1979), 83–6.

The First Crusade and the Idea of Crusading. London, 1986.

Rowe, J. G. 'Paschal II and the Relations between the Spiritual and Temporal Powers in the Kingdom of Jerusalem', *Speculum*, XXXII (1957), 470–501.

'The Papacy and the Ecclesiastical Province of Tyre (1100–1187)', *Bulletin of the John Rylands Library*, XLIII (1960–1), 160–89.

Runciman, S. 'The Visit of King Amalric I to Constantinople in 1171', in B. Z. Kedar, H. E. Mayer and R. C. Smail (eds.), *Outremer: Studies in the History of the Crusading Kingdom of Jerusalem*. Jerusalem, 1982, pp. 153–8.

Schwinges, R. C. 'Kreuzzugsideologie und Toleranz im Denken Wilhelms von Tyrus', *Saeculum*, XXV (1974), 367–85.

Kreuzzugsideologie und Toleranz. Studien zu Wilhelm von Tyrus. Monographien zur Geschichte des Mittelalters, 15. Stuttgart, 1977.

Siberry, E. *Criticism of Crusading, 1095–1274*. Oxford, 1985.

Smail, R. C. 'Latin Syria and the West, 1149–1187', *TRHS*, 5th ser. XIX (1969), 1–20.

'The International Status of the Latin Kingdom of Jerusalem, 1150–1192', in P. M. Holt (ed.), *The Eastern Mediterranean Lands in the Period of Crusades*. Warminster, 1977, pp. 23–43.

Smalley, B. 'Sallust in the Middle Ages', in R. R. Bolgar (ed.), *Classical Influences on European Culture. A.D. 500–1500*. Cambridge, 1971, pp. 165–75.

Historians in the Middle Ages. London, 1974.

Southern, R. W. 'Aspects of the European Tradition of Historical Writing. 1. The Classical Tradition from Einhard to Geoffrey of Monmouth', *TRHS*, 5th ser. XX (1970), 173–96.

'The Schools of Paris and the School of Chartres', in R. L. Benson and G. Constable (eds.), *Renaissance and Renewal in the Twelfth Century*. Oxford, 1982, pp. 113–37.

Stevenson, W. B. *The Crusaders in the East*. Cambridge, 1907.

Sybel, H. von. *The History and Literature of the Crusades*. Trans. Lady Duff Gordon. London, n.d.

Vessey, D. W. T. C. 'William of Tyre and the Art of Historiography', *Mediaeval Studies*, XXXV (1973), 433–55.

Bibliography

'William of Tyre: Apology and Apocalypse', in G. Cambier (ed.), *Hommages à André Boutemy*. Collection Latomus, 145. Brussels, 1976, pp. 390–403.

Werweke, H. Van. *Filips van de Elzas en Willem van Tyrus*. Mededelingen van de Koninklijke Vlaamse Academie voor Weterschappen, Letteren en Schone Kunsten van Belgie. Klasse de Letteren. Brussels, 1971.

INDEX

Index

Augustine, 32, 40, 154

Baldric of Dol, 46, 47
Baldwin, archbishop of Caesarea, 126
Baldwin of Boulogne: *see* Baldwin I,
 king of Jerusalem
Baldwin of Ibelin, 18
Baldwin I, king of Jerusalem (Baldwin
 of Boulogne), 61, 69, 72, 168;
 character, 71, 73–5, 77–8;
 coronation, 50, 67, 68, 104;
 military activities, 38, 74–5, 137,
 156, 158; relations with church,
 29, 49, 88, 89, 90, 100–2, 110–12,
 113, 116–18, 123; ruler of Edessa,
 66, 74
Baldwin II, king of Jerusalem, 50n, 64,
 66, 71, 74, 80–1, 82, 105, 118, 156,
 168; accession, 69–70
Baldwin III, king of Jerusalem, 24, 30,
 44, 56–7, 68, 71–2, 74, 79, 99,
 157, 160–1; association with
 Melisende, 68, 80–2, 167; relations
 with Byzantium, 141–3, 145, 146;
 relations with church, 88, 90, 106
Baldwin IV, king of Jerusalem, 1–2,
 17–20, 21, 24, 29, 30, 39, 54, 68,
 71–2, 87, 128, 147, 163–5; *Historia
 Ierosolymitana* as *apologia* for, 61,
 62–5, 76–7, 78–80, 82–4, 93, 172
Baldwin V, king of Jerusalem, 68, 84
Balian of Ibelin, 18
Banyas, 57, 113n, 117, 157
Barbeaux, Cistercian abbey of, 3
Beatrice, countess of Edessa, 141
Bede, 34
Beirut, 116, 118, 121, 122, 124n, 146–7;
 bishops of: *see*, Mainard, Odo,
 Raymond
Benedict of Nursia, 32
Berengar, bishop of Orange, 112
Bernard of Valence, patriarch of
 Antioch, 89, 115, 117–18, 119–22,
 123
Bethlehem: bishopric, 29, 89, 95,
 113–14; bishops: *see* Albert,
 Aschetinus, Ralph; church of the
 Nativity, 91n
Bible, books of: *see* Daniel, Ezekiel,
 Isaiah, Matthew; *see also Historia
 Ierosolymitana*, biblical
 references
Boethius, 32, 33
Blois, count of: *see* Stephen
Bohemond I, prince of Antioch, 49–50,
 69, 89, 100, 102–4, 111, 136–7; on
 First Crusade, 61, 73, 97, 134, 135
Bohemond II, prince of Antioch, 46,
 66, 69
Bohemond III, prince of Antioch,
 63–4, 77, 83, 90, 93, 106–7, 146,
 147, 163–4, 169
Bologna, 15
Bostra, 42, 160–1, 163
Bulgars, 98
Byzantine empire, 18, 26, 47, 130–50
 passim, 167, 173; emperors: *see*
 Alexius I Comnenus, Alexius II
 Comnenus, Andronicus I
 Comnenus, Constantine IX
 Monomachus, Heraclius, John II
 Comnenus, Manuel I Comnenus,
 Maurice, Michael VII, Nicephorus
 I, Nicephorus III, Phocas,
 Romanus III, Romanus IV
 Diogenes; empress: *see* Maria of
 Antioch

Caesarea, archbishops of: *see* Baldwin,
 Ebremar, Ernesius, Monachus;
 lord: *see* Hugh
Calcidius, 33
Canterbury, 104; archbishop of: *see*
 Thomas Becket
Carthage, 36
Cassiodorus, 32, 34
Castalian Spring, 36
Castile, king of: *see* Alphonso X
Caxton, William, 5
Châlons-sur-Marne, 3
Charlemagne, 25, 34, 43, 131, 132n
Charles 'the Good', count of Flanders,
 83n
Chosroes II, 65
Chrétien de Troyes, 83n
Chronique d'Amadi, 5
Cicero, 32, 33, 37, 38n
Cilicia, 69, 74, 78, 137–8, 139, 142–3,
 144, 145, 146
Clement III (anti-pope) (Guibert of
 Ravenna), 86, 109
Clermont, Council of, 47, 152
Coloman I, king of Hungary, 73
Conrad III, western emperor, 141, 158
Constance, princess of Antioch, 66, 80
Constantine, bishop of Lydda, 126
Constantine IX Monomachos
 (Byzantine emperor), 131
Constantinople, 138, 141, 146; Council
 of, 36; First Crusade in, 73, 132–3,

182

Index

Ovid, 32, 33–4, 36

papacy, 67, 86, 109–29 *passim*, 172, 173; schisms: of 1080, 47, 109; of 1130, 109; of 1159, 28, 38, 86, 99, 106, 109; *see also* popes, Rome
papal legates, 88, 96–7, 110, 113, 114; *see also* Adhemar, bishop of Le Puy, Alberic of Ostia, Berengar, bishop of Orange, Gibelin of Arles, Giles of Tusculum, Robert of Paris, John of St John and St Paul
Paris, 15
Paschal II, Pope, 89, 101, 111–13, 117–18, 120, 122, 123
Persia, 146
Persius, 32
Peter, archdeacon of Lydda, 20, 22
Peter of Barcelona, archbishop of Tyre, 96, 98–9, 104–5, 126
Peter Bartholomew, 48
Peter of Blois, 15
Peter the Hermit, 47, 49, 131–2, 155
Peter of Narbonne, bishop of Albara, archbishop of Apamea, 88, 115
Peter, prior of the Holy Sepulchre, 94
Peter des Roches, bishop of Winchester, 3
Peter, Saint, 114, 139
Petra, 113n
Philip II Augustus, king of France, 64
Philip, count of Flanders, 19, 54, 63–4, 82–3, 148, 163–4, 165, 172, 173
Philomelium, 133
Phocas (Byzantine emperor), 65
Plato, 33–4
Plautus, 32
Pontigny, Cistercian abbey of, 3
Popes: *see* Adrian IV, Alexander III, Eugenius III, Gregory the Great, Honorius II, Innocent II, Lucius III, Paschal II, Urban II; anti-popes: *see* Clement III, Victor IV
Proverbs, Book of, 37
Prudentius, 32
Pseudo-Isidore, 117

Quintilian, 32

Rainald of Dassel, 15
Ralph: archbishop-elect of Tyre, 88, 92; bishop of Bethlehem, chancellor of Jerusalem, 95, 116

Ralph of Domfront, patriarch of Antioch, 14, 46, 53, 66, 86, 87, 90, 104, 114–15, 116, 122, 167, 169
Ralph (brother of William II, archbishop of Tyre), 14
Ramla, 163
Raymond of Aguilers, 45, 47–8, 49–50, 88n, 97n
Raymond, bishop of Beirut, 94
Raymond IV, count of Toulouse, count of Tripoli, 47–8, 61, 66n, 73, 88, 97, 134–5, 154
Raymond III, count of Tripoli, 21, 63–4, 72, 77, 83, 90, 146, 163; regent of Jerusalem, 18–19, 29–30, 84, 166, 174
Raymond of Poitiers, prince of Antioch, 66, 87, 90, 104, 114–15, 116, 137–9, 140, 141, 146
Raynald, abbot of Mount Zion, 94
Raynald of Châtillon: prince of Antioch, 90, 93, 142–3, 144, 146, 173; lord of Oultrejourdain, 17, 18, 77
Renier, bishop of Sebastea, 126
Rheims, 104
Riblah, 36
Robert, archbishop of Nazareth, 160
Robert, count of Flanders, 83n
Robert Guiscard, 135
Robert of Paris (papal legate), 110, 111n
Robert Pullen, 15
Rochester: priory of St Andrew, 3
Roger, prince of Antioch, 69
Romanus III (Byzantine emperor), 131
Romanus IV Diogenes (Byzantine emperor), 65n
Rome, 16, 20, 25, 95, 100, 111–16; *see also* papacy
Rufinus, 34, 36, 40–1

Sa'īd ibn Baṭrīk, patriarch of Alexandria, 23, 45
St Albans, abbey of, 3, 24
St Mary Major (abbey in Jerusalem), abbess of: *see* Stephany of Courtenay
St Mary of the Valley of Josaphat (abbey), 82
Saladin, 2, 16, 17, 57n, 76, 84, 148, 151, 153, 155, 157, 163–5, 171
Sallust, 32, 33, 39, 40n
Sebastea, bishop of: *see* Renier
Seljük dynasty, 66–7, 77